3615495400

University of Stirling Library, FK9 4LA
Tel: 01786 467220

LONG LOAN

Please **RETURN** or **RENEW**
no later than the date on the receipt
Subject to recall if requested

Motivational Aspects of Prejudice and Racism

THE NEBRASKA SYMPOSIUM ON MOTIVATION

SERIES TITLES:

Cynthia Willis-Esqueda (Ed.) *Motivational Aspects of Prejudice and Racism*

Cynthia Willis-Esqueda

Editor

Motivational Aspects of Prejudice and Racism

 Springer

Editor

Cynthia Willis-Esqueda
Institute of Ethnic Studies
Department of Psychology
University of Nebraska
336 Burnett Hall
Lincoln, NE 68588-0308
USA
cwillis@unlserve.unl.edu

ISBN: 978-0-387-73234-3   e-ISBN: 978-0-387-73233-6

Library of Congress Control Number: 2007934983

Printed on acid-free paper.

9 8 7 6 5 4 3 2 1

springer.com

Preface

The 53rd Nebraska Symposium on Motivation developed under the past Series Editor, Richard A. Dienstbier. Prof. Dienstbier oversaw the symposium for many years and he is largely responsible for its continued success. His broad and thoughtful view of the field of psychology has guided the symposium into the twenty-first century. Everyone connected to the symposium is extremely grateful for his leadership. With his retirement, the University of Nebraska-Lincoln, Department of Psychology developed a new administrative structure for oversight of the symposium and selected Debra A. Hope as the new series editor for a 6-year term. Publication of the 53rd volume has fallen under Prof. Hope's watch.

As the new series editor, one of the first tasks that the symposium committee and I undertook was to evaluate the current needs of the symposium. As a result, we began an extended process to find a new publisher for the symposium volumes who would respect and support the intellectual freedom and rigor of the series as well as promote it broadly in traditional print and electronic formats. We are very pleased that Springer has agreed to be our publisher, starting with Volume 53.

The volume editor for this 53rd volume of the Nebraska Symposium on Motivation is Cynthia Willis-Esqueda. The volume editor coordinated the symposium that led to this volume including selecting and inviting the contributors and coordinating all aspects of editing. My thanks to our contributors for excellent presentations and chapters.

This symposium series is supported by funds provided by the Chancellor of the University of Nebraska-Lincoln, Harvey Perlman, and by funds donated in memory of Prof. Harry K. Wolfe to the University of Nebraska Foundation by the late Prof. Cora L. Friedline. We are extremely grateful for the Chancellor's generous support of the Symposium series and for the University of Nebraska Foundation's support via the Friedline bequest. This symposium volume, like those in the recent past, is dedicated to the memory of Prof. Wolfe, who brought psychology to the University of Nebraska. After studying with Prof. Wilhelm Wundt, Prof. Wolfe returned to this, his native state, to establish the first undergraduate laboratory in psychology in the nation. As a student at Nebraska, Prof. Friedline studied psychology under Prof. Wolfe.

Debra A. Hope
Series Editor

v

Contents

Preface... v
Debra A. Hope

Contributors.. ix

1   Introduction: Motivational Aspects of Prejudice and Racism 1
Cynthia Willis-Esqueda

2   Social Cognition, Ethnic Identity, and Ethnic Specific Strategies
    for Coping with Threat due to Prejudice and Discrimination........ 7
Amado M. Padilla

3   New Directions in Aversive Racism Research:
    Persistence and Pervasiveness 43
John F. Dovidio and Samuel L. Gaertner

4   The Role of Race and Racial Prejudice
    in Recognizing Other People 68
John C. Brigham

5   Addressing Contemporary Racism:
    The Common Ingroup Identity Model 111
Samuel L. Gaertner and John F. Dovidio

Author Index 134

Subject Index 141

Contributors

John C. Brigham, *Florida State University*

John F. Dovidio, *University of Connecticut*

Samuel L. Gaertner, *University of Delaware*

Debra A. Hope, *University of Nebraska – Lincoln*

Amado M. Padilla, *Stanford University*

Cynthia Willis-Esqueda, *Institute of Ethnic Studies, Department of Psychology, University of Nebraska, 336 Burnett Hall, Lincoln, NE 68588-0308 USA*

1
Introduction: Motivational Aspects of Prejudice and Racism

Cynthia Willis-Esqueda

> *Racial categories did not emerge simply as the products of energy – and time-saving cognitive devices, but as functional entities constructed in the service of social power and cultural domination.* (Eberhardt & Randall, 1997)
>
> *But suppose God is black, I replied. What if we go to Heaven and we, all our lives, have treated the Negro as an inferior, and God is there, and we look up and He is not white? What then is our response?* (Kennedy, 1966)

Introduction

As the two quotes above demonstrate, in the United States we are motivated to organize our social life around racial categories, and yet, at the same time, there is anxiety attached to the use of race, particularly when one is a beneficiary of one's racial group membership.[1] Since both prejudice and racism have such a tremendous impact on the lives of both the perpetrators and targets of racism, a symposium based on the psychological investigation of motivational issues is an appropriate forum to hear from expert scholars on prejudice and racism. In 2005, the University of Nebraska-Lincoln's 53rd Annual Symposium on Motivation brought together experts in the motivational aspects of prejudice and racism. It was clearly time to hear from such experts.

In the United States, prejudice and racism take on a pivotal meaning. The United States was founded with ethnic confrontations (Tischauser, 2002) and the development of a "racially" based social hierarchy. Within the first 70 years of English settlement in colonial America, the son of Massasoit, the Powhatan Chief that shared the first "thanksgiving" ceremony with the Pilgrims, was dismembered and beheaded by the Plymouth settlers. Massasoit's daughter-in-law and grandson were sold into slavery in the Caribbean (Tischauser, 2002). Within the

---

[1] The use of the term race is not meant to signify that the term is a valid indicator of human variation. Rather, it is used to indicate the social construction of categories that are based on presumed phenotypic features and actual historical, legal, and psychological issues.

C. Willis-Esqueda (ed.), *Motivational Aspects of Prejudice and Racism.*
© Springer 2008

first 60 years from time of arrival, African Americans' were legally classified as slaves for life (McLemore & Romo, 2005), and the United States has never enjoyed a time when African Americans' lived in equal parity with European Americans. Mexican Americans, by virtue of their race, were believed inferior to European Americans, and their lands and rights were usurped during the colonization of the southwestern parts of the United States (Perea, 2003). Known as the "Yellow Peril" during the 1800s, Asians, particularly the Chinese, were not allowed citizenship and were legally barred from entering the country with the Chinese Exclusion Act (1882–1943). Indeed, the first border patrols along the United States/Mexican border were not designed to keep Mexican nationals from entering the United States, but to deter any Chinese from entering the United States via Mexico (Tischauser, 2002). Thus, every ethnic group of color in the United States has experienced, and may still experience, the effects of prejudice and racism. Such experiences give psychological meaning to the current intergroup relationships we encounter today.

Within United States' culture, there is no other social concept with the power of race to mold and determine our behavior. As the late Gould (1994) stated:

> The shift from a geographic to a hierarchical ordering of human diversity must stand as one of the most fateful transitions in the history of Western Science – for what, short of railroads and nuclear bombs, has had more practical impact, in this case almost entirely negative, upon our collective lives? (p. 66)

Indeed, even today, no other socially constructed phenomenon has had the power to determine:

1. One's self definition as a member of a particular racial/ethnic group
2. The concept of history and its meaning for your ethnic/racial group
3. Who one marries and where one lives
4. What one does for employment and to live – including the acceptability of one' research work on ethnic minority issues
5. Chances for schooling and chances for participation in the political process, including voting rights
6. Chances for social networks that shape and mold present and future success
7. Membership in social organizations and participation in the social and economic fabric of one's community, state, and nation

Moreover, as Essie Mae Washington-Williams, daughter of the late US Senator Strom Thurmond, has shown us, even the right to claim one's parentage can be determined by the dominant culture's racial classifications and where one fits in that system (*Essie Mae on Strom Thurmond*, 2003). All of this is based on a socially constructed concept called race.

For those who harbor the notion that race is biologically determined, it should be noted that human variation is sophisticated and can not be fitted to a clean taxonomy. The cultural and "scientific" notion of race has changed in both definition and meaning over time, regionally, nationally, and even internationally. Consequently, those who pursue the investigation of race as a biological determinant of human behavior fail to comprehend the cognitive processes and motivational forces that create and maintain the social order and promote the use of race as a meaningful categorization of humans.

Within psychology, the changing race definitions, the meaning of race, and racial biases within the discipline have been noted by several scholars (Yee, Fairchild, Weizmann, & Wyatt, 1993; Zuckerman, 1990). For example, the late Robert Guthrie's (1976/2004) notable book, *Even the Rat Was White*, outlines psychology's historical issues with race, particularly for African Americans, the measurement of race, and the place of race in historical and current research endeavors. While race now plays an important component in both conceptual and explanatory areas of scholarship, researchers often fail to examine the meaning of the race concept. Race and ethnicity are used interchangeably (Yee et al.), and research findings which use one "racial" group are generalized to other "racial" groups. Thus, the conceptual power and veracity of research findings is compromised when race has no consensual, scientific definition.

As a central issue of interest within the psychological understanding of human behavior, the study of prejudice and racism has waxed and waned. Fifty years ago (in 1955), at the very beginnings of the Nebraska Symposium on Motivation series, the scholarship concerning prejudice and racism was in its theoretical infancy. A review of the psychology literature (and the social sciences literature) indicates the increasing importance of scholarship on the topics of prejudice and racism since 1955, due in part to the emerging, preferred view of the United States as an egalitarian society, the advent of the civil rights era, changes in the social and legal acceptability of being a blatant racist, and the increasing sophistication of measurement instruments and technology. Thus, as a discipline, psychology embarked on the task of addressing prejudice and racism long ago, and our scholars for the 2005 symposium provided a demonstration of the sophistication of that research journey.

For those who believe prejudice and racism are no longer social issues worthy of scholarly attention, please remember that inequality and bias are a constant problem for most people of color, particularly in the United States, on a daily basis. The lessons of our racial and ethnic histories are still alive in our psychological understandings, and societal preferences for the attributes of the dominant culture remain strong. We know racial inequality exists, and members of the dominant culture do not want to be treated like members of minority groups. As Robert Staples has aptly stated: "Despite the color-blind theory, white claims of reverse racism, and preferential treatment for blacks, there is no queue of whites claiming black heritage to qualify for the 'benefits' of black membership." (1993, p. 121) Two of the poorest counties in the US (Shannon County in South Dakota and Cameron County in Texas) are predominantly inhabited by American Indians and Mexican Americans, yet there is no ground-swell of indignation to change that fact – no funding campaigns, food drives, or national media images of the struggle for existence.

At the same time, psychological investigations into the ramifications for targets of prejudice and racism are present, but limited. We know very little about minority group members' experiences and perceptions of prejudice and racism. There is a dearth of knowledge concerning minority group members' psychological responses to racial/ethnic bias as perpetrators or as victims, particularly as it is experienced in relation to various racial/ethnic groups. In this volume, the chapter by Amado Padilla (p. 7) provides a much needed overview of the psychological issues surrounding cognitive processing and identity for Mexican Americans, the largest Latino group in the United States, and the only in situ Latino group in the United States. His synthesis of research concerning the myriad of issues that Mexican Americans face in claiming and maintaining an ethnic voice is timely, important, and serves to call attention to an approach to the study of minority groups that is essential. Padilla's scholarly study concerning Mexican American identity and psychological issues in the United States demonstrates the importance of research on specific minority groups. Each racial/ethnic group's psychological issues are grounded on historical, legal, and situational events that are unique to that group. Mexican Americans' cultural place in the United States and their singular and common psychological issues highlight the profound benefit of approaching scholarship on prejudice and racism from the perspective of a minority group and its members.

The research on European Americans' prejudice and racism has been the foundation for much of the scholarship in the field. The chapter by John Dovidio and Samuel Gaertner provides the quintessential review of where this approach has been and the level of understanding we currently have concerning White Americans' ethnic and racial bias from a combination of both cognitive and motivational features. In addition, an overview of the theory of aversive racism is provided that highlights the premises of the theory and its explanatory power. One of the benefits of the theory is its reliance on the motivation to appear nonprejudiced, which can produce anxiety in interracial encounters. This aspect of the theory makes it of infinite value in the quest for understanding how social information concerning race is handled, as well as the consequences for everyday interactions. Moreover, the implications for implicit and explicit bias, as outlined in the chapter, will certainly make this chapter of interest in the area of "double attitudes" and the relationship between what we "know" at the deepest levels of our cognitive lives, and what we wish to "show" at the public, conscious level of our lives.

Pettigrew (2004) has reminded us that we should not abandon a focus on and the study of actual behavior of majority group members toward minority group members in our quest to comprehend the nuances of racially biased behavior. John Brigham's chapter returns us to the study of such behavior, and how it is tied to ideology.

John Brigham's preeminent work on issues of prejudice and racism is noteworthy for both its breadth and pioneering approaches. The chapter in this volume provides the synthesis of two areas of Brigham's work. The chapter includes a review of the theoretical underpinnings and applied work on one of the more onerous ramifications of our racially constructed social world – the cross race effect in identification (or CRE). The cross race effect in identification has real and negative consequences for our daily social lives. From being the targets of mistaken identification during embarrassing social encounters to miscarriages of justice resulting in years of imprisonment, the cross race effect has been a major outcome of our motivation to live in a racially stratified social world.

In addition, Brigham reminds us that the cross race effect is embedded in an ideology that includes racial prejudice within its structure. In this chapter, the various approaches to study racial prejudice are explicated. Moreover, a comprehensive understanding of racial prejudice is crucial for advancing the best method to eliminate the cross race effect. Brigham makes it clear that we have overlooked the importance of interracial contact and the elemental function it will play in future research on changing our racially structured social relationships.

If we know racism exits, how do we eliminate it? In groundbreaking scholarship, Gaertner and Dovidio have moved beyond theorizing about the "Why?" of the motivational aspects of prejudice and racism, and they have developed a theory for the elimination of such bias. The chapter, titled *Addressing Contemporary Racism: The Common Ingroup Identity Model*, focuses on unique aspects of the motivations for prejudice and racism. We are grounded in our identity with a particular racial/ethnic group, and we exclude those groups to which we are not psychologically attached. Gaertner and Dovidio provide a review of how we socially categorize others and then come to identify with the group that best represents us, or the group we have been taught is our ingroup. According to Gaertner and Dovidio, we tend to over value and favor our ingroup and its members and, perhaps, devalue and discriminate against those in an outgroup. Various theories related to how best to eliminate such self categorizations are outlined in the chapter. However, the elimination of racial/ethnic bias must come from engaging in an alternate orientation toward the self categorization that produces bias – namely a recategorization of self. This recategorization of self involves identification with a more multiracial group that incorporates persons of diverse racial memberships. This would appear to be a particularly effective method for eliminating racial/ethnic bias in the United States, which harbors an ethnically diverse population. In addition, as global mobility and immigration becomes more commonplace, it may behoove a society to reinvent an inherent concept of a nationhood populace. A societal recategorization that incorporates a multiracial/ethnic population may serve to reinforce what a national polity resembles and reduce societal discord and discrimination.

In 1964 Ashley Montegu (1964) gave a lecture at the University of Nebraska, Lincoln, where he opined that "the social construction of race is so antihuman, and individually and socially destructive, that it demands our most earnest attention." (p. 6) Forty years later, I have been very proud to introduce our speakers for the symposium and their writings for this volume. These scholars were chosen with care. Their work signifies the highest achievements in the study of the motivational aspects of prejudice and racism, and they have made tremendous inroads into our understanding of these issues. In American Indian culture the value of individual achievement is acknowledged with an honoring ceremony. We honor the scholars of the symposium. We know their continued achievements will provide us with a clearer understanding of what it means to live in a social world that is divided by prejudice and racism and to work toward the elimination of such bias.

References

Eberhardt, J. L., & Randall, J. L. (1997). The essential notion of race. *Psychological Science, 8*, 198–203.

Essie Mae on Strom Thurmond. (2003). Interview with Dan Rather. Retrieved November 14, 2004 from http://www.cbsnews.com/stories/2003/12/17/60II/main589107.shtml.

Gould, S. J. (1994). The geometer of race. *Discover, 15*, 65–69.

Guthrie, Robert V. (2004). *Even the rat was White: A historical view of psychology.* New York: Allyn Bacon.

Kennedy, R. F. (1966). Suppose God is Black. *Look, 30*, 45.

McLemore, S. D., & Romo, H. D. (2005). *Racial and ethnic relations in America.* New York: Allyn & Bacon.

Montegu, A. (1964). *The concept of race.* Lincoln, NE: University of Nebraska Press.

Perea, J. (2003). A brief history of race and the U.S.-Mexican border: Tracing the trajectories of conquest. *UCLA Law Review, 51*, 283–312.

Pettigrew, T. (2004). The social science study of American race relations in the 20th century. In C. S. Crandall & M. Schaller (Eds.), *The social psychology of prejudice: Historical and contemporary perspectives.* Seattle, WA: Lewinian Press.

Tischauser, L. V. (2002). *The changing nature of racial and ethnic conflict in United States history.* New York: University Press of America.

Yee, A. H., Fairchild, H. H., Weizmann, F., & Wyatt, G. E. (1993). Addressing psychology's problems with race. *The American Psychologist, 48*, 1132–1140.

Zuckerman, M. (1990). Some dubious premises in research and theory on racial differences: Scientific, social, and ethical issues. *The American Psychologist, 45*, 1297–1303.

2

Social Cognition, Ethnic Identity, and Ethnic Specific Strategies for Coping with Threat due to Prejudice and Discrimination

Amado M. Padilla

> *Psychology has been generally remiss in explaining the*
> *relationship between ethnic minority and majority groups and*
> *even more so in propounding models for explaining the*
> *psychology of ethnic minority identity.* (Hutnik, 1991, p. 37)

> *The way we perceive others will influence indirectly how we*
> *act towards them.* (Turner, 1982, p. 29)

Diversity is a much used term in the United States. Diversity means the existence of peoples from different cultures, who speak different languages, hold different religious beliefs, rituals and practices, celebrate different holidays, take pleasure in different forms of entertainment, interact with family and friends in different ways, and enjoy different types of food and food preparation. Diversity also implies that people, because of the color of their skin color and physical appearance, are easily identifiable as different from the majority group. Although, historians note that diversity is not new in America, something has changed the discourse of diversity (Takaki, 1993). At least three macrochanges are in part responsible for how we view diversity today. These changes include the Civil Rights movement that began in the 1960s, the large increase in Hispanic and Asian populations due to changes in immigration policy beginning in 1965, and economic and political upheavals in developing countries that have resulted in large-scale migration to America. Collectively, these forces have changed the racial and ethnic landscape of this country.

While we hear frequent accolades to the value of diversity, there is at the same time much acrimony about diversity. Diversity has stirred up much resentment on issues such as affirmative action, racial profiling, bilingual education, and immigration policy. While this chapter is not about diversity per se, it does address how one large and heterogeneous ethnic group finds itself in the center of the conversation about diversity on a daily basis. I am referring specifically to Latinos, and while I will not engage in an overview of this groups' demographic representation in the United States, it is important to make three points to properly contextualize Latinos in the United States. First, Latinos are a diverse group consisting of peoples from Mexico, Central and South America, and the Caribbean. Members of this group may be of any race, they come from Spanish speaking countries, and they share

C. Willis-Esqueda (ed.), *Motivational Aspects of Prejudice and Racism.*
© Springer 2008

many cultural similarities. Second, Latinos number more than 39 million people and constitute 13% of the US population, making them the largest ethnic minority group in the United States. Further, whereas Latinos once lived in specific geographic areas – Mexican Americans in the West and Southwest, Puerto Ricans in the Northeast, and Cubans in the Southeast, Latinos are increasingly evident in every geographic region. Finally, historically Latinos are not newcomers to this country. Their roots run deep and their history predates the Mayflower, the American Revolution, and the rush to California in search of gold (Takaki, 1993). At the same time, immigrants from various countries in Latin America are still arriving daily with the same dream that brought all peoples to this country; that is, the dream of a better future.

My purpose in this chapter is to offer a theoretical framework for understanding how prejudice, discrimination, and racism affect how Latinos perceive intergroup relationships. The goal too is to explain why Latinos are more tenacious in maintaining their ethnicity than some other ethnic groups. I will first frame my analysis within the main tenets of social cognition and social identity theory (SIT). Then I will offer a theory for ethnic threat that incorporates features from SIT, reactions to stigmatization and perceived discrimination, and motivation factors that contribute to maintenance of cultural uniqueness despite pressures to assimilate. Another important feature of my analysis is that it is framed from the perspective of the recipients of discrimination and racism, not from a majority White group perspective that seeks to examine why and how Whites are racist (e.g., Dovidio & Gaertner, 1986). In addition, often in the social psychology of racism the discourse is on White–Black relationships, with the focus on lessening White racism. The objective in this chapter is to understand how racism affects Latinos and how they respond to the threat that racism poses to their ethnic identity.

Social Psychology of Minority Group Identification

Social Cognition

Social cognition is a meta-theoretical approach to the study of social behavior. Its focus is on the psychological processes that guide social interactions between people. Fiske and Taylor (1991) define social cognition as "how ordinary people think about people and how they think they think about people." (p. 1) In this chapter on ethnic identity, I will follow the tradition of pragmatism in social cognition research (Fiske, 1993) that emphasizes the motivational and intentional bases of perception and cognition (e.g., Heider, 1958; James, 1890).

According to social cognition researchers, cognitive processes stem from people's pragmatic goals, which derive from multiple sources, including person-level variables, situational constraints, societal structure, and evolutionary mechanisms (e.g., Fiske, 1993; James, 1890). Simply put, "thinking is for doing," a message from James (1890) positing that cognition follows from people's goals. These goals vary according to the social situation.

Because of my interest in the acculturation process of immigrants (Padilla, 1980, 1986; Padilla & Perez, 2003), I am interested in merging social cognition theory with issues involved in the immigration-adjustment process. Individuals who transition from one culture to another, due to migration, experience new cultural–societal standards of behavior that they must adjust to in order to be successful. They are obliged to make sense of their new social environment and decide how and/or to what extent they are going to integrate into the host culture. How do they develop situated behavior patterns that are adaptive within the larger societal–cultural context (Markus & Kitayama, 1991; Markus, Kitayama, & Heiman, 1996)? Pragmatism and cultural competence play critical roles in how we theorize about individual and group acculturation. Today, social cognition researchers have used the metaphor "motivated tactician" (Fiske & Taylor, 1991) to describe social perceivers. According to this theoretical view, people choose among a wide range of pragmatic cognitive tactics based on their goals, motives, and needs, as determined by the power of the situation and, as a result, most significant cognitive activity results from motivation. Put plainly, people think for the purpose of satisfying their pragmatic motives, and they tend to think with less effort when their goals are satisfied (Fiske, 1993). This is equally true for people transported to a new culture, who are typically highly motivated to be successful in the new country.

To utilize a social cognition model to its fullest, we need to understand what it means to be culturally competent in one or more cultural contexts. Most simply, cultural competence refers to the learned ability to function in a culture in a manner that is congruent with the values, beliefs, customs, mannerisms, and language of the majority of members of the culture. When members of the culture come to view the person as an "insider," then we can say that the person has attained complete competence in the new culture. However, acceptance as an "insider" is not a prerequisite for cultural competence per se. The important consideration is for the person to behave within a rather narrow cultural band of normative behavior that conforms to the host culture. When a newcomer's behavior is outside the acceptable range of behavior, he is likely to encounter sanctions by members of the dominant group. In sum, social cognition guides newcomers in their adaptation to their new environment and at the same time determine how they will be perceived and received by members of the host group.

Social Categorization

It is a fundamental adaptive process of human existence to want to organize our world. In fact, the cognitive process that enables us to categorize our experiences brings order to our daily existence. In other words, the cognitive process of categorization simplifies our perceptions and renders our world less chaotic (Hogg & Abrams, 1988). Over time people have developed highly elaborate classification systems for every living and inanimate object. These systems serve as one of the foundations on which modern science is built. Categorization serves to accentuate the similarities within and between categories. The categorization of people-by-people is no exception. For example, we have seen throughout history how racial and ethnic categories have been used to determine the innate value of other human beings. Any social or physical trait that is meaningful to a person and/or group can be the basis for social categorization, and in turn, the categorization can serve as the foundation for social identity. Importantly, in self-categorization the in-group is motivated to highlight positive attributes to their membership and use these to differentiate themselves from others who do not share in these "positive" attributes. Individuals, in other words, are vested in wanting to be associated with positive categories because these confer positive self-evaluation and create feelings of self-esteem.

Two important psychological processes are embedded in social categorization. The first is that we use social categorization to make decisions about how we see ourselves and how we wish others to see us. Once an individual assumes a particular social category, the person sees the self and others in terms of that category membership. The second process is that social categorization and the striving for positive self-esteem at both the individual and group levels results in intergroup relations marked by ethnocentrism and competition (Tajfel, 1978). This is followed by in-group favoritism and intergroup discrimination. In essence, social categorization is the process whereby the individual finds meaning in the group (Hogg & Abrams, 1988) and distinctiveness between their social group and others.

Social Comparison

Social comparison goes hand-in-hand with social categorization. In social comparison, individuals evaluate who they are in relationship to others in their environment and self-evaluate themselves as smarter, richer, more attractive, a better athlete, etc. We use social comparisons to organize our social world and to process information about other individuals or groups. When we do this, we also accentuate intergroup distinctiveness as much as possible and on as many dimensions as possible (Hogg & Abrams, 1988). Social comparisons are overwhelmingly evaluative in nature. Thus, people viewed as smarter, richer, or more attractive are evaluated positively and are imbued with positive characteristics whereas those evaluated as less smart, poor, and not as attractive are more likely to be stigmatized negatively. An important outcome of social comparisons and heightened intergroup distinctiveness is elevated self-esteem and the determination of status hierarchies that result in power and prestige to those individuals imbued with more positive social, intellectual, or physical characteristics. The converse is the fate of those individuals who lack the "positive" characteristics.

Social Dominance

Sidanius (1993) and Sidanius and Pratto (1999) posit that throughout history all societies and cultures have evolved some form of social hierarchy with one or a small number of groups at the top and one or a small number of groups at the bottom. This structure lends itself to an analysis of dominant and subordinate social groups. According to social dominance theory (SDT), dominant groups enjoy a disproportionate share of political authority, power, wealth, prestige, and all the benefits that come with high social status. On the other hand, subordinate groups have disproportionately little political authority, power, and wealth. Members of subordinate groups are also subject to a larger array of negative life outcomes as seen in lower education levels, higher rates of unemployment, more crime, and disproportionate rates of prison and death sentences.

Generally societies determine social dominance based on age, gender, and an arbitrary set of characteristics. Older members of society generally enjoy greater social dominance than children and young adults. Men more often enjoy greater power and status than women. The final way in which dominance is established is more dependent on socially constructed differentiations between groups based on such things as ethnicity, race, social class, religious sect, regional group, immigration status, and social caste. Invariably, one or several groups are politically and/or materially superior to the other groups.

According to SDT, all forms of intergroup conflict and oppression, such as ethnocentrism and racism, are manifestations of basic human predispositions to form group-based social hierarchies. In essence, SDT explains all forms of prejudice, stereotypes, and categorizing of groups as superior or inferior. Finally, as societies evolve there is always a tension between producing hierarchal systems that foster social inequality and forces that counteract strict hierarchy setting and which permit greater social mobility and equality between groups. Legitimizing myths (LMs) provide the moral and intellectual justification for the social practices that distribute social value within a society (Sidanius & Pratto, 1999). According to Sidanius and Pratto, LMs include, but are not limited to, such beliefs as the superiority of some races over others (i.e., racism), meritocracy, individualism, belief in manifest destiny, and the Protestant work ethic. There are also LMs that serve the purpose of moving a group in the direction of greater social equality. These LMs may include religious beliefs of equality, the Civil Rights movement and its resulting legislation, and beliefs in the value of multiculturalism.

In addition, there are also certain personal and group traits that are associated with social dominance. A social domination orientation (SDO) describes individuals who support a group-based hierarchy that sponsors domination of "inferior" groups by "superior" groups. Not surprisingly, Sidanius and Pratto (1999) report that Whites, men, and heterosexuals score higher on measures of SDO. In addition, education, gender, and a religious orientation serve to moderate SDO. In keeping with this, individuals with greater education, women, and deeply religious people score lower on SDO and are more willing to engage in equality balancing behaviors.

A final aspect of social dominance that is important for this analysis has to do with hierarchical consensuality. This simply means that there is generally a high degree of consensus among both dominant and subordinate group members of who belongs to which group and why. Importantly, the subordinates are especially knowledgeable of their place in the social hierarchy.

Unlike most other social identity theories that focus on situational explanations of intergroup relations, the theory here rests on individual differences in social dominance. Individual orientations toward social dominance are pragmatic insofar as hierarchies are functional for the collective unit. Social hierarchies are validated through cultural ideologies that sustain the legitimacy and centrality of a hierarchy within the larger society. This theory accounts for large-scale examples of intergroup dominance that occur in the absence of overt conflict, such as ethnic, religious, or gender oppression. SDT differs in form from the cognitive and motivational analysis of self-categorization and optimal distinctiveness theories (Brewer, 1991), stressing both the inevitability and functionality of consensual hierarchies, such as legitimized social class distinctions and gender roles, as a function of individual differences in social dominance.

The socially derived constructs (i.e., social cognition, social categorization, social comparison, and social dominance) are critical to the theory that I will advance in this chapter to explain the processes involved in ethnic identity. I maintain that acculturation and adjustment are more difficult for Latinos who are more distinct (e.g., by skin color, physical features, and language) from the dominant in-group, White majority. Consequently, they are more likely to be compelled by situational factors and the pressures emanating from social comparisons and social dominance to maintain their identity with their ethnic group. In order to complete this analysis, we need to address the question of social stigma in understanding ethnic identification. This is because persons who are more identifiable as outsiders are more likely to be targets of prejudice, discrimination, and racism by the socially dominant and powerful in-group. Accordingly, outsiders who hold little social power may endure more physical and psychological hardships that call into question their motives for wanting to adapt to the ways of the dominant host group. Outsiders may experience fewer opportunities for contact with "insiders" thereby limiting their chances for successful adaptation. Finally, outsiders may be prohibited either implicitly or explicitly from entry into groups and/or institutions that offer privileges to their members (McIntosh, 1988; Tatum, 1997). In other words, how we perceive others will influence, indirectly, how we act towards them (Turner, 1982). I will now turn to a discussion of how individuals form their social identity.

Social Identity

SIT (e.g., Tajfel & Turner, 1986) stresses that an individual's behavior reflects the individual's larger societal unit. This means that overarching societal structures such as groups, organizations, cultures, and most importantly the individual's identification, and the value and emotional significance attached to that membership, is what guides cognitive structures and processes (Tajfel, 1982).

Cultural competence lies at the heart of this SIT, since collective group membership influences and frequently determines an individual's thoughts and behaviors (Markus et al., 1996). Accordingly, an individual is not a self-contained unit of psychological analysis. There is the social milieu that always plays a role in social interactions. Thus, people think, feel, and act as members of collective groups, institutions, and cultures. SIT reinforces the idea that an individual's social cognitions are socially construed, depending on their group or collective frame of reference. For instance, a Latino who perceives himself as negatively stigmatized because of his darker skin color or accented English speech may be less willing to acculturate because of his belief that he is judged not by his cultural competence as an American, but as an outsider of lower social status, merely because of his skin color or speech.

As originally formulated, SIT explains intergroup relations in general and social conflict in particular. The theory incorporated three main points: (1) people are motivated to maintain a positive self-concept; (2) the self-concept derives largely from group identification; and (3) people establish positive social identities by favorably comparing their in-group against an out-group (Operario & Fiske, 1999). As such, social identity theorists assume that internal social comparison processes drive intergroup conflict, even in the absence of explicit rivalry or competition between groups. Structural variables, such as power, hierarchy, and resource scarcity increase the individual's natural tendency to perceive the in-group more favorably than the out-group.

An influential component of social identity has to do with how an individual uses self-categorization to frame their identity. Turner, Hogg, Oakes, Reicher, and Wetherell (1987) argue that social contexts create meaningful group boundaries, and social identities are socially construed categories that shift depending on situational pragmatics. In this way, an individual can have somewhat different identities depending on the social context. The salience of social categories provides the raw material necessary for organizing out-groups and in-groups. The consequence is that situational factors guide cognitive processes and as such, self-categorization theory suggests that these pragmatic cognitive processes form the basis for ensuing intergroup interaction including prejudice and intergroup conflict.

Related to self-categorization is the work of Brewer (1991) on optimal distinctiveness. According to Brewer, a person's social identity is guided by two core human motives: the need to be unique and the need to belong. Having a social identity (e.g., ethnic, religious, or national) satisfies an individual's simultaneous needs for inclusion and differentiation. In other words, we need simultaneously to fill the need to belong to a social group (e.g., Latino, Catholic, and Spanish/English bilingual) while also maintaining our distinctiveness from another group (e.g., Euro-American, Protestant, and English monolingual). In this way, we are motivated to identify with social groups that we feel an emotional kinship with and to separate from groups that we do not feel a part of, and we strive to remain detached through a manifestation of distinctiveness. Importantly, according to optimal distinctiveness theory animosity toward the out-group occurs only when dimensions that are particularly relevant to the in-group's collective self-worth are challenged. For instance, in recent years we have seen considerable conflict between some Latino groups (e.g., National Association for Bilingual Education) and majority group organizations and leaders on issues of Spanish use in school and in the workplace. This conflict has been organized by large nativist groups through national efforts, such as English-only, or has been generated by legislative actions at the state level with laws banning bilingual education in public education.

Collectively through the processes of social cognition, social categorization, social dominance, and social identity, individuals who hold membership in consensually dominant and powerful social groups are not negatively evaluated because of stigma. In fact, Tajfel (1981) stated that because dominant group members do not suffer any stigma, their social identities are so natural as to be almost invisible or "privileged" (McIntosh, 1988). However, what about individuals who are stigmatized and categorized into the out-group?

Social Stigma

Goffman (1963) in an early work on stigma argued that because of certain stigmas an individual's identity is "spoiled." By this Goffman meant that if a person possesses what others perceive to be a stigma, that person is disqualified from full social acceptance. Accordingly, if other people's reactions influence our behavior and identity, then we try to control the reactions of others by manipulating what we reveal about ourselves. Goffman further stated that in their interactions with others, people often expose or hide certain beliefs, ideas, or behaviors in order to manipulate the perceptions that others hold of them. This is why, historically, when homosexuals decided to reveal their sexual orientation publicly, they called such an announcement "coming out of the closet." By "coming out," homosexuals risk their social status even if they are members of the privileged dominant social group. In the past, such stigmatized people often displayed traits of victimization – low self-esteem, defensiveness, passivity, in-group hostility, and identification with the oppressor (Allport, 1954). Today the affects of negative stigmatization are often challenged by social movements that call attention with pride to membership in gay and lesbian groups or to ethnic organizations that sponsor community and social activism.

Crocker, Major, and Steele (1998) maintained that it is not unexpected to envision a person possessing a social stigma to be negatively evaluated in one context, but not in another. Thus, stigmatization is not inextricably linked to something essential to the stigmatized attribute, or the person who possesses that attribute. The essential distinction is in the unfortunate circumstance of possessing an attribute that, in a given social context, leads to devaluation. In other words, a stigma will be negatively evaluated as determined by the situational context.

Ascribed and actual characteristics that are frequently associated with negative stigmatization include skin color, other physical features (e.g., indigenous vs. European physiognomy), recognizable accent when speaking in the nonnative language, certain religious apparel, obesity, homosexuality, homelessness, physical disabilities, mental illness, etc. The attributes that result in negative stigmatization are generally associated with minority groups, low social status, and powerlessness. An important consideration here is that people who use stigmas to stereotype come to believe that the stigmatized group really deserves their misfortune (e.g., poverty, homelessness, poor health) because they are lazy, lack intelligence, or are morally corrupt. By explaining others misfortune in this way, without examining the effects of prejudice and discrimination, dominant group member, are able to rationalize their elevated social status without feeling guilt or remorse.

In addition, high social standing and power is associated with decreased vulnerability to being negatively stigmatized (Fiske, 1993). It is important to recognize though that "high social standing and power" is relative and may vary from one society or culture to another. For example, a low status minority person of color may be devalued because of his employment as a maintenance worker during the day in an office building where the majority of workers are White professionals. At the same time, that minority individual in another context may be a respected member of his community and enjoy high social status through his community volunteerism as a youth soccer coach or because of his ministry on weekends at a local church. Fiske (1993) has suggested that when stigmatized individuals who are devalued in one or more contexts are able to enjoy situational contexts where they are valued for their positive attributes, the psychological consequences of being negatively stigmatized are mitigated.

A dimension of social stigma of critical importance in understanding the subjective experience of stigmatized individuals is *salience* or *visibility*. Salient stigmas such as race, ethnicity, certain physical handicaps, accented speech, obesity, or severe malnourishment due to poverty cannot be hidden easily from others. For people with a visible attribute, the stigma can provide the primary schema through which others believe that they know everything about the person (Goffman, 1963; Jones et al., 1984) and how they then set about to label the person who possesses the stigma. Thus, the stigma comes to stand for, or signify, the person. For example, a friend of mine related how she frequently finds herself stigmatized when she hears herself being referred to as the African American German language teacher. To make her point she related an experience where she overheard someone saying, "You know the African American woman who teaches German." Upon hearing this, she wondered whether the person who made the remark meant:

Aren't you surprised that an African American teaches German?
She's a teacher and she's African American!
How good do you suppose her German is, after all she is African American?

My friend noted that if a teacher were White the issue of race would not even be embedded in the statement "You know the woman who teaches German" or simply "The German teacher." Further, my friend went on to say that when she hears things like this her racial antennas go up and she finds herself feeling uncomfortable because of her heightened sense of "ethnic threat." The point is that often socially dominant individuals are not even aware of how their use of language to label ethnic group members reflects their negative evaluation of the person. Further, to be stigmatized often results in feelings of dehumanization or depersonalization by the target. The person with stigma becomes an object, and a devalued one at that. The situation is made worse when the depersonalizing statement is followed by other discriminatory behaviors.

The importance of this for the stigmatized person is that possessing awareness that others may be judging her because of her visibility may influence her thoughts, feelings, and behavior (Steele & Aronson, 1995). Visibly stigmatized individuals cannot use concealment of the stigma to cope with stereotypes and prejudice that their stigma may trigger. For example, a person with dark skin and American indigenous features may be a second or third generation American, yet in the eyes of nonracially stigmatized Americans, he may be perceived as a Mexican foreign national and discriminated against. Takaki (1993) captures the feeling experienced by many ethnic Americans in the following opening excerpt from his book:

> The rearview mirror reflected a White man in his forties. "How long have you been in this country?" he asked. "All my life," I replied wincing. "I was born in the United States." With a strong southern drawl, he remarked: "I was wondering because your English is excellent!" Then, as I had many times before, I explained: "My grandfather came here from Japan in the 1880s. My family has been here, in America, for over a hundred years." He glanced at me in the mirror. Somehow I did not look "American" to him; my eyes and complexion looked foreign. (p. 1)

People with nonvisible stigmas, such as members of certain ethnic groups, religious groups, or gay/lesbians have different concerns. Because their stigma is not visible, they can interact with others without their negative social identity filtering how everything about them is understood. Nevertheless, they are aware that they could be stigmatized if their devaluing attribute is discovered – they know that they are "discreditable" (Goffman, 1963). Thus, some individuals may carefully monitor the way they speak, dress and behave in order to maximize their chances of "passing" with the dominant group (Breakwell, 1986). Other individuals may actually make a conscious decision to display their stigma by wearing signs or symbols that convey their stigmatized identities, or engage in collective manifestations that demonstrate their identity with a stigmatized group (e.g., taking part in a gay pride parade or a United Farm Workers march).

In general, stigmatized individuals are aware of the negative connotations of their social identity in the eyes of members of the dominant group. For example, Casas, Ponterotto, and Sweeney (1987) reported that Mexican Americans believe that many non-Hispanic Whites hold negative views of their group. The age at which this awareness develops is not always clear, but it is likely to be well established by early adolescence (Quintana, Castaneda-English, & Ybarra, 1999). Although having a negative social identity may threaten both collective and personal self-esteem, it does not have to result in low personal or collective self-esteem (Crocker & Major, 1989). For example, Crocker, Luhtanen, Blaine, and Broadnax (1994) found that both Asian and especially Black college students believed their racial groups were evaluated negatively by members of the majority group; nonetheless, both Asian and Black students were as likely to evaluate their respective groups as positively as White students. Thus, while having a devalued social identity may create a challenge, stigmatized individuals respond to this predicament in a variety of ways. For instance, some "stigmatized" individuals can effectively defend their self-esteem from external threat while affirming their social identity with the group, but other individuals seek strategies to minimize their stigma.

In sum, Tajfel's theory of intergroup relations has served the purpose of generating considerable research on social identification among ethnic minority individuals. In addition, social cognition theory has provided powerful tools for understanding how different social groups interact with one another; aspects of this theoretical framework will guide the remainder of this chapter. In order to understand some of the complexity that surrounds ethnic identity and why it persists and where SIT fits, I will turn to a more detailed discussion of some critical elements that help explain how perceived discrimination plays a crucial role in the ethnic identity formation and maintenance that Latinos assume.

Effects of Social Stigma on the Individual

Stigmatized individuals are sensitive to information in their environment that affects the likelihood that negative reactions or evaluations from others are due to prejudice and discrimination (Crocker, Voekl, Testa, & Majors, 1991). In addition, attributions to discrimination may be very costly to interpersonal and working relationships (Crosby, 1982), such as the process that immigrants undergo to acquire competence in a new culture. Immigrants may be less motivated to engage in behaviors that will lead to acculturation if they have experienced discrimination directly or know other members of their group who were discriminated against by members of the dominant social group. When an immigrant becomes resistant to accommodation because of discrimination, unfortunately they lessen their opportunities for social mobility in the new culture.

One factor that may influence the willingness of stigmatized individuals to attribute negative outcomes to prejudice and discrimination is the perceived controllability of the stigma itself. Crocker and Major (1994) argued that individuals who believe that their stigmatization condition is under their control, or is their own fault, are less likely to blame negative outcomes associated with stigma on prejudice and discrimination because they feel they deserve those outcomes. Crocker et al. (1998) suggest that ideologies related to personal responsibility may predict which stigmatized individuals and groups are unwilling to blame negative outcomes on prejudice and discrimination. For example, Majors, Gramzow, McCoy, Levin, & Schmader (2002) found that the more Black, Latino, and Asian students believed that the American system is just (i.e., believed in individual social mobility, that hard work pays off, and that group differences in social status are fair), the less likely they were to perceive both themselves personally, and members of their ethnic group, as experiencing discrimination due to their ethnicity.

Salience of the stigmatized group identity, and the degree to which stigmatized individuals are highly identified with their group, also affect the extent to which they perceive themselves as targets of discrimination based on their group

membership Majors et al. (2002). Stigmatized individuals who are highly identified with their group are more likely to make intergroup comparisons, notice
intergroup inequalities, and label them as unjust. Consistent with this observation,
Majors et al. (2002) also found that the more highly identified students were with
their ethnic group, the more they said that they personally, and members of their
group, experienced discrimination based on their ethnicity. However, it is important to recognize that their consciousness of discrimination may have contributed
significantly to their enhanced social identity as a member of a stigmatized ethnic
group. Thus, feelings of perceived discrimination may be the fuel that triggers the
search for greater affinity to a heritage culture among later generation ethnics.
This mechanism then may explain the adherence to a Mexican heritage identity
found even among third and fourth generation Mexican Americans (Keefe &
Padilla, 1987).

One way in which members of stigmatized groups may protect their personal
self-esteem from the potentially painful consequences of upward social comparisons with advantaged out-group members is by restricting their comparisons to
others who share their stigmatized status. By coping in this way, the person is more
likely to compare with others whose outcomes are also likely to be relatively poor
(Crocker & Major, 1989; Gibbons, 1986; Jones et al., 1984; Major, 1987, 1994;
Tajfel & Turner, 1986). For example, there is substantial evidence that women who
work are more likely to compare their personal outcomes (e.g., lower wages) with
those of other women, rather than with those of men (Major, 1994; Zanna, Crosby,
& Lowenstein, 1986). Importantly, this has the effect of reducing perceptions of
wage discrimination between males and females and preserving some semblance of
self-esteem for women.

One reason people tend to make interpersonal comparisons with in-group rather
than out-group members is simple proximity – people who are similar to us tend to
be more readily available in our environments and hence more salient for social
comparison purposes (Runciman, 1966; Singer, 1981). The greater prevalence of
similarly stigmatized individuals in the immediate environment occurs both
because of forced segregation due to discrimination (e.g., in housing, schooling, or
employment), and because of preferences to affiliate with similar others (Schacter,
1959). Affiliation with others who are similarly stigmatized not only furnishes a
potentially less threatening comparison environment, but also provides the stigmatized with opportunities to be "off duty" from the attribution ambiguity, stereotype
threat, anxiety, and mindfulness that are likely to accompany interactions with the
nonstigmatized, socially dominant group.

The opportunity to be "off duty" while also meeting a variety of social needs
is probably one of the underlying reasons for why Latinos and other ethnic groups
gather in neighborhoods (e.g., Latino barrios, China towns, or little Saigons)
where there is proximity to people of the same group. University administrators
understand this well and make accommodations under the name of multiculturalism for the ever popular ethnically oriented theme houses and social clubs that
are no doubt due, in part, to the benefits accrued by ethnic students of affiliating
with others who share a stigmatizing attribute. Tatum (1997) shows that same

group affiliation allows individuals to relax from the stress of having to be vigilant about their behavior because of being on display as members of a minority group.

In an investigation of the contextual nature of social stigma and its effects, Brown (1998) assessed self-esteem and "possible selves" (Markus & Nurius, 1986) of students of color (Latino and African-American) and White students. Brown reported (Study 1) that the students of color had higher self-esteem and envisioned more positive future selves than did White students. However, in a follow-up study (Study 2) Brown asked students to imagine that they would be in a semester-long course with a White student or a student of color as the teaching assistant (TA). In this condition, students of color indicated more positive possible selves when they imagined having a TA who was ethnically similar than dissimilar to them. White students did not show a similar pattern when the hypothetical TA was also White, or when the expected interaction was of more limited duration (a single class).

Brown's study suggests that the effects of stigma on self-concept may be much more dependent on the particular features of the social context, resulting in temporary changes in the aspects of the self-concept that are activated. This may help explain why some stigmatized individuals make greater efforts to identify with their ethnic group if they experience long-term positive encounters with same ethnic group role models (e.g., teachers, counselors, physicians) and mentors.

The stigmatized person may also experience attribution ambiguity on occasion. That is, the stigmatized individual may be uncertain whether friendly or unfriendly behavior directed at them by a majority group member is a response to his or her social identity, or to personal, individual qualities (Crocker & Major, 1989; Crocker et al., 1991; Major & Crocker, 1993). In addition to these negative effects of attribution ambiguity, ambiguity about the causes of positive and negative outcomes may contribute to the motive to be reserved or to cope, by holding back in interpersonal interactions until the causes of the other person's positive or negative signals are known. Often individuals who are cautious about revealing or displaying their social identity remain "in the closet" in a manner of speaking. In other contexts (e.g., classroom) teachers have mistakenly labeled such individuals as shy and/or possessing a poor self-concept when the only thing operating was the student trying to determine how "safe" the teacher or the environment was for being ethnic. The likelihood of this mislabeling occurring is even more probable when students and teachers of the dominant social group surround the minority student who then feels overwhelmed and "unsafe."

Thus, negative stigma represents a potential threat to a person's sense of safety. Coping strategies such as in-group social comparisons, attributions to prejudice, and disengagement from the source of discrimination may enable stigmatized individuals to maintain a sense of self-worth in the face of devaluation. Stigma also denotes how we construe our social world. The construction of social identities, and the meanings associated with them, is a cognitive, sense-making process. The stereotypes that drive impressions, judgments, and behaviors toward stigmatized individuals are mental representations that make order of one's social world. Many of the predicaments of being stigmatized involve a self-consciousness of how one is thought of by others, and construal of the meaning and causes of others' behavior. Likewise, many of the strategies that the stigmatized use to cope with their predicaments emerge from interpretations of social contexts and social events.

I turn now to a social analysis of how Latinos experience their minority status and how they cope with stigma, prejudice, and discrimination. I will use the social cognition and identity framework summarized here. The goal is to present a fuller analysis of the social barriers faced by many Latinos as they strive to take their place as Americans along side other Americans who makeup the multicultural fabric that is America today.

Social Status of Latinos in the United States

Padilla (1980) and Keefe and Padilla (1987) in a study of acculturation of Mexican Americans described a model of acculturation characterized by two major constructs: *cultural awareness* (CA) and *ethnic loyalty* (EL). In the model, *CA* is the cognitive knowledge dimension that indicates what a person knows about his culture. This construct was made up of questions that assessed a respondents knowledge of history, art, and music of both Mexico and the United States; knowledge of current events that shape culture; and self-rated proficiency in Spanish and English. Differing from the awareness component is EL, which is the behavioral component of the acculturation model. This construct was measured with questions assessing a respondent's prefer-ences for using Spanish and English, language preference when listening to radio and television, Mexican oriented vs. American oriented leisure activities, food prefer-ences, ethnicity of friends, and preferred ethnicity in mate selection. The rationale was that the emotional affect that a person expresses toward a social group dictates the preferences a person holds toward activities and members of the ethnic group.

Based on data collected from a community sample of Mexican Americans span-ning four generations, Keefe and I tracked CA and EL across generations. This was important at the time because most work on acculturation had concentrated on only immigrants or their immediate offspring. Using our cross-sectional generational design, we found that CA decreased markedly between the first and second genera-tion and continued to decrease so that by the fourth generation our respondents possessed little knowledge of the culture of their great grandparents. However, we found that although there was a small decrease in *EL* between the first and second generation, there was almost no decrease in loyalty through the fourth generation. Interestingly, with the loss of specific cultural knowledge including a language shift to English, parents and grandparents had little heritage culture to transmit to their children and grandchildren. Thus, our later generation respondents compen-sated by transmitting more messages about EL and ethnic identification and less about actual cultural content. Arbona, Flores, and Novy (1995) and Montgomery (1992) replicated these findings with a college student population of Mexican American respondents in South Texas.

A major question of theoretical significance is why EL persists across generations in the face of decreasing or near total loss of Mexican oriented cultural knowledge. In our work, Keefe and I created typologies based on our respondents' scores on *CA* and *EL*. This enabled us to describe how respondents of different generations change in *CA* and how these individuals, nevertheless, manifest EL to a social group that they have been removed from physically in some cases by as much as 75–100 years when their great grandparents immigrated to the United States. Using cluster analysis, we identified five subgroups based on their scores on CA and EL. We called these five groups, respectively, La Raza, Changing Ethnics, Cultural Blends, Emerging Americans, and New Americans.

Extensive interviews carried out with the two groups that we designated as Cultural Blends and Emerging Americans revealed that these respondents held generally positive attitudes toward both Mexican and American culture and saw benefits in being active members of both cultures. These individuals reported varying degrees of proficiency in Spanish, but were mostly dominant English speakers. They spoke about the benefits of knowing two languages and some wished that they were more proficient in Spanish. They also spoke about the richness of their biculturalism in being able to celebrate American holidays such as July 4th, as well as Mexican holidays such as *Dia de los Muertos* (Day of the Dead). Our informants also shared how they actively transmitted information about their dual cultural membership to their own children. These informants discussed how they encouraged their children to be bilingual and how they modeled pride in their biculturalism. In the homes of these informants, we noted many Mexican cultural artifacts (e.g., statues of the Virgin of Guadalupe, the patroness saint of Mexico) along with displays of the American flag.

More importantly for purposes of our discussion here, informants spoke about experiences where they felt discriminated against by non-Hispanic Whites. Our respondents related experiences where they or close acquaintances had been the objects of negative stereotypes and prejudice. In support of our interview data, the quantitative analysis revealed that the higher our respondents scored on a measure of *perceived discrimination*, which was one of several subscales making up the EL dimension, the higher the respondents scored on EL. Our study also revealed that regardless of how seemingly bicultural and/or Americanized our respondents appeared, they were still relatively insulated within their ethnic group. For example, few had intimate friendships outside their ethnic group and most had only limited social contacts with non-Hispanics. This was true even though the more acculturated or bicultural an informant was the more likely he was to have coworkers from other ethnic groups. Therefore, while acculturation served to move our informants in the direction of American culture and to distance them from family and friends who were less acculturated, acculturation did not serve the purpose of enabling our respondents to become incorporated into a broader social network of nonethnics.

In order to explain why EL persists across generations, I propose a theory of ethnic identity based on social cognition, categorization, comparison, and dominance. This theory is an extension of a model William Perez and I proposed to explain how social cognition theory and stigma contribute to differential acculturation rates of Latinos (Padilla and Perez, 2003). Central to the theory is the role played by social stigma and perceived discrimination that give rise to a feeling of ethnic threat experienced by stigmatized peoples. The theory holds that the consequence of perceived discrimination is ethnic threat that motivates one person to identify as a member of an ethnic group and which leads another person to seek membership in the dominant group. In order to understand how perceived discrimination and ethnic threat operate in the theory some comments about stigma and the consequences of negative stigmatization are in order.

Stigma – skin color and phenotype. Unfortunately, in our acculturation research Keefe and I did not collect data on the skin color or phenotype of our respondents. We have no way to confirm our general impression that respondents who were more "Mexican" in their physical appearance also scored higher on our measure of perceived discrimination. However, such data do exist in a similar study of Mexican American ethnicity. In this study, Arce, Murguia, and Frisbie (1987) hypothesized that Mexican Americans with a European physical appearance (phenotype) would have more enhanced life opportunities as measured by socioeconomic status than Mexican Americans with an indigenous Native American phenotype. To test their hypothesis, Arce and colleagues gathered skin color and phenotype information as part of a national survey of nearly one thousand respondents of Mexican heritage. In this face-to-face survey, the interviewer rated the interviewee's skin color on a 5-point scale from "Very Light" to "Very Dark." Interviewee's phenotype was judged as "Very European," "European," "Medium," "Indian," and "Very Indian." The findings supported the hypothesis that respondents classified as light skinned and European in phenotype reported more total years of education, higher income, and a lower perception of past discrimination than respondents classified as dark skinned and Indian in phenotype. Arce et al. noted that the darker and more Indian the phenotype of the respondents, the more likely they were to report incidents of discrimination from the majority group against them directly or toward other Mexican Americans. Importantly, these individuals also reported that they were more aligned socially and politically with their Mexican heritage, regardless of their generation. Analysis of these same data revealed that among US born Latino males, those with dark skin and a more Indian phenotype reported higher depression even after controlling for education, family income, and proficiency in English (Codina & Montalvo, 1994).

In another study, Vazquez, Vazquez, Bauman, and Sierra (1997) examined the effects of skin color on acculturation. The participants in their study were 102 Mexican American undergraduate students at a southwestern university. Results indicated that students with the darkest skin (as *self-reported*) had significantly lower levels of acculturation (on the heritage-culture/mainstream culture continuum) than those with lighter skin. Vasquez et al. hold that if a Mexican American experiences discrimination, the incentives to master English and the opportunities to interact with non-Hispanics may be limited. Interestingly, among the Mexican-oriented students, those with the darker skin were more interested in the Latino community, while the darker skinned Anglo-oriented Mexican students showed the least interest in the Latino community. Vazquez et al. interpreted these findings to mean that individuals who identify with the mainstream group and whose physical appearance is dissimilar from the mainstream group may adopt a strategy to ensure their assimilation into the dominant social group by exhibiting few other traits (such as adherence to the Latino culture) that could mark them as outsiders.

Gómez (2000) analyzed data from the Boston Social Survey Data of Urban Inequality, conducted in 1993 and 1994. Of the total 1,820 respondents in the study, 353 were Latinos. As in the Arce et al. (1987) study, interviewers rated the skin color of their interviewees. Gómez found that lighter skinned Latinos had more education, were more likely to own their homes, were more likely to be married, and used Spanish more often as a language for communication than their darker skinned counterparts. This last finding is similar to Vasquez et al., if a dark skinned Latino wants to "fit into the dominant group" it is best to minimize stigmatizing conditions. Since little can be done about skin color, it is possible to use more English to not draw attention to oneself. However, the only statistically significant variable was hourly wage. This difference was still significant after controlling for education. Thus, the results from the Gómez study affirm that skin color matters in the life chances of Latinos in the United States, with darker skin color negatively influencing earnings.

Two studies (Espino & Franz, 2002; Mason, 2004) used data from the Latino National Political Survey (LNPS) to report on the occupational status and income differentials of Latinos of different phenotype and skin coloration. The LNPS is a probability sample of the three largest Latino groups and consisted of 1,546 Mexicans, 589 Puerto Ricans, and 682 Cubans interviewed in 1989–1990. In this study, respondents agreed to a face-to-face interview that explored a number of social and political issues. At the conclusion of the study the interviewer also recorded the skin color of the respondent using a 1–5 scale: one being "very dark" and five being "very light."

Espino and Franz (2002) reported that Mexican and Cuban individuals who are lighter skinned had higher occupational prestige jobs than their darker skinned counterparts. Although a similar finding was found for Puerto Ricans the difference was not statistically significant. Using the same LNPS survey, Mason (2004) analyzed for differences in earnings among the three Latino groups using skin color, acculturation, and language as predictor variables. Mason reported that light skin Mexican Americans on an annual basis earned $4,065 more than medium-skin-color Mexican Americans, while dark skinned persons earned $2,285 less than medium-skin colored persons. Similar statistically significant earning differentials were found for Cuban Americans, but not for Puerto Ricans. Mason also found that there was a significant earnings incentive for Mexican and Cuban Americans favoring acculturation (adopting English as the preferred language) and adopting a non-Hispanic White racial identity. However, the incentive for abandoning Spanish and a specific Hispanic racial self-identity was not sufficient to overcome the penalties associated with having a dark complexion and non-European phenotype.

Tafoya (2004) reported on an analysis of 2,000 census data and a national study of Hispanics conducted in 2002 by the Pew Foundation. The census counted 35 million Hispanics and asked them to identify along racial lines: White, Black, Asian, American Indian, or some other race. Approximately, 48% or 17 million people indicated that they were White, and 42% or nearly 15 million individuals indicated that they were of "some other race." Importantly, among US born Latinos, those individuals who indicated their race was "White" on the census had higher social status, higher levels of civic participation, and a stronger sense of acceptance. On the other hand, those individuals who replied "some other race" typically had lower socioeconomic status than self-reported White Hispanics. For instance, among respondents 25 years and older, 54% of the "some other race" group had less than a high school education, compared with 44% of "White" Latinos. Further, Latinos who chose "some other race" were more likely than White Hispanics to be in poverty (24% vs. 20%). According to the Pew national survey data, 23% of White Hispanics reported that they only spoke English, compared with 16% of "some other race" Hispanics. The survey also found that more White Hispanics (81%) than "some other race" Hispanics (66%) had ever voted.

Whether a person was born in the United States or immigrated was important in knowing if a person identified as White or some other race – 46% of foreign-born Latinos identified as "some other race" compared to 40% for US born Latinos. Interesting too was the fact that the Pew national survey data revealed that US born children of immigrants more often identified as White than their foreign born parents, and the percent who indicate White for race was higher still among the grandchild of immigrants.

To summarize, the available research on the impact of skin color on the life chances of Latinos indicates that, even after controlling for background variables such as education, age, and English proficiency, darker skinned and more Indian-looking Latinos had lower educational and economic attainment than lighter skinned Latinos. This may also explain why Twenge and Crocker (2002) in a meta-analysis of race and self-esteem found that Black and Hispanic self-esteem was higher in groups with high socioeconomic status.

The findings here support the contention made by Portes and Rumbaut (2001) that newcomers pay a penalty for being immigrants or later generation ethnics, especially if they differ in phenotype from the host society, and even a greater penalty for being darker and more Indian-looking (or Asian or African) in phenotype. The cost is both *psychological* and *economic*. The psychological cost involves stigmatization and the ensuing perception of discrimination. The economic cost means that because of greater stigma the lower the human capital that the person is able to acquire that is necessary for social mobility in the American context of structural assimilation. Tafoya (2004) sums up her findings in this way:

> For Latinos the concept of race appears to extend beyond biology, ancestral origins or a history of grievance in this country. The differences in characteristics and attitudes between those Hispanics who call themselves White and those who identity as some other race, suggests they experience racial identity as a measure of belonging: Feeling White seems to be a reflection of success and a sense of inclusion. The fact that changeable characteristics such as income help determine racial identification among Latinos, versus permanent markers such as skin color does not necessarily mean that color lines in American society are fading. On the contrary, these findings show that color has a broader meaning. The Latino experience demonstrates that Whiteness remains an important measure of belonging, stature and acceptance. And, Hispanic views of race also show that half of this ever larger segment of the U.S. population is feeling left out (p. 3)

This leads naturally to a discussion of perceived discrimination. Were the informants in the Keefe and Padilla (1987) study justified in reporting discrimination in their environment? In addition, how do individuals assess perceived discrimination and cope with instances of discrimination directed at them or other members of their ethnic community?

Perceived Discrimination and Ethnic Threat

When a stigmatized person becomes aware of his/her stigma and how it is used by others to evaluate him/her or other members of the group negatively, this has adverse psychological affects on the individual. If the stigmatized person assesses the discriminatory act as negative and hurtful, the person may experience a range of emotions such as feelings of depersonalization, lack of belonging, anger, frustration, and depression. In addition, if the person experiences negative evaluations because of the stigma associated with their ethnic group from multiple sources – peers, teachers, mass media – the person may also experience an increased arousal level in similar social contexts in which they have felt threatened on other occasions. Thus, highly stigmatized individuals may experience generalized threat in many social contexts.

Because stereotyping is associated with self-identity and group membership through the common underlying process of social categorization and comparison, social identity must inevitably be influenced by motivational factors involved in self-conceptualization and identity construction. Thus, it is clear why in-group stereotypes tend to be favorable and out-group ones derogatory and unfavorable: self-categorization imbues the self with all the attributes of the group, and so it is important that such attributes are ones that reflect well on the self. Thus, people (and social groups) are highly motivated to achieve wide social acceptance and to emphasize those dimensions which reflect well on the in-group and which differentiate them from the out-group.

The effects of perceived discrimination and ethnic threat may increase if friends and acquaintances who are members of the dominant group do not validate the stigmatized person's perceptions. It is not uncommon for the stigmatized person who is conscious of how his/her stigma is used to categorize and/or compare him/her unfavorably to hear disclaimers about his feelings of perceived discrimination by friends who do not share their stigma. Beschloss (2002) relates a good example of this in his account of Eleanor Roosevelt's interaction with her Jewish friend Elinor Morgenthau, the wife of Henry Morgenthou, Jr. The Morgenthaus were friends and neighbors of the Roosevelts, and Mr. Morgenthou was Secretary of the Treasury under President Roosevelt. Although the women were good friends, Beschloss writes:

> Having shed the genteel anti-Semitism of her class, Mrs. Roosevelt took care to shield her Jewish friend from social slights. She once wrote to another friend, who was Protestant, "You are worse than Elinor Morgenthau and haven't the reason!" When Mrs. Morgenthau was blackballed from membership in the elite Colony Club of New York, Mrs. Roosevelt

resigned in protest. ... Still, Mrs. Roosevelt was exasperated that Elinor felt social discrimination that the First Lady considered to be only in her head. "I have always felt you were hurt often by imaginary things and have wanted to protect you." She once wrote her. "But if one is to have a healthy relationship ... it must be on some kind of equal basis. You simply cannot be so easily hurt. Life is too short to cope with it." (p. 47–48)

Thus, while Mrs. Roosevelt was trying to be helpful on the one hand, she also offered up the suggestion that much of what Mrs. Morgenthau believed was mere "imaginary." The idea that anti-Semitism and other racist behaviors never occurred or were taken out of context is a common occurrence and often offered by very well intentioned individuals. Denials of the existence of discrimination directed at a person directly or to members of one's ethnic group can heighten the person's anxiety because it is easily possible to believe that perhaps one is being too sensitive and that friends and acquaintances are correct that one is just imaging discrimination where none exists. Also operating is the matter of self-evaluation and the need to evaluate one's self in positive terms against the conflicting feelings of discrimination and the messages that the stigmatized person is just imaging racism where none exists.

According to the theory proposed here the continuation of perceived discrimination creates a condition of ethnic threat. Ethnic Threat comes about when the person has a heightened awareness of the salience of his or her "stigma" and how members of the dominant group use stigma to make negative evaluations of self, other members of a person's ethnic group, and the ethnic group itself. Ethnic threat occurs because the discriminatory acts challenge the integrity of a person's self-esteem and their relationship to their ethnic group. The threat challenges the self-worth of the person and their group.

Importantly, perceived discrimination and feelings of ethnic threat do not come about merely through overt or explicit acts of discrimination against the self or members of one's group. Some ethnic individuals state that they sometimes "just know that another person" is evaluating them negatively because of their stigma. This heightened awareness of discrimination is often downplayed as mentioned earlier in the case of Mrs. Roosevelt. It is one thing to be able to point to explicit or overt acts of discrimination, but what about the more subtle messages that members of minority groups sometimes claim that they sense in their interactions with nonminority individuals. Is there any basis for such claims?

Explicit and Implicit Bias

Although acts of blatant discrimination are less common today, discriminatory practices are still prevalent. Evidence of racism abounds in the stereotypical images of people of color in the media, housing discrimination, documented racial bias in lending practices, and racial tracking in schools. Research has found that the majority of African Americans report experiencing discrimination in the last year and most reported negotiating daily discrimination (Feagin, 1991; Feagin & Sikes, 1994;

Landrine & Klonoff, 1996; Swim, Cohen, & Hyers, 1998). Sellers and Shelton (2003) report that for the majority of people of color racial discrimination is still pervasive.

Though private beliefs about race have improved (Schuman, Steeh, Bobo, & Krysan, 1997), people still associate African Americans with low intelligence, hostility, aggression, and violence (Devine & Elliot, 1995) and describe Latinos as unintelligent, antisocial, and lacking ambition (Cowan, Martinez, & Mendiola 1997; Neimann, Pollack, Rogers, & O'Connor, 1998). Kao (2000), through her conversations with African American, Asian, White, and Latino high school students received similar reports of stereotypic group images from adolescents. These youth described African Americans as poor in academics and Latinos as manual laborers with little academic ambition, yet described Whites and Asians as educated and ambitious. These youth tended to categorize Whites and Asians together while combining Blacks and Latinos in their thinking about group stereotypes. These recent studies provide clear evidence that racial stereotypes persist. Today political correctness likely masks how people really feel about members of different ethnic and racial groups. Often people do not want to appear biased when they actually are, or they might not realize the extent of their own biases.

Studies are beginning to show that in today's climate of political correctness a person's self-presentational concerns may inhibit them from revealing prejudicial feelings and stereotyped thoughts on self-report measures that are straightforward and transparent (Fazio, Jackson, Dunton, & Williams, 1995; Greenwald & Banaji, 1995). So rather than relying on explicit measures of bias (e.g., social distance), more accurate assessments of prejudice and stereotyping can be obtained from measures that are less influenced by the conscious control of test takers. These more indirect, or implicit, measures include techniques that involve cognitive priming and, the implicit association test (IAT) (Greenwald, McGhee, & Schwartz, 1998). The IAT involves making quick judgments about stimuli-flashed on a computer screen. On some critical trials, the judgments made are congruent with a hypothesized bias, such as prejudicial feelings toward, or stereotyped beliefs about, members of an ethnic group. For example, in one version of the test respondents press one key if a word that appears on the computer screen is either unpleasant (e.g., assault) or a typical first name of a Hispanic male (e.g., Miguel). They press another key if the word is either pleasant (e.g., peace) or a common first name of a White male (e.g., John). On other critical trials, the judgments to be made are incongruent with the hypothesized bias. For example, the respondents are to press one key if the word on the screen is either unpleasant or a name commonly given to a person who is White and to press another key if the word is either pleasant or a name commonly given to Latino. The assumption underlying the test is that if a respondent is biased then he or she should take less time to make judgments that are congruent with their bias than to make judgments that are incongruent with the bias. For example, providing evidence for prejudice against Blacks, White college students were quicker to respond on judgments congruent with prejudicial feelings than they were on judgments incongruent with such feelings (Greenwald et al.).

In a recent study, Weyant (2005) employing non-Hispanic White college students adapted the IAT to test for belief in a stereotype that Hispanics are, compared to Whites, relatively unintelligent. Respondents were exposed to words that are either indicative of intelligence (e.g., brainy) or lack of intelligence (e.g., dull) and to first names that are commonly given to Hispanics or to non-Hispanic Whites. In the study, respondents also received an explicit measure of social distance when they completed a modified version of the Bogardus Social Distance Scale that asked about the respondent's willingness to associate with Hispanics through marriage, dating, close friendships, as neighbors, or as coworkers. The findings revealed that the IAT successfully detected stereotypic beliefs that Hispanics were less intelligent than Whites were and high scores on the IAT were also associated with greater preferred distance from Hispanics.

In a review of implicit measures in social cognition research, Fazio and Olson (2003) discuss microbehaviors that have been found to be associated with various implicit procedures used to assess racial attitudes. Some of the microbehaviors that have been detected when more biased Whites are observed with Blacks include: less touching, greater sitting distance from target, less eye contact, less smiling, less extemporaneous social comments, more speech errors, more speech hesitations, and greater body tension. In one such study Vanman, Paul, Ito, and Miller (1997) showed that by using an explicit and an implicit technique for assessing racial bias they produced contradictory findings. When Vanman et al. asked White participants to rate photos of Whites and Blacks for friendliness there was an apparent bias in favor of Blacks. With the photos of Blacks rated as friendlier than photos of White. However, when an implicit measure of bias was carried out by recording facial electromyography (EMG) which measures activity of muscles used in facial expressions at the same time as the respondents completed an explicit rating task on the photos a different finding revealed racial bias. In this case, facial EMG activity showed a contradictory finding indicating a bias in favor of the White photographs. Thus, White participants in this study were saying one thing overtly, but possibly unconsciously signaling a different message through their facial expressions. In a followup study, Vanman, Saltz, Nathan, and Warren (2004) followed a similar procedure, but in addition asked their White respondents to decide on who should be awarded a teaching fellowship. In this experimental study, vignettes containing similar qualifications for the fellowship were prepared for White and black "applicants." In addition, photos of White and black applicants were included with the bogus application files. The findings showed that White participants who exhibited higher levels of EMG activity in the facial cheek region (i.e., White bias) when they viewed pictures of White rather than black fellowship applicants were more likely to choose the White "applicant" for the teaching fellowship. Interestingly, this finding was obtained with White students who exhibited little apparent prejudice against African Americans on an explicit measure of bias.

In a recently published study, Wheeler and Fiske (2005) used functional magnetic resonance imaging (fMRI) to compare brain activity in the amygdala region of the brain with White participants during presentation of black and White faces. During the presentation of the facial stimuli subjects were asked to perform three different types of tasks: social neutral visual search (find a dot on the face), social categorization (judge whether the person is over age 21), and social individuation (decide whether the person likes a particular type of vegetable). In a second experiment words were used to prime racial stereotypes (African American positive and negative stereotypes: musical, athletic, loud, and lazy). Wheeler and Fiske found that when subjects processed the photos as simple visual stimuli or for the individuation task, the response of the amygdala was essentially the same for the White and black photos. However, when subjects viewed White and black photos and were required to make social categorization judgments a different pattern of amygdala activity emerged with different parts of the amygdale "turning on" to the different photos. The relevance is that the amygdala is involved in sensing, relaying, and learning about potential danger represented by stimuli, regardless of whether the learning occurs through direct experience with the aversive stimulus or indirectly by expressed fear or anger through others' facial expressions. This type of amygdala activation, however, occurs only when deep cognitive processing is required as seen in the social categorization task (Wheeler & Fiske).

The importance of distinguishing here between explicit and implicit measures of racial attitudes and microbehaviors is that it is common knowledge that ethnic people are often aware of these more subtle indices of intergroup relations. Although they may not be able readily to describe what cues they are attending to when they sense threat, the person who says that they perceive discrimination is likely reporting accurately. Clearly, it is important to find an empirical methodology for studying what cues ethnic individual are attending to when they report discomfort due to subtle forms of discrimination. The challenge too is to understand how well intentioned people who may quite truthfully report that they are not biased still manage to communicate their subconscious feelings of in-group and out-group bias. Further, when including this fact in the context of perceived discrimination and ethnic threat, these microbehaviors are what the ethnic person is detecting when they believe Whites evaluate them negatively. There is still no empirical basis for this assertion, but there is anecdotal evidence for this in the life experiences of minority individuals.

In today's climate of political correctness, it is these much more subtle microbehaviors that give a person's true racial attitudes away. However, it also places a much more difficult burden on the ethnic person to "prove" that they are justified in feeling that they are being discriminated against. These feelings of being the target of negative evaluations are also more likely to be present in the experiences of individuals who carry more stigmas attached to their ethnicity and/or race. Simultaneously, stigmatized individuals are more likely to have their feelings that Whites are judging them negatively denied by both less stigmatized and more assimilated coethnics and by sympathetic Whites. However, this is an area of future research that remains to be investigated. There is some suggestion in the ethnic socialization literature that parents enable children to detect both explicit and implicit forms of racial bias.

Socialization Around Race and Prejudice

African American parents transmit information about racism to their children that they received from their own parents (e.g., Hughes & Johnson, 2001; Spencer, 1983; Thornton, 1997). Moreover, if parents have experienced overt racism and if they also felt that their children had been treated unfairly because of their race, they were significantly more likely to engage in cultural transmissions about race group history and heritage, while also teaching about prejudice and discrimination – a form of socialization for racism (Hughes & Jackson).

In a similar fashion, Phinney and Chavira (1995) report that Mexican American, African American, and Japanese American parents stated that in their ethnic socialization of children they felt compelled to instill pride in their heritage while also having conversations with them about ethnic discrimination that they might confront in the future. Also Knight et al. (1993), in a study of 45 dyads of Mexican American English speaking mothers and their 6–10-year-old children, reported that mothers discussed issues of ethnic discrimination and prejudice with their children. However, the way in which these cultural and discrimination focused messages occurred was not straightforward, but was very much connected to a bundle of variables associated with the mothers' cultural and familial circumstance. Specifically, mothers who were more comfortable with their Mexican cultural background and less comfortable with the majority culture and whose husbands' families had resided in the United States for fewer generations were more likely to instill Mexican culture in their children while also transmitting more messages about ethnic pride and discrimination in their young children. As for the children in these dyads, Knight et al. found that children whose mothers were comfortable with their Mexican background used more ethnic labels to describe themselves and importantly knew more about their culture, reported engaging in ethnic behaviors, and were more likely to prefer ethnic foods, friends, and social activities.

In a study that used a similar methodology to that of Knight et al. (1993) and Quintana and Vera (1999) found that their 7–11-year-old children had a sophisticated understanding of the ethnic prejudice they faced. This in turn was associated with higher levels of ethnic knowledge and ethnic identification. Parental ethnic socialization was not predictive of understanding prejudice in this study, but it did relate significantly with ethnic knowledge. Thus, the developmental process suggests that children learn about their cultural heritage from their parents. Further, as they mature cognitively, they are increasingly able to understand the meaning of prejudice and how their ethnic group may be the target of discrimination. The result of this process is that young persons emerge with a sharpened sense of their ethnic identity that takes form through ethnic-related socializing experiences with parents, family members, and peers.

In a related study that examined the role of ethnic and social perspective taking abilities and parental ethnic socialization, Quintana et al. (1999) found that parental ethnic socialization was positively correlated with ethnic identity achievement among a population of mostly third and later generation Mexican American adolescents. However, the ability to take a different perspective was linked developmentally to cognitive processes, and not to ethnic socialization. Quintana et al. speculate that higher levels of ethnic perspective taking reflect higher cognitive processing and that these are related to self-protective properties found among stigmatized groups. Specifically, adolescents with a high level of ethnic perspective taking understand that negative feedback about their ethnicity or ethnic group is likely due to ethnic prejudice on the part of members of the dominant social group. It is still not well understood how an adolescent's higher cognitive processing, and not ethnic socialization, comes to offer this self-protective function. In addition, research on ethnic identity among children and adolescents has not included skin color and other measures of observable stigma as variables to determine their relationship to ethnic identity. At least one tenable hypothesis is that more stigmatized Latino parents will engage in more socializing of children on themes of race, ethnicity, and discrimination and this in turn will culminate in children who are more astute in recognizing the explicit and implicit prejudicial types of behaviors.

Coping Strategies to Minimize Ethnic Threat

A person's social identity is threatened if he believes he has been or will be evaluated negatively because of his racial and/or ethnic group. This is the most frequent outcome of perceived discrimination. Breakwell (1986) describes intrapsychic and intergroup coping strategies that a person engages in when her identity is threatened. According to Breakwell intrapsychic coping strategies include deflection (e.g., denial, adoption of an unreal self, fantasy), acceptance (e.g., anticipatory restructuring of identity, compartmentalism, compromise), and reevaluation (e.g., reevaluate the content of identity, change the criteria for judging identity characteristics, challenge the right of other people to make judgments about one's identity). In this last strategy, the stigmatized individual takes the position that negative social cognitions and evaluations of his/her group would be different if the persons holding the negative evaluation possessed the stigma themselves. This is akin to the saying "don't criticize me unless you intend to walk in my shoes." Here, the member of a stigmatized ethnic group may be involved in activities aimed at recasting the image of the ethnic group held by the majority group.

Perspectives that rely on intrapsychic coping strategies are not new. For many years, Stonequist's (1937) theory of the marginal person, based on an examination of intrapsychic coping strategies he observed among Jews, Blacks, and immigrants, was widely cited. According to Stonequist, the person who experienced threat to his social identity because of stigma and/or lower social status was prone to psychological instability if she/he could not easily assimilate into the high status group. Historically, this analysis is important because it varies to a considerable extent from the contemporary analysis of the motivation, context, and outcome of ethnic identity discussed here. The "marginal" person model advanced by Stonequist was the generally accepted view for more than half a century. Despite repeated criticisms about the lack of scientific evidence for marginality and the vagueness of the concept (e.g., Green, 1947; Mann, 1973); the ideas emanating from the concept of marginality are still present in some current models of accul- turation (Berry, 2003). However, Del Pilar and Udasco (2004) in a critique of the concept of marginality conclude:

> Marginality has endured because it seems logical and reasonable and makes common sense. This may explain the resistance in the field to contrary evidence about marginality's valid- ity. We found whole lines of investigation that are anchored by slender threads of theory. Being caught between cultures frequently does result in difficulties and adjustment prob- lems. The marginality investigators failed to note that these difficulties and adjustment problems can take as many negative forms as are discussed in the voluminous diagnostic manual of psychiatric problems or as many positive forms as are reflected in the biographies of successful immigrants. Despite the wishes of the marginality researchers, one concept cannot hope to cover all these variables. (p. 11)

Thus, it is important to recognize intrapsychic coping strategies when examining individual and collective efforts to minimize ethnic threat; however, to pathologize these coping strategies by labeling the person or group as "marginal" is to overly simplify a complex process of intergroup interactions between dominant and sub- ordinate individuals.

It is important to place our understanding of intrapsychic strategies for coping with ethnic threat in the broader context of intergroup relations between Latinos and majority group members. The theory of ethnic threat presented here argues that Latinos generally show one of three strategies in coping with discrimination and racism: social activism, assimilation (passing), and multiple group memberships/ biculturalism. Importantly, these coping strategies do not exist in a zero-sum man- ner and their associated social identities are not necessarily mutually exclusive. However, the theory maintains that person characteristics such as skin color and physical features (i.e., stigma) may predispose the person toward one strategy more than another. This is because individuals who are darker and more indigenous look- ing experience greater explicit and implicit forms of discrimination and have fewer options available to them in terms of social identity (Arce et al., 1987; Keefe & Padilla, 1987; Tafoya, 2004).

Ethnic Identity With and Without Social Activism

One strategy for coping with prejudice and discrimination that challenge a person's self-esteem or the integrity of the social group to which a person belongs is to assert one's ethnic identity. In addition to this, the person can also decide whether to con- front those individuals or groups that are discriminating against them. Confrontation can move from the level of individual action against the aggressor to a group or collective social movement. Social movements occur when a large number of peo- ple who are bound together by a common purpose or "essence," like ethnicity and race, join together to solve a collective problem such as unequal treatment, discriminatory practices and policies, and racism. The goal of a social movement is to bring about social change. We can point to the Civil Rights Movement generally and in the context of people of Mexican heritage to the Chicano Movement for examples of this behavior.

Social activism is energized because ethnic threat is aversive, especially if the ethnic group's core values are attacked. Further, social activists are likely to become more secure in their ethnic identity and activism if three conditions are met: (1) the person experiences racism directly, (2) there is a supportive group of coethnics who gather for mutual social support, and (3) the activism results in some measurable positive social change. Importantly, persons who choose social activism as their primary strategy for confronting injustice and discrimination against them or their ethnic group may also prefer to associate with other members of their ethnic group. It is a mistake, however, to label such ethnics as possessing a "separatist" orientation (e.g., Berry, 2003).

A coping strategy involving social activism and an orientation of exclusivity for the ethnic group to which one belongs can be explained in two ways. First, as mentioned earlier, individuals who are easily categorized because of skin color and physiognomy experience more instances of real or perceived discrimination and understandably feel more comfortable with members of their own ethnic group where they do not have to be on guard for attacks on their group (Tatum, 1997). Thus, just because the ethnic person expresses a preference to be with members of her own group does not mean that the person completely endorses an exclusive separatist orientation. In this same fashion, a White person whose primary social support group consists of other Whites is not espousing a racist philosophy because of their same racial group friendships (Tatum, 1997).

Another perspective on social activism as a coping strategy is that the label "social activist" can be the basis for another way of categorizing people negatively. Ironically, the US Constitution guarantees justice and equality for all, but often when minority individuals seek social change to remedy injustices they are labeled radicals, leftist, communist, or separatists. We do not have to look very hard to see how some members of the dominant social group denigrated the social activism of Martin Luther King, Jr. or Cesar Chavez. According to Brewer (1993) and optimal distinctiveness theory, minority group members who embrace their minority identity in response to feeling overly distinctive risk losing whatever positive evaluation was being accorded them by the majority group. In sum, the person who meets ethnic threat via social activism is likely to experience even greater discrimination and threat because of their actions. This is why social support from like-minded individuals becomes so important for maintaining self-esteem and ethnic pride.

There are individuals who because of ethnic threat identify strongly with their ethnic group, but who either do not engage in social activism or do so only sporadically. There are several interpretations for their behavior. First, these individuals may not enjoy a support group that reinforces the idea of activism, and therefore, they may feel greater reluctance to protest discrimination in fear of even greater reprisal because of their ethnicity. Second, such individuals may not have the human capital in the form of education and knowledge of the legal and political system to know how to assert their civil rights. However, once they are taught their civil rights and how to obtain support from others they are likely to increase their orientation toward greater social activism. Finally, there are likely personality traits related to whether or not a person has the capacity to confront prejudice and discrimination. Research is lacking on personality variables associated with social activism.

In sum, there is still much that we must learn about social activism as a coping strategy for dealing with ethnic threat. Although there is a long history of social activism among Latinos to social injustices directed at them, there is a scarcity of research on the psychology of threat and coping. We will now turn to another form of coping that is the opposite of social activism.

Assimilation and Efforts to "Pass"

A second coping strategy for overcoming ethnic threat is to seek ways to integrate into the dominant social group. There is a long history, for example, of people using "passing" as one strategy for coping (Winter & DeBose, 2003). According to Breakwell (1986), passing "refers to the process of gaining access to a group or social category ... by camouflaging one's group origins." (p. 116) How success-fully a person is able to camouflage his/her group origin depends obviously on the stigma s/he manifests (e.g., skin color and physical features). Thus, very light skinned, mixed race individuals have the best chance of "passing," if they chose to do, so because their stigma is less visible than other members of their group (Goffman, 1963). Passing can be a suitable strategy for some individuals; however, it also entails risks if the person's "true identity" is discovered. Thus, the potential for fear of discovery that is engendered by "passing" as a coping response may be as harmful, psychologically, to the person as enduring the negative social evalua-tions that occur in a race conscious society.

Another strategy in this same domain is for the person to assimilate culturally and socially into the dominant group. There are two forms of assimilation. In the first, a person passes into the group by "blending in" and not calling attention to their ethnic heritage. This may include not speaking the heritage language, chang-ing one's name, and acquiring all the behaviors of the dominant group. In the sec-ond, the person does not deny their racial/ethnic heritage, but rather seeks to set it aside in order to acquire the dominant culture; thereby, attempting to gather social acceptance and inclusion from the dominant group. This conformity to the domi-nant group is a predicted outcome of optimal distinctiveness theory (Brewer, 1991, 1993; Tafarodi, Kang, & Milne, 2002) where the self-perceived physical distinc-tiveness induces in the minority person the need for belonging to the dominant group. In this situation, acculturation to the dominant group represents a form of conformity to the high status group.

Immigrants predominantly from Europe (Feagin & Feagin, 2003) used this strat-egy of conforming to the dominant group successfully during the early part of the twentieth century. The question often heard today is why immigrants from Asia and Latin America have not adopted this strategy. According to the theory of ethnic threat posited here assimilation works well when the stigma of skin color and physiognomy deviate very little from the majority group. The greater the disparity in color and physical features between the minority and majority group, the more difficult complete assimilation is, even when the person has conformed completely to the values, behaviors, and life style of the majority culture (Tafarodi et al., 2002). Remember the conversation between Ron Takaki and his taxi cab driver (refer to p. 16) where because of the shape of his eyes and complexion, the taxi cab driver asked Takaki how long he had been in the United States. Obviously, Takaki, who is an American citizen by birth, did not look "American" enough for the cab driver.

In a discussion of assimilation, Schaefer (2004) notes that assimilation is difficult for the minority individual because while it is encouraged by the dominant group it comes with a conflicting message. As Schaefer states:

> In the United States, dominant White society encourages assimilation. The assimilation perspective tends to devalue alien culture and to treasure the dominant. For example, assimilation assumes that whatever is admirable among Blacks was adapted from Whites and that whatever is bad is inherently Black. The assimilation solution to Black–White conflict is the development of a consensus around White American values. (p. 25)

Thus, while not impossible to assimilate, some ethnic minority individuals are able to overcome the odds and assimilate, but the majority group often views them as the exception. Interestingly, these "exceptions" often internalize the negative stereotypes attributed to their group and are as likely to discriminate against members of their own group, as are members of the majority group. Schaefer points out that "Members of the subordinate group who choose not to assimilate look on those who do as deserters." (p. 26) There is some justification in this labeling as shown by Vazquez et al. (1997) who reported that highly acculturated dark-skinned Mexican American students had little ethnic community involvement, suggesting that the more salient a person's physical features, the more they have to overcompensate by disregarding most, if not all vestiges of the culture of origin. In sum, assimilation is not easy, as Schaefer states. Assimilation involves having to gain acceptance from the majority group while at times enduring disparaging comments about one's origins. At the same time, it also may engender distrust from members of the ethnic group, especially if the person attempting assimilation is at the same time deliberating placing social distance between himself and his ethnic heritage community.

Multiple Group Membership and Biculturalism

The third intergroup coping strategy is what Breakwell (1986) terms multiple group membership. Because most people are members of different social groups simultaneously, the belief is that with a carefully balanced mix of social group memberships, a person can be protected from the threat that may occur because of the stigma attached to any one of the groups. Biculturalism builds on the idea of multiple group membership. Many ethnic individuals, especially second and later generation individuals, find that biculturalism is an appropriate strategy for coping with discriminatory practices directed at one's ethnic group. Biculturalism is a more adaptable strategy for confronting ethnic threat than is assimilation because it allows the person the flexibility to be both a member of their ethnic heritage culture while also having the cultural competence to profit from their knowledge of the dominant social group (LaFromboise, Coleman, & Gerton, 1993; Padilla, 1994).

Biculturalism is not as easy a road to travel as it might seem. The bicultural person must keep a mental calculus of different social groups and their members (e.g., family, peer groups, clubs, coworkers, etc.) and operate within the acceptable cultural style of behavior of each. Biculturalism too is easier when the boundaries between cultural groups are more permeable and when conflict between groups is minimal. In fact, the truly bicultural person is often capable of bringing members of different racial and/or ethnic groups' together and minimizing conflict because the bicultural person understands the value and behavioral systems of each group and knows how to transverse the sensitive intersects between the various groups. The personal effectiveness is even greater when these cultural brokers are trusted members of both the dominant and subordinate social groups. Thus, the bicultural person is often able to make the social boundaries between distinct groups more permeable by bringing different people together to talk and learn about each other without categorizing and engaging in negative social evaluations.

Hong, Morris, Chiu, and Benet-Martinez (2000) in a study with Chinese–American biculturals showed how cultural meaning systems guide sociocognitive processes that allow biculturals to switch between their different cultural orientations. In addition, Haritatos and Benet-Martinez (2002) have expanded this view of biculturalism by identifying two forms of bicultural integration. Bicultural individuals high on integration envision their two cultural orientations in nonconflictual terms and move with fluidity between both worlds with ease. On the other hand, biculturals who are low in integration see their two cultural orientations in opposition to each other and although they are competent in both cultures, they are less confident in the role of cultural broker.

According to Padilla (1994; 2006) motives for biculturalism are different depending on generational status. For first-generation individuals, acculturation to the dominant "American" culture is a necessity for success in the United States. The newcomer must learn English and culturally appropriate behaviors. Generally, it is more difficult for adult immigrants, especially if they do not possess much education (i.e., human capital) to acculturate to the level where they are competent enough in the language and culture of the dominant group to be completely bicultural. For the children of immigrants (i.e., second generation) or immigrant children, on the other hand, biculturalism often occurs because of the demand to serve as a bridge between the culture of the parents and that of the majority group at school and in the community (Morales & Hanson, 2005). These individuals often become competent biculturals because they have more opportunities to move between the language and culture of the home and that of the mainstream group. Importantly, the motivation for third and later generation individuals to develop bicultural skills may be due to their higher awareness to social inequities and astuteness in recognizing more subtle forms of discrimination directed at them personally or at other members of their ethnic group. No studies have yet been conducted to assess how stigmas such as accents, skin color, and physiognomy interact with a person's perceptions of ethnic threat to determine to what extent he or she will engage in multiple group memberships.

Conclusion

The theory of ethnic identity advanced here is based on earlier theories of social cognition and social identity. The theory explains why Latinos, who have become the largest ethnic group in the United States, manifest different orientations toward their ethnic identity. The core of the theory suggests that the processes of social categorization, social comparison, and social dominance are driven in large measure by skin color in determining social status. Skin color represents a primary stigma that influences intergroup interactions between the majority group and Latinos. Thus, a central construct in the theory is social stigma.

Latinos are a heterogeneous ethnic group comprised of different races and mixtures of race, and vary from light-skinned European in their features to very dark and indigenous in their physiognomy. Evidence is accumulating to indicate that lighter skinned, more European-looking Latinos fare better socioeconomically than their darker skinned Latino counterparts. The dynamics that seem to advantage fairer skinned Latinos suggest the maintenance of race-based preferences despite Civil Rights legislation and efforts toward social equity in education and employment.

The theory of Latino ethnic identity posits that when individuals experience overt or implicit threats to their ethnic group, they are motivated by the social context to act upon such threats by employing one of several different coping strategies that will mitigate the threat. The coping strategy employed is determined by several considerations. These considerations include: (a) the extent of actual and perceived personal and social group discrimination a person experiences; (b) the social cognitions the person forms about their ethnic group including the self-evaluations they hold about themselves and their group; and (c) the ethnic socialization a person receives from parents and other family members. Individuals who are socially categorized as possessing more of the stigma experience more negative social evaluations and consequently have fewer options in the coping responses available to them.

The three major intergroup coping strategies for dealing with ethnic threat are social activism, assimilation, and multiple group membership/biculturalism. Each of these strategies is in turn associated with particular social identities that enable the person to meet ethnic threat while also safe guarding personal and ethnic group self-esteem. However, because social identities are malleable, the identities can change because of two properties – identities are largely social constructions, and they are not zero-sum and consequently, the existence of one identity at one point in time or in one situational context does not negate the existence of another identity at another time or in another context.

Acknowledgments I would like to thank my graduate students Graciela Borsato, Noah Borrero, and Cristina Leal (Stanford University School of Education) for their many helpful comments on earlier versions of this chapter. I also want to thank Professor Rosemary Gonzalez (California State University, Northridge) for her thoughtful suggestions, large and small, that helped in my final reworking of the chapter. Finally, I owe much gratitude to Professor Cynthia Willis-Esqueda, the organizer, of the 53rd Annual Symposium on Motivation, for her assistance in preparing this chapter and for her dedication in bringing this symposium on the motivational aspects of prejudice and racism to fruition.

References

Allport, G. W. (1954). *The nature of prejudice*. Cambridge, MA: Addison-Wesley.

Arbona, C., Flores, C. L., & Novy, D. (1995). Cultural awareness and ethnic loyalty: Dimensions of cultural variability among Mexican American college students. *Journal of Counseling and Development, 73*, 610–614.

Arce, C. H., Murguia, E., & Frisbie, W. P. (1987). Phenotype and life chances among Chicanos. *Hispanic Journal of Behavioral Sciences, 9*, 19–32.

Berry, J. W. (2003). Conceptual approaches to acculturation. In K. M. Chun, P. Balls Organista, & G. Marin (Eds.), *Acculturation: Advances in theory, measurement, and applied research* (pp. 17–37). Washington, DC: American Psychological Association.

Beschloss, M. (2002). *The conquerors*. New York: Simon Schuster.

Breakwell, G. M. (1986). *Coping with threatened identities*. London: Methuen.

Brewer, M. B. (1991). The social self: On being the same and different at the same time. *Personality and Social Psychology Bulletin, 17*, 475–482.

Brewer, M. B. (1993). The role of social distinctiveness in social identity and group behavior. In M. A. Hogg & D. Abrams (Eds.), *Group motivation: Social psychological perspectives* (pp. 1–16). Hertfordshire, UK: Harvester Wheatsheaf.

Brown, L. M. (1998). Ethnic stigma as a contextual experience: A possible selves perspective. *Personality and Social Psychology Bulletin, 24*(2), 163–172.

Casas, J. M., Pontero, J. G., & Sweeney, M. (1987). Stereotyping the stereotyper: A Mexican American perspective. *Journal of Cross-Cultural Psychology, 18*, 45–57.

Codina, G. E., & Montalvo, F. F. (1994). Chicano phenotype and depression. *Hispanic Journal of Behavioral Sciences, 16*, 296–306.

Cowan, G., Martinez, L., & Mendiola, S. (1997). Predictors of attitudes toward illegal Latino immigrants. *Hispanic Journal of Behavioral Sciences, 19*, 403–415.

Crocker, J., Luhtanen, R., Blaine, B., & Braodnax, S. (1994). Collective self-esteem and psychological well being among White, Black, and Asian college students. *Personality and Social Psychology Bulletin, 20*, 502–513.

Crocker, J., & Major, B. (1989). Social stigma and self-esteem: The self-protective properties of stigma. *Psychological Review, 96*, 608–630.

Crocker, J., & Major, B. (1994). Reaction to stigma: The moderating role of justification. In M. P. Zanna & J. M. Olsen (Eds.), *The psychology of prejudice: The ontario symposium* (pp. 289–314). Hillsdale, NJ: Erlbaum.

Crocker, J., Major, B., & Steele, C. (1998). Social Stigma. In D. T. Gilbert, S. T. Fiske, & G. Lindzey (Eds.), *The handbook of social psychology* (pp. 504–553). New York, NY: McGraw-Hill.

Crocker, J., Voekl, K., Testa, M., & Major, B. (1991). Social stigma: The affective consequences of attributional ambiguity. *Journal of Personality and Social Psychology, 60,* 218–228.

Crosby, F. (1982). *Relative deprivation and working women.* New York: Oxford University Press.

Del Pilar, J. A., & Udasco, J. O. (2004). Marginality theory: The lack of construct validity. *Hispanic Journal of Behavioral Sciences, 26,* 3–15.

Devine, P. G., & Elliot, A. J. (1995). Are racial stereotypes really fading?: The Princeton trilogy revisited. *Personality and Social Psychology Bulletin, 21,* 1139–1150.

Dovidio, J. F., & Gaertner, S. L. (1986). *Prejudice, discrimination, and racism.* San Diego: Academic Press.

Espino, R., & Franz, M. M. (2002). Latino phenotypic discrimination revisited: The impact of skin color on occupational status. *Social Science Quarterly, 83,* 612–623.

Fazio, R. H., Jackson, J. R., Dunton, B. C., & Williams, C. J. (1995). Variability in automatic activation as an unobtrusive measure of racial attitudes: A bona fide pipeline? *Journal of Personality and Social Psychology, 69,* 1013–1027.

Fazio, R. H., & Olson, M. A. (2003). Implicit measures in social cognition research: Their meaning and use. *Annual Review of Psychology, 54,* 297–327.

Feagin, J. R. (1991). The continuing significance of race: Antiblack discrimination in public places. *American Sociological Review, 56,* 101–116.

Feagin, J. R., & Feagin, C. B. (2003). *Racial and ethnic Relations* (7th ed.). Upper Saddle River, NJ: Prentice Hall.

Feagin, J., & Sikes, M. P. (1994). *Living with racism: The Black middle-class experience.* Boston: Beacon Press.

Fiske, S. T. (1993). Social cognition and social perception. In M. R. Rosenzweig & L. W. Porter (Eds.), *Annual review of psychology* (pp. 155–194). Palo Alto, CA: Annual Reviews, Inc.

Fiske, S. T., & Taylor, S. E. (1991). *Social cognition* (2nd ed.). New York, NY: Mcgraw-Hill Book Company.

Gibbons, F. X. (1986). Stigma and interpersonal relationships. In S. C. Ainlay, G. Becker, & L. M. Coleman (Eds.), *The dilemma of difference* (pp. 123–156). New York: Plenum Press.

Goffman, E. (1963). *Stigma: Notes on the management of spoiled identity.* Englewood Cliffs, NJ: Prentice-Hall.

Gómez, C. (2000). The continual significance of skin color: An exploratory study of Latinos in the Northeast. *Hispanic Journal of Behavioral Sciences, 22,* 93–103.

Green, A. W. (1947). A re-examination of the marginal man concept. *Social Forces, 26,* 167–171.

Greenwald, A. G., & Banaji, M. R. (1995). Implicit social cognition: Attitudes, self-esteem, and stereotypes. *Psychological Review, 102,* 4–27.

Greenwald, A. G., McGhee, D. E., & Schwartz, J. L. K. (1998). Measuring individual differences in implicit cognition: The implicit association test. *Journal of Personality and Social Psychology, 74,* 1469–1480.

Haritatos, J., & Benet-Martinez, V. (2002). Bicultural identities: The interface of cultural, personality, and socio-cognitive processes. *Journal of Research in Personality, 6,* 598–606.

Heider, F. (1958). Perceiving the other person. In R. Tagiuri & L. Petrullo (Eds.), *Person perception and interpersonal behavior* (pp. 22–26). Palo Alto, CA: Stanford University Press.

Hogg, M. A., & Abrams, D. (1988). *Social identifications: A social psychology of intergroup relations and group processes.* New York: Routledge.

Hong, Y. Y., Morris, M., Chiu, C. Y., & Benet-Martinez, V. (2000). Multicultural minds: A dynamic constructivist approach to culture and cognition. *American Psychologist, 55,* 709–720.

Hughes, D., & Johnson, D. (2001). Correlates in children's experiences of parents' racial socialization behaviors. *Journal of Marriage and Family, 63,* 981–995.

Hutnik, N. (1991). *Ethnic minority identity: A social psychological perspective.* New York: Oxford University Press.

James, W. (1890). *The principles of psychology.* Cambridge, MA: Harvard University Press.

Jones, E. E., Farina, A., Hastorf, A. H., Markus, H., Miller, D. T., & Scott, R. A. (1984). *Social stigma: The psychology of marked relationships.* New York: Freeman.

Kao, G. (2000). Group images and possible selves among adolescents: Linking stereotypes to expectations by race and ethnicity. *Sociological Forum, 15*, 407–430.

Keefe, S., & Padilla, A. M. (1987). *Chicano ethnicity*. Albuquerque, NM: University of New Mexico Press.

Knight, G. P., Bernal, M. E., Cota, M. K., Garza, C. A., & Ocampo, K. A. (1993). Family socialization and Mexican American identity and behavior. In M. E. Bernal & G. P. Knight (Eds.), *Ethnic identity: Formation and transmission among hispanics and other minorities* (pp. 105–129). Albany, NY: State University of New York Press.

LaFromboise, T., Coleman, H. I. K., & Gerton, T. (1993). Psychological impact of biculturalism: Evidence and theory. *Psychological Bulletin, 114*, 395–412.

Landrine, H., & Klonoff, E. A. (1996). The schedule of racist events: A measure of racial discrimination and a study of its negative physical and mental health consequences. *The Journal of Black Psychology, 22*, 144–168.

Major, B. (1987). Gender, Justice, and the psychology of entitlement. In P. Shaver & C. Hendrick (Eds.), *Review of personality and social psychology* (Vol. 7, pp. 124–148). Beverly Hills, CA: Sage.

Major, B. (1994). Gender, Justice, and the psychology of entitlement: The role of social comparisons, legitimacy appraisals, and group membership. In M. P. Zanna (Ed.), *Advances in experimental social psychology* (pp. 293–348). San Diego: Academic Press.

Major, B., & Crocker, J. (1993). Social stigma: The affective consequences of attributional ambiguity. In D. M. Mackie & D. L. Hamilton (Eds.), *Affect, cognition, and stereotyping: Interactive processes in intergroup perception* (pp. 345–370). New York: Academic Press.

Majors, B., Gramzow, R. H., McCoy, S. K., Levin, S., & Schmader, T. (2002). Perceiving personal discrimination: The role of group status and legitimizing ideology. *Journal of Personality and Social Psychology, 82*, 269–282.

Mann, J. W. (1973). Status: The marginal reaction – Mixed-bloods and Jews. In P. Watson (Ed.), *Psychology and Race* (pp. 213–223). Upper Saddle River, NJ: Penguin Education.

Markus, H., & Nurius, P. (1986). Possible selves. *American Psychologist, 41*, 954–969.

Markus, H. R., & Kitayama, S. (1991). Culture and the self: Implications for cognition, emotion, and motivation. *Psychological Review, 98*, 224–253.

Markus, H. R., Kitayama, S., & Heiman, R. J. (1996). Culture and "basic" psychological principles. In E. T. Higgins & A. W. Kruglanski (Eds.), *Social psychology: Handbook of basic principles* (pp. 857–913). New York: Guilford.

Mason, P. L. (2004). Annual income, hourly wages, and identity among Mexican Americans and other Latinos. *Industrial Relations, 43*, 817–834.

McIntosh, P. (1988). White privilege and male privilege: A personal account of coming to see correspondences through work in women's studies. In M. L. Andersen and P. Hill Collins (Eds.), *Race, class, and gender: An anthology*. Belmont, CA: Wadsworth Publishing Co.

Montgomery, G. T. (1992). Comfort with acculturation status among students from south Texas. *Hispanic Journal of Behavioral Sciences, 14*, 201–223.

Morales, A., & Hanson, W. E. (2005). Language brokering: An integrative review of the literature. *Hispanic Journal of Behavioral Sciences, 27*, 471–503.

Neimann, Y., Pollack, K., Rogers, S., & O'Connor, E. (1998). Effects of physical context in stereotyping of Mexican-American males. *Hispanic Journal of Behavioral Sciences, 20*, 349–362.

Operario, D., & Fiske, S. T. (1999). Integrating social identity and social cognition: A framework for bridging diverse perspectives. In D. Abrams & M. A. Hogg (Eds.), *Social identity and social cognition* (pp. 26–54). Malden, MA: Blackwell Publishers, Inc.

Padilla, A. M. (1980). The role of cultural awareness and ethnic loyalty in acculturation. In A. M. Padilla (Ed.), *Acculturation: Theory, models and some new findings* (pp. 47–84). Boulder, CO: Westview.

Padilla, A. M. (1986). Acculturation and stress among immigrants and later generation individuals. In D. Frick (Ed.), *The quality of urban life: Social, psychological, and physical conditions* (pp. 101–120). Berlin: Walter de Gruyter.

Padilla, A. M. (1994). Bicultural development: A theoretical and empirical examination. In R. G. Malgady & O. Rodriguez (Eds.), *Theoretical and conceptual issues in Hispanic mental health* (pp. 20–50). Malabar, FL: Krieger Publishing Co.

Padilla, A. M. (2006). Bicultural social development. *Hispanic Journal of Behavioral Sciences, 28,* 467–497.

Padilla, A. M., & Perez, W. (2003). Acculturation, social identity, and social cognition: A new perspective. *Hispanic Journal of Behavioral Sciences, 25,* 35–55.

Phinney, J., & Chavira, V. (1995). Parental ethnic socialization and adolescent coping with problems related to ethnicity. *Journal of Research on Adolescence, 51,* 31–53.

Portes, A., & Rumbaut, R. (2001). *Legacies: The Story of the Immigrant Second Generation.* Berkeley, CA: University of California Press.

Quintana, S. M., Castaneda-English, P., & Ybarra, V. C. (1999). Role of perspective-taking abilities and ethnic socialization in development of adolescent ethnic identity. *Journal of Research on Adolescence, 9,* 161–184.

Quintana, S. M., & Vera, E. M. (1999). Mexican American children's ethnic identity, understanding of ethnic prejudice, and parental ethnic socialization. *Hispanic Journal of Behavioral Sciences, 21,* 387–404.

Runciman, W. G. (1966). *Relative deprivation and social justice: A study of the attitudes to social inequality in 20th century England.* Berkeley: University of California Press.

Schacter, S. (1959). *The psychology of affiliation.* Stanford, CA: Stanford University Press.

Schaefer, R. T. (2004). *Racial and ethnic groups* (9th ed.). Upper Saddle River, NJ: Pearson/ Prentice Hall.

Schuman, H., Steeh, C., Bobo, L., & Krysan, M. (1997). *Racial attitudes in America: Trends and interpretations.* Cambridge, MA: Harvard University Press.

Sellers, R. M., & Shelton, J. N. (2003). The role of racial identity in perceived racial discrimination. *Journal of Personality and Social Psychology, 84,* 1079–1092.

Sidanius, J. (1993). The psychology of group conflict and the dynamics of social oppression: A social dominance perspective. In S. Iyengar & W. McGuire (Eds.), *Explorations in political psychology* (pp. 183–219). Durham, NC: Duke University Press.

Sidanios, J., & Pratto, F. (1999). *Social dominance: An intergroup theory of social hierarchy and oppression.* Cambridge, UK: Cambridge University Press.

Singer, E. (1981). Reference groups and social evaluations. In M. Rosenberg & R. Turner (Eds.), *Social psychology* (pp. 66–93). New York: Basic Books.

Spencer, M. B. (1983). Children's cultural values and parental child rearing strategies. *Developmental Review, 3,* 351–370.

Steele, C., & Aronson, J. (1995). Stereotype threat and the intellectual test performance of African Americans. *Journal of Personality and Social Psychology, 69*(5), 797–811.

Stonequist, E. V. (1937). *The marginal man: A study in personality and culture conflict.* New York: Russell & Russell, Inc.

Swim, J., Cohen, L., & Hyers, L. (1998). Experiencing everyday prejudice and discrimination. In J. Swim & C. Stangor (Eds.), *Prejudice: The target's perspective* (pp. 37–60). San Diego, CA: Academic Press.

Tafarodi, R. W., Kang, S., & Milne, A. B. (2002). When different becomes similar: Compensatory conformity in bicultural visible minorities. *Personality and Social Psychology Bulletin, 28,* 1131–1142.

Tafoya, S. (2004). *Shades of belonging. Pew Hispanic Center Report.* Washington, DC: Pew Research Center.

Tajfel, H. (1978). Social categorization, social identity and social comparison. In H. Tajfel (Ed.), *Differentiation between social groups* (pp. 61–67). London: Academic Press.

Tajfel, H. (1981). *Human groups and social categories: Studies in social psychology.* Cambridge, UK: Cambridge University Press.

Tajfel, H. (Ed.). (1982). *Social identity and intergroup relations.* Cambridge, UK: Cambridge University Press.

Tajfel, H., & Turner, J. C. (1986). The social identity theory of intergroup behavior. In S. Worchel & W. Austin (Eds.), *The social psychology of intergroup behavior* (pp. 7–24). Chicago: Nelson-Hall.

Takaki, R. (1993). *A different mirror: A history of multicultural America.* Boston: Little, Brown and Co.

Tatum, B. (1997). *Why are all the black kids sitting together in the cafeteria?* New York: Basic Books.

Thornton, M. C. (1997). Strategies of racial socialization among Black parents: Mainstream minority, and cultural messages. In R. J. Taylor, J. S. Jackson, & L. M. Chatters (Eds.), *Family life in black America* (pp. 201–215). Thousand Oaks, CA: Sage Publications.

Turner, J. C. (1982). Towards a cognitive redefinition of the social group. In H. Tajfel (Ed.), *Social identity and intergroup relations* (pp. 15–40). Cambridge, UK: Cambridge University Press.

Turner, J. C., Hogg, M. A., Oakes, P. J., Reicher, S. D., & Wetherell, M. S. (1987). *Rediscovering the social group: A self-categorization theory.* Oxford: Blackwell.

Twenge, J. M., & Crocker, J. (2002). Race and self-esteem: Meta-analysis comparing Whites, Blacks, Hispanics, Asians, and American Indians. *Psychological Bulletin, 128,* 371–408.

Vanman, E. J., Paul, P. Y., Ito, T. A., & Miller, N. (1997). The modern face of prejudice and structural features that moderate the effect of cooperation on affect. *Journal of Personality and Social Psychology, 73,* 941–959.

Vanman, E. J., Saltz, J. L., Nathan, L. R., & Warren, J. A. (2004). Racial discrimination by low-prejudiced Whites. *Psychological Science, 15,* 711–714.

Vazquez, L. A., Garcia-Vazquez, E., Barman, S. A., & Sierra, A. (1997). Skin color, accultura-tion, and community interest among Mexican American students: A research note. *Hispanic Journal of Behavioral Sciences, 19,* 377–386.

Weyant, J. M. (2005). Implicit stereotyping of Hispanics: Development and validity of a Hispanic version of the implicit association test. *Hispanic Journal of Behavioral Sciences, 27,* 355–362.

Wheeler, M. E., & Fiske, S. T. (2005). Controlling racial prejudice: Social-cognitive goals affect amygdale and stereotype activation. *Psychological Science, 16,* 56–63.

Winters, L. I., & DeBosse, H. L. (2003). *New faces in a changing America: Multiracial identity in the 21st century.* Thousand Oaks, CA: Sage Publications.

Zanna, M. P., Crosby, F., & Lowenstein, G. (1986). Male reference groups and discontent among female professionals. In B. A. Gutek & L. Larwood (Eds.), *Women's career development* (pp. 28–41). Newbury Park, CA: Sage.

3
New Directions in Aversive Racism Research: Persistence and Pervasiveness

John F. Dovidio and Samuel L. Gaertner

Over 100 years ago, in his classic book, *The souls of Black folk*, W. E. B. DuBois (1903/1986) prophesized, "The problem of the twentieth century is the problem of the color line." (p. 372) DuBois offered this observation before the Wright brothers took the first powered flight, before automobiles were common, and before most households in the United States had electricity. The advances that have occurred in transportation and technology over the past century could not be envisioned at the time. However, DuBois clearly identified the social and political issue that has dominated US society for the past 100 years and the problem that threatens to extend far into the future.

Significant progress has obviously been made socially and politically over the past century with respect to the "problem of the color line." Racism has increasingly been recognized as immoral by large segments of the US population over time (Schuman, Steeh, Bobo, & Krysan, 1997). The Civil Rights legislation of the 1960s made racial discrimination not simply immoral but also illegal. Nevertheless, because the issue of race is a complex one, it is an enduring issue. Politics and social change, particularly in democratic societies, is complicated. Progress is often slow, following circuitous paths. Barriers to racial equality are often embedded in cultural values (Jones, 1997) and institutional policies (Feagin & Sikes, 1994; Sidanius & Pratto, 1999). We contend that another critical element is the complexity of Whites' racial attitudes. In this chapter, we explore the nature of contemporary racial attitudes. We focus specifically on one form of racial prejudice, aversive racism, and we consider its causes and consequences for Whites' behaviors toward Blacks, for interracial interactions, and ultimately for race relations more broadly. We first define the concept of aversive racism and describe how it can operate to produce subtle forms of discrimination. We then present initial evidence documenting the operation of aversive racism, followed by more recent research illustrating its persistence and pervasiveness. After that, we review recent advances in understanding and assessing implicit attitudes and illustrate their role in aversive racists' interracial interactions. We conclude by considering the implications for race relations currently and in the future.

C. Willis-Esqueda (ed.), *Motivational Aspects of Prejudice and Racism*.
© Springer 2008

The Nature of Aversive Racism

Much of the psychological research on prejudice from the 1920s through the 1950s portrayed it as psychopathology (Dovidio, 2001; Duckitt, 1992). Prejudice was viewed as a type of "social cancer." For example, stimulated politically by the Nazis' rise to power in Germany, historically by the holocaust, and intellectually by the classic work on the authoritarian personality (Adorno, Frenkel-Brunswik, Levinson, & Sanford, 1950), psychologists of the 1950s typically viewed prejudice and other forms of bias as dangerous aberrations from normal thinking. One implication of this perspective is that if the attitudes of this "abnormal" minority could be changed or their influence on others constrained, the effects of prejudice on society would be significantly reduced.

While acknowledging the contribution of authoritarianism and other abnormal psychological influences (e.g., such as low self-esteem; Allport, 1954; Fein & Spencer, 1997), scholars began to recognize that racial bias was woven into the basic fabric of American society. Myrdal (1944), a Swedish political economist commissioned by the Carnegie Corporation, identified the paradox between historical egalitarian values and racist traditions in the United States, which he represented in the title of his classic book, *An American dilemma*. According to Myrdal, the dilemma involves

> the ever-raging conflict between, on the one hand, the valuations preserved on the general plane which we call the "American creed," where the American thinks, talks, and acts under the influence of high national and Christian precepts and, on the other hand, the valuations on the specific planes of individual and group living, where personal and local interests; economic, social, and sexual jealousies; consideration of community prestige and conformity; group prejudice against particular persons or types of people; and all sorts of miscellaneous wants, impulses, and habits dominate his outlook. (p. xliii)

By the 1960s, a decade that was characterized by great civil unrest in the United States and the successful passage of Civil Rights legislation, social psychologists widely acknowledged sociocultural influences in prejudice, stereotyping, and bias (Duckitt, 1992). Elements related to the American dilemma, described by Myrdal (1944), such as sympathy for the underdog and racial prejudice, were recognized as components of an ambivalence that many "normal" White Americans experienced toward Blacks (Katz, Wackenhut, & Hass, 1986). In 1970, Kovel distinguished between dominative and aversive racism. Dominative racism is the "old-fashioned," blatant form. According to Kovel, the dominative racist is the "type who acts out bigoted beliefs – he represents the open flame of racial hatred" (p. 54). Aversive racists, in contrast, sympathize with victims of past injustice, support the principle of racial equality, and regard themselves as nonprejudiced, but at the same time possess negative feelings and beliefs (which may be unconscious) about Blacks.

Building on Kovel's (1970) distinction, over the past 35 years we have explored the existence and operation of aversive racism among White Americans. Aversive racism is hypothesized to be qualitatively different than blatant, "old-fashioned," racism, is more indirect and subtle, and is presumed to characterize the racial attitudes of most well-educated and liberal Whites in the United States. Nevertheless, the consequences of aversive racism (e.g., the restriction of economic opportunity) are as significant and pernicious as those of the traditional, overt form (Dovidio & Gaertner, 1998; Gaertner & Dovidio, 1986).

In this chapter, we briefly review our initial empirical evidence about aversive racism, and then, in more detail, we discuss the recent developments: the persistence and prevalence of aversive racism, the relationship of aversive racism to research on implicit attitudes, and the influence of aversive racism on interracial interaction.

Early Evidence

As we noted earlier, overt expressions of prejudice in the United States have declined significantly over the past 40 years. As Bobo (2001) concluded in his review of trends in racial attitudes, "The single clearest trend in studies of racial attitudes has involved a steady and sweeping movement toward general endorsement of the principles of racial equality and integration." (p. 269) Nevertheless, at the same time racial disparities in fundamental aspects of life, such as income and health persist, and in some spheres of life are increasing (Blank, 2001). Moreover, discrimination has been identified as a critical element creating and sustaining these disparities (Elvira & Zatzick, 2002; Smedley, Stith, & Nelson, 2003).

One explanation for the discrepancy between the decline in overt racial prejudice and the persistence of racial disparities is that the nature of prejudice and its expression in discrimination has changed over time. New forms of prejudice have emerged. Although other forms of contemporary racism have been identified, such as modern racism (McConahay, 1986) and symbolic racism (Sears, Henry, & Kosterman, 2000), these conceptions typically share the basic proposition that although most White Americans *consciously* endorse egalitarian principles and sincerely believe that they are not prejudiced, they continue to harbor, often *unconsciously*, negative feelings and beliefs toward Blacks and other people of color (Dovidio & Gaertner, 2004). These negative feelings may develop through early socialization coupled with almost unavoidable biases associated with categorizing people into different groups. Measures of implicit (unconscious) prejudice suggest that, despite the dramatic decrease in explicit (self-reported) prejudice, the vast majority of White Americans have these relatively negative unconscious associations with Blacks (Blair, 2001). The existence of conscious egalitarian values along with unacknowledged negative racial feelings and beliefs produces systematic patterns of interracial behavior and discrimination. Specifically, in contrast to the direct and overt pattern of discrimination exhibited by traditionally prejudiced people, the expression of discrimination by aversive racists is more complex and typically influenced by a number of factors.

One key element is the nature of the situation. From the perspective of aversive racism (Dovidio & Gaertner, 2004; Gaertner & Dovidio, 1986), because aversive racists consciously recognize and endorse egalitarian values and because they truly aspire to be nonprejudiced, they will *not* discriminate in situations with strong social norms when discrimination would be obvious to others and to themselves. Consciously, aversive racists are motivated to avoid acting inappropriately in interracial contexts. However, the unconscious negative feelings and beliefs that aversive racists also possess will produce discrimination in situations in which normative guidelines are weak or when negative actions toward a Black person can be justified or rationalized on the basis of some factor other than race. Under these circumstances, aversive racists may engage in behaviors that ultimately harm Blacks but in ways that allow Whites to maintain their self-image as nonprejudiced and that insulate them from recognizing that their behavior is not colorblind. Support for this pattern of outcomes has been obtained across studies involving a wide variety of actions (Crosby, Bromley, & Saxe, 1980; Dovidio & Gaertner; Gaertner & Dovidio).

Our first empirical evidence of aversive racism was obtained over 30 years ago, in a largely serendipitous finding (Gaertner, 1973). We began this research on racism naively with a simple assumption: Based on differences in their expressed racial attitudes (see Adorno et al., 1950), conservative Whites would behave in a more racially discriminatory way than would liberal Whites. This hypothesis was tested by selecting White participants residing in Brooklyn, New York, on the basis of their liberal or conservative orientations, as indicated by their political party affiliations (i.e., Liberal or Conservative parties in New York State) that were a matter of public record for a field experiment on helping. Both the liberal and the conservative households received ostensibly wrong-number telephone calls that quickly developed into requests for assistance. The callers, who were clearly identifiable from their dialects as being Black or White, explained that their car was disabled and that they were attempting to reach a service garage from a public phone along the parkway. The callers further claimed that they had no more change to make another call and asked the participant to help by calling the garage. If the participant agreed to help and called the number, ostensibly of the garage, the participant was thanked for helping and a "helping" response was scored. If the participant refused to help or hung up after the caller explained that he or she had no more change, a "not helping" response was recorded. If the participant hung up before learning that the motorist had no more change, the response was recorded as a "premature hang-up."

The first finding from this study was direct and predicted. Conservatives showed a higher "helping" response to Whites than to Blacks (92% vs. 65%), whereas liberals helped Whites somewhat, but not significantly, more than Blacks (85% vs. 75%). By this measure, conservatives were more biased against Blacks than were liberals. Additional inspection of the data, however, revealed an unanticipated finding. Liberals "hung up prematurely" significantly more often on Blacks than they did on Whites (19% vs. 3%). Conservatives did not discriminate in this way (8% vs. 5%). From the perspective of Black callers, the consequence of a direct "not helping" response and of a "premature hang-up" was the same: they would be left without assistance. From the perspective of the participants, however, the consequences were different. Whereas a "not helping" response was a direct, intentional form of discrimination because it should have been clear to participants that their help was needed, a "premature hang-up" was a more indirect form because participants disengaged from the situation before they learned of the other person's dependence on them, and thus participants never overtly refused assistance. Indeed, to refuse help that is perceived to be needed clearly violates the social responsibility norm, whereas the appropriateness of hanging-up prematurely on a wrong-number caller is unclear. Therefore, both conservative and liberal Whites discriminated against Blacks but in different ways.

Another one of our early experiments (Gaertner & Dovidio, 1977) demonstrates how aversive racism can operate in fairly dramatic ways. The scenario for the experiment was inspired by an incident in the mid-1960s in which 38 people witnessed the stabbing of a woman, Kitty Genovese, without a single bystander intervening to help. What accounted for this behavior? Feelings of responsibility play a key role (see Darley & Latané, 1968). If a person witnesses an emergency knowing that he or she is the only bystander, that person bears all of the responsibility for helping and, consequently, the likelihood of helping is high. In contrast, if a person witnesses an emergency but believes that there are several other witnesses who might help, then the responsibility for helping is shared. Moreover, if the person believes that someone else will help or has already helped, the likelihood of that bystander taking action is significantly reduced.

We created a situation in the laboratory in which White participants witnessed a staged emergency involving a Black or White victim. We led some of our participants to believe that they were the only witness to this emergency, while we led others to believe that there were other White people who also witnessed the emergency, each isolated in a separate room within the laboratory. We predicted that, because aversive racists do not act in overtly bigoted ways, Whites would not discriminate when they were the only witness and the responsibility for helping was clearly focused on them. However, we anticipated that Whites would be much less helpful to Black than to White victims when they had a justifiable excuse not to get involved, such as the belief that one of the *other* witnesses would take responsibility for helping.

The results clearly reflected these predictions. When White participants believed that they were the only witness, they helped both White and Black victims very frequently (over 85% of the time) and equivalently. There was no evidence of blatant racism. In contrast, when they thought there were other witnesses and they could rationalize a decision not to help on the basis of some factor other than race, they helped Black victims only half as often as White victims (37.5% vs. 75%). Thus, these results illustrate the operation of subtle biases in highly consequential, spontaneous, and life-threatening circumstances involving a failure to help, rather than an action intentionally aimed at doing harm. This research, therefore, shows that although the bias may be subtle and the people involved may be well-intentioned, its consequences may be severe.

Whereas the previous study illustrates the operation of aversive racism in a fairly dramatic way, other studies demonstrate the more "mundane," albeit still significant, effects of aversive racism. For example, to examine how aversive racism relates to questionnaire or survey responses, we conducted an experiment in which we asked people on 1–7 scales (e.g., good–bad) to describe Blacks and Whites (Dovidio & Gaertner, 1996; see also Gaertner & McLaughlin, 1983). These White respondents demonstrated no racial difference in their evaluative ratings. A biased response (e.g., "bad") is obvious, and respondents consistently rated both Blacks and Whites on the positive ends of the scales. However, when we varied the instrument slightly by placing positive (e.g., good) and negative characteristics (e. g., bad) in separate scales (responses from "not at all" to "extremely"), we found that bias does exist, but in a subtle form.

Although the ratings of Blacks and Whites on the negative scales showed no racial bias, the ratings on the positive scales did reveal a significant difference. Whereas Blacks were not rated *more negatively* than Whites, Whites were evaluated *more positively* than Blacks. Apparently, aversive racists resist reporting that Blacks are bad or even that they are worse than Whites, remarks easily interpreted as racial bias. Subtle bias is displayed, however, in respondents' willingness to indicate that Blacks may be quite good, but Whites are better. Again, this is not the old-fashioned, overt type of bias associated with the belief about Black inferiority. Instead, it is a modern, subtle form of bias that reflects a belief about White superiority. Thus, whereas the traditional form of racial preju- dice is primarily anti-Black, aversive racism may have a significant pro-White component (Gaertner et al., 1997).

Appreciating the impact of pro-White attitudes in contemporary racism also offers important insight into legal, social, and personal actions that can eliminate racial bias. Current antidiscrimination laws are based largely on the premise that racial discrimination by Whites is the result of anti-Black attitudes and actions. Laws designed to protect disadvantaged individuals and groups from anti-outgroup actions may be ineffective for addressing biased treatment based on ingroup favoritism. For example, the first author of this chapter served as an expert witness for the plaintiff in an employment discrimination case. The plaintiff, a Black man, was one of two employees placed on probationary status by his employer because of some deficiencies in his performance. The other employee, one with a compara- ble record, was a White man. During the probationary period, both employees' performances remained comparably marginal by company standards. At the end of the period, however, the company terminated the position of the Black man but retained the White man as an employee.

Our side's argument in court was that that the decision to terminate the employ- ment of the Black defendant represented different and unfair treatment for equiva- lent performance. The defense argued that although the plaintiff was indeed treated differently for equivalent performance, he was not treated unfairly. His case was handled in accordance with the procedures of the company. It was acknowledged that, perhaps because of a closer personal relationship between the other worker and the supervisor, the White employee was given an *extra* opportunity within the company. However, this special and favorable treatment toward the White (ingroup) worker, the defense claimed, is not valid *legal* grounds for demonstrating unfair and discriminatory treatment toward the Black (outgroup) employee. The position of the defense was upheld and the case was dismissed. Awareness of the changing nature of contemporary racism may thus lead to the recognition of the need for new policies and types of laws to ameliorate the consequences of racism.

Persistence of Aversive Racism

Like a virus that has mutated, contemporary racism has evolved in a way that produces behaviors that are not directly prohibited by current laws but still contribute to the persistence of racial disparities in essential qualities of life. Even well-meaning Whites who genuinely endorse egalitarian values may discriminate against Blacks and other minorities unintentionally. Without personal awareness or public recognition aversive racism may operate with little resistance. As a consequence, whereas blatant expressions of prejudice, such as hate crimes, are readily identified and inhibited by social sanctions, aversive racism is likely to persist unchallenged over time.

A number of experimental findings converge to support the idea that, whereas overt expressions have declined over time, aversive racism continues to operate in a relatively consistent fashion. In the previous section, we described our early helping behavior experiments that provided initial evidence for the aversive racism framework. Recently, Saucier, Miller, and Doucet (2005) performed a meta-analysis of 31 experiments conducted over the past 40 years that examined race and Whites' helping behavior, specifically testing implications of the aversive racism framework. Across these studies, Saucier et al. found "that less help was offered to Blacks relative to Whites when helpers had more attributional cues available for rationalizing the failure to help with reasons having nothing to do with race" (p. 10). Moreover, the pattern of discrimination against Blacks remained stable over time; the effect for year of study was nonsignificant ($p > 0.40$). Saucier et al. summarized, "The results of this meta-analysis generally supported the predictions for aversive racism theory" (p. 13), and concluded, "Is racism still a problem in our society? Racism and expression of discrimination against Blacks can and will exist as long as individuals harbor negativity toward Blacks at the implicit level." (p. 14)

Additional evidence of the persistence of the effects of aversive racism comes from studies using other paradigms, such as experiments of simulated juror decision-making. Traditionally, Blacks and Whites have not been treated equally under the law (Sidanius, Levin, & Pratto, 1998). Across time and locations in the United States, Blacks have been more likely to be perceived by jurors as guilty (Fairchild & Cowan, 1997), more likely to be convicted of crimes, and, if convicted, sentenced to longer terms for similar crimes, particularly if the victim is White (see Robinson & Darley, 1995). Although there is some evidence that disparities in judicial outcomes are declining (Sommers & Ellsworth, 2001), aversive racism appears to have a continuing, subtle influence.

The first study of the role of aversive racism in juridic decisions was conducted over 25 years ago. Faranda and Gaertner (1979) investigated the hypothesis that, whereas the racial biases of those who are likely to have traditionally racist attitudes (high authoritarians) would reflect primarily anti-Black biases, the racial biases of those who are likely to exhibit aversive racism (low authoritarianism) would mainly represent pro-White biases. White participants, classified as low or high in authoritarianism based on a pretest at the beginning of the semester, read a transcript from a trial in which a Black or White defendant was accused of murdering a storekeeper and the storekeeper's grandchild while committing a robbery. In one condition, participants were presented with the prosecution's evidence, which pilot evidence demonstrated was weak. In a second condition, participants were presented with the same weak case against the defendant, but with an extremely damaging statement introduced by the prosecution attorney that indicated that the defendant confessed to the crimes to a third party. The defense attorney objected to this statement as hearsay because the prosecution was not able to produce the third party in court. Sustaining the motion by the defense, the judge instructed the jurors to ignore this inadmissible evidence. We explored whether this damaging inadmissible evidence would differentially influence the decisions of guilt for Black and White defendants.

Both high- and low authoritarian participants displayed racial biases in their reactions to the inadmissible evidence, but they did so in different ways. In their ratings of certainty of guilt, high authoritarians did not ignore the inadmissible testimony when the victim was Black: They were more certain of the Black defendant's guilt when they were exposed to the inadmissible evidence than when they were not presented with this testimony. For the White defendant, however, high authoritarians followed the judge's instructions appropriately. Low authoritarian participants, in contrast, followed the judge's instructions about ignoring the inadmissible testimony when the defendant was Black. However, they were biased in favor of the White defendant when the inadmissible evidence was presented. That is, low authoritarians were less certain of the White defendant's guilt when the inadmissible evidence was presented than when it was omitted. Thus, low authoritarian participants demonstrated a pro-ingroup bias. It is important to note that the anti-outgroup bias of high authoritarians and the pro-ingroup bias of low authoritarians both disadvantage Blacks relative to Whites, but in fundamentally different ways.

Over 15 years later, Johnson, Whitestone, Jackson, and Gatto (1995) further explored how the introduction of an apparently nonrace-related factor suggesting guilt can differentially impact juridic decisions in ways that discriminate against Black defendants. In particular, in another laboratory simulation study, Johnson et al. examined the impact of the introduction of inadmissible evidence, which was damaging to a defendant's case, on Whites' judgments of a Black or White defendant's guilt. No differences in judgments of guilt occurred as a function of defendant race when all the evidence presented was admissible. However, consistent with the aversive racism framework, the presentation of inadmissible evidence increased judgment of guilt when the defendant was Black but not when the defendant was White. Furthermore, suggesting the unconscious or unintentional nature of the bias, participants' self-reports indicated that they believed that the inadmissible evidence had less effect on their decisions when the defendant was Black than when the defendant was White. Johnson et al. conclude that these results "are clearly consistent with the modern racism perspective, which suggests that discriminatory behavior will occur only when it can be justified on nonracial grounds." (p. 896)

Recently, we conducted another study along these lines in the United Kingdom. In this study (Hodson, Hooper, Dovidio, & Gaertner, 2005), White participants were exposed to DNA evidence that was damaging to the case of a White or Black defendant accused of a robbery. In one condition, the DNA evidence was ruled inadmissible by the judge; in another condition the admissibility of the evidence was not challenged. Consistent with our predictions, we found that White participants appropriately corrected their judgments for White defendants by effectively discounting the inadmissible evidence, judging the defendant as less guilty when the damaging evidence was inadmissible than when it was admissible. In contrast, White participants had difficulty suppressing the inadmissible evidence when the defendant was Black; they demonstrated a rebound effect, tending to judge the Black defendant as more guilty when the evidence was inadmissible than when it was admissible. Thus, consistent with the previous research, the presentation of damaging inadmissible evidence had a stronger negative impact on the judgments of Black defendants than of White defendants.

Thus, three experiments that used using similar paradigms over a span of 35 years obtained evidence of a subtle but persistent pattern of discrimination predicted by the aversive racism framework. Several other studies of legal decision-making have also yielded evidence consistent with the proposition that Whites' biases against Blacks will be more pronounced when they have an apparently non-race-related justification for judging a Black defendant guilty or sentencing them more severely (Knight, Guiliano, & Sanchez-Ross, 2001). However, also consistent with the aversive racism framework, when testimony is included that suggests that racial bias may be involved in the allegations against a Black defendant, Whites no longer racially discriminate (Sommers & Ellsworth, 2000).

Moreover, the processes of aversive racism are not limited to the United States; there is increasing evidence that they are reflected in the attitudes and actions toward a number of different groups in other countries when overt forms of discrimination are recognized as inappropriate (see Esses, Dovidio, Jackson, & Armstrong, 2001; Kleinpenning & Hagendoorn, 1993; Pettigrew & Meertens, 1995).

Whereas the evidence indicating the persistence of the effects of aversive racism in Whites' helping behavior and juridic decisions have relied on conceptual replications across time and different locations, we have further evidence involving a direct procedural replication (Dovidio & Gaertner, 2000). We used exactly the same paradigm with students from the same college in 1989 and 1999. Participants at these two different points in time were asked to assist in deciding which applicants should be hired as a Resident Advisor in one of the college's large dormitories. They were given background information, including a résumé and excerpts from an interview, that indicated (as pretested) that the applicant had very weak, moderate (arguably qualified), or very strong qualifications for the position. Information on the résumé revealed the race of the candidate as Black or White. Our prediction, based on the aversive racism framework, was that bias would not be expressed when the candidate was clearly qualified or unqualified for a position, because the appropriate decision would be obvious. However, bias was expected when the appropriate decision was unclear, when the candidate had moderate qualifications.

Consistent with the aversive racism framework, when the candidates' credentials clearly qualified them for the position (strong qualifications) or the credentials clearly were not appropriate (weak qualifications), there was no discrimination against the Black candidate. However, when candidates' qualifications for the position were less obvious and the appropriate decision was more ambiguous (moderate qualifications), White participants recommended the Black candidate significantly less often than the White candidate with exactly the same credentials. Moreover, when we compared the responses of participants in 1989 and 1999, whereas overt expressions of prejudice (measured by items on a self-report prejudice scale) declined over this 10-year period, the pattern of subtle discrimination in selection decisions remained essentially unchanged. As depicted in Fig. 1, we obtained a nearly identical pattern of results for hiring recommendations in 1989 and 1999.

Recently, Otero and Dovidio (2005) conceptually replicated this research with human resource professionals in Puerto Rico, focusing on the moderate qualifications and strong qualifications conditions. The findings illustrate the generalizability and persistence of these effects even among experienced professionals in the field. When the applicant had strong qualifications, Blacks and Whites received equivalently strong recommendations for hiring (M_s=6.17 and 6.39). However, when the applicant had only moderate qualifications, Black candidates were recommended significantly less strongly than White candidates (M_s=2.88 vs. 3.78). This effect was mainly due to a devaluation of the Black candidate. In a condition in which no information about the race of the applicant was given, participants recommended candidates with no information about race the same as those who indicated that they were White on the application (M_s=3.64 vs. 3.78).

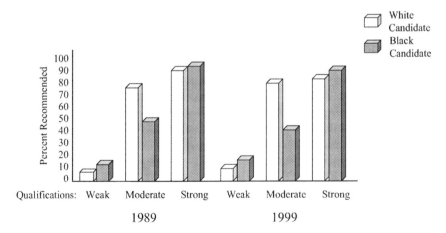

Fig. 1 Recommendations for Hiring as a Function of the Strength of the Candidate's Qualifications and Race (Dovidio & Gaertner, 2000)

Overall, these studies show that in contrast to the dramatic decline in overt expressions of prejudice, subtle forms of discrimination outlined in the aversive racism framework continue to exist, apparently largely unabated. As we noted earlier, one reason for this persistence is that these types of bias may not be fully recognized as discrimination under the law, and therefore they cannot be prosecuted successfully. Even though appropriate structural changes, such as revisions of legal codes, can potentially have dramatic impact on even subtle forms of bias (Dovidio, Gaertner, & Bachman, 2001), more informal forces, such as social norms (Crandall & Stangor, 2005) and personal standards (Devine, 2005; Devine & Monteith, 1993) can also bring about significant social change. We propose, in fact, that aversive racism can influence interracial behaviors at the relatively microlevel of behavior in interracial interactions, which can subsequently subtly shape specific outcomes for Blacks and the general climate of racial relations. The root of this type of bias in action is the unconscious attitudes that aversive racists harbor. Thus, we next consider the nature of these unconscious attitudes, informed by research in social cognition on implicit attitudes.

Implicit Attitudes and Interracial Behavior

A cornerstone of the aversive racism framework is the conflict between the denial of personal prejudice (i.e., explicit attitudes) and the underlying unconscious negative feelings and beliefs (i.e., implicit attitudes and stereotypes). Beginning in the 1970s and 1980s (e.g., Shiffrin & Schneider, 1977) but substantially in the 1990s, the field of cognitive psychology offered an important distinction between implicit and explicit memory processes. Implicit memory processes involve lack of awareness and are unintentionally activated, whereas explicit processes are conscious, deliberative, and controllable.

A similar distinction emerged in the social psychological literature on attitudes and stereotyping (Devine, 1989; Greenwald & Banaji, 1995). Explicit attitudes and stereotyping operate in a conscious mode and are exemplified by traditional, self-report measures of these constructs. Implicit attitudes and stereotypes, in contrast, are evaluations and beliefs that are automatically activated by the mere presence (actual or symbolic) of the attitude object. They commonly function in an unconscious fashion. Implicit attitudes and stereotypes are typically assessed using response latency procedures, memory tasks, physiological measures (e.g., galvanic skin response, GSR; see Nail, Harton, & Decker, 2003), and indirect self-report measures (e.g., involving attributional biases). These techniques for assessing automatic activation offer conceptually and empirically different perspectives on both attitudes and stereotypes than traditional self-report measures.

Evidence of implicit negative racial attitudes of Whites toward Blacks has been generally consistent and strong. Response latency procedures, in particular, have demonstrated that racial attitudes and stereotypes may operate like other stimuli to facilitate responses and decision-making about related concepts (e.g., doctor–nurse).

In general, the greater the associative strength between two stimuli for participants, the faster they can make decisions about them (e.g., Dovidio, Evans, & Tyler, 1986; Gaertner & McLaughlin, 1983). Convergent evidence has been obtained with a variety of different priming procedures (see Blair, 2001; Dovidio, Kawakami, & Beach, 2001), as well as with other response latency techniques such as the Implicit Association Test (Greenwald, McGhee, & Schwartz, 1998). For example, we have found, using subliminally presented schematic faces of Blacks and Whites as stimulus primes, that White participants have faster response times to negative traits after Black than White primes and faster response times to positive traits after White than Black primes (Dovidio, Kawakami, Johnson, Johnson, & Howard, 1997, Study 1; see also Wittenbrink, Judd, & Park, 1997).

Moreover, consistent with the aversive racism framework, Whites' implicit attitudes, which are negative on average, are largely dissociated from their explicit attitudes, which are frequently relatively positive and egalitarian (Dovidio et al., 2001). Implicit and explicit (i.e., self-report) attitudes may thus reflect the components of a system of "dual attitudes." According to Wilson, Lindsey, and Schooler (2000), dual attitudes commonly arise developmentally. With experience or socialization, people change their attitudes. However, the original attitude is not replaced, but rather it is stored in memory and becomes implicit, whereas the newer attitude is conscious and explicit. Because Whites are exposed to negative images of Blacks through the media and to pervasive stereotypes about Blacks through common socialization experiences (Devine, 1989), they may initially develop largely negative attitudes toward Blacks. Later, when as social norms change to become more egalitarian or an individual is exposed to new normative proscriptions that dictate that people should *not* have these negative feelings toward Blacks, people may adopt explicit unbiased or positive attitudes. Nevertheless, these negative implicit attitudes linger. It is this combination of explicit egalitarian attitudes and implicit negative attitudes that can then characterize the racial attitudes of aversive racists.

The disassociation between the explicit and implicit attitudes of aversive racists can subtly shape the ways that Whites and Blacks interact and further contribute to the different perceptions that Whites and Blacks develop about their interactions. Specifically, implicit and explicit attitudes can influence behavior in different ways and under different conditions (Dovidio & Fazio, 1992; Fazio, 1990; Wilson et al., 2000). Explicit attitudes shape deliberative, well-considered responses for which people have the motivation and opportunity to weigh the costs and benefits of various courses of action. Implicit attitudes influence responses that are more difficult to monitor and control (e.g., some nonverbal expressions of feelings) or responses that people do not view as an indication of their attitude and thus do not try to control. Thus the relative impact of implicit and explicit attitudes is a function of the context in which the attitudinal object appears, the motivation and opportunity to engage in deliberative processes, and the nature of the behavioral response.

Consistent with the work of other researchers in this area (Fazio, Jackson, Dunton, & Williams, 1995), we have also found evidence in a series of experiments that implicit and explicit attitudes influence different types of race-relevant behaviors of Whites (Dovidio et al., 1997). One study (Dovidio et al., 1997, Study 3), for example, involved two ostensibly unrelated parts: (a) measures of racial attitudes and (b) interaction with a Black and a White interviewer sequentially. The measures of racial attitudes included a response latency task and two self-report measures, McConahay's (1986) Old-Fashioned and Racism Modern Racism Scales. Measures of deliberative and spontaneous behaviors were assessed during the interaction. As a measure of deliberative behavior, participants were asked to evaluate both other interactants (i.e., the Black and White interviewers) on a series of rating scales. As measures of spontaneous behavior, the nonverbal behaviors of eye contact and blinking were coded from videotapes of the interactions. Higher levels of visual contact (i.e., time spent looking at another person) reflect greater attraction, intimacy, and respect. Higher rates of blinking have been demonstrated to be related to higher levels of negative arousal and tension (Exline, 1985). Both of these types of nonverbal behaviors are particularly difficult to monitor and control. It was predicted that explicit measures of prejudice would primarily relate to bias in the evaluations of Black relative to White interviewers by White participants. In contrast, the response latency measure of implicit negative racial attitude was expected to be the best predictor of nonverbal reactions – specifically higher rates of blinking and less visual contact with the Black relative to the White interviewer.

The results supported the predictions. Bias in terms of more negative judgments about Black than White interviewers was correlated with the two explicit measures of prejudice, Old-Fashioned Racism ($r=0.37$) and Modern Racism ($r=0.54$), but was uncorrelated with implicit prejudice ($r=0.02$). In contrast, implicit prejudice predicted lower levels of visual contact ($r=-0.40$) and higher rates of blinking ($r=0.43$), but Old-Fashioned Racism ($r_s=0.02$, -0.04) and Modern Racism ($r_s=0.20,0.07$) did not.

One reason why Whites' implicit attitudes relate to nonverbal behaviors relating to both attraction (eye contact) and anxiety (blinking) is that interracial interaction is a highly demanding activity for Whites, particularly those who are motivated to behave in an unbiased manner and who genuinely strive to be nonprejudiced (Dovidio & Gaertner, 2004; Shelton & Richeson, 2006). Richeson, Shelton, and colleagues have found that interracial interactions are very cognitively demanding experiences for Whites in general, which depletes their cognitive resources for subsequent intellectual tasks (Richeson et al., 2003; Richeson & Shelton, 2003). These effects are especially pronounced when evaluative concerns are high, such as among Whites who are high in implicit prejudice (Richeson & Shelton, 2003). Moreover, Whites' concerns with appearing prejudiced often result in their having more negative affective reactions during interracial encounters (Devine, Evett, & Vasquez-Suson, 1996; Plant & Devine, 2003). Shelton (2003), for example, demonstrated that Whites who were instructed to try not to be prejudiced during an interracial interaction reported experiencing more anxiety compared to those who were not given these instructions. The enhanced cognitive demand and increased anxiety that accompany the heightened evaluative concerns, such as those experienced by aversive racists, can lead these individuals to behave in ways that are the opposite of their desired response, ultimately creating confusion and problems in communication in interracial interactions (Vorauer & Turpie, 2004), in part through their effects on nonverbal behavior.

Although nonverbal behaviors, such as eye contact and blinking, may seem inconsequential relative to more overt behaviors, such as evaluations of the performance of Blacks relative to Whites, nonverbal behavior can have a substantial impact on the impressions that Blacks and Whites form of each other during interactions. The impressions formed in these specific interactions then readily generalize to the racial groups as a whole (Henderson-King & Nisbett, 1996). People typically rely heavily on nonverbal behaviors when interpreting others' behaviors (Dovidio & Ellyson, 1982), and the information conveyed through the nonverbal behavior of others is weighed more heavily than verbal behaviors in forming impressions of others when there is an inconsistency between verbal and nonverbal behavior or when the perceiver is suspicions of the trustworthiness of the other person (Mehrabian, 1972). In the United States, Blacks and Whites are often wary of the true intentions of each other (Dovidio, Gaertner, Kawakami, & Hodson, 2002). In addition, because of the history of tensions and contemporary distrust between the groups (Crocker, Luhtanen, Broadnax, & Blaine, 1999), Blacks and Whites may tend systematically to confuse nonverbal behaviors generated by anxiety with cues of dislike in their interactions with each other. Indeed, many of the nonverbal behaviors elicited by anxiety, such as reduced eye contact and more closed postures, are the same as those associated with negative attitudes.

To examine this possibility, in a set of two studies (Dovidio, Pearson, Smith-McLallen, & Kawakami, 2005) we had White and Black participants view a silent videotape of Black and White confederates. The nonverbal behaviors of the confederates were patterned after differences observed in pilot testing of participants who presented a speech either as informal practice to one other person (low anxiety) or in front of an audience that they believed would evaluate them (high anxiety). In the high anxious situation, compared to the low anxious situation, participants exhibited less eye contact, more closed posture, more smiling, and higher rates of blinking, and more self-touching. We had our Black and White confederates model these high and low anxious behaviors, which were generated from situations independent of race, in brief (2-min) interactions with another person (who could not be see on the video screen).

Our results revealed that both White and Black participants perceived the confederates of both races as more tense and anxious in the high anxious video condition compared to the low anxious video condition. However, when they were viewing confederates of the other race, both White and Black participants also perceived the confederates in the high anxious condition as showing more negative feelings and attitudes to their interaction partner than those in the low anxious condition. Thus, the behaviors that were interpreted accurately as anxiety for a member of their own racial group were seen as anxiety accompanied by dislike when they were displayed by a member of the other racial group. These biases occurred to a comparable degree for Black and White participants. This pattern of findings suggests that nonverbal behavior in interracial interactions, particularly involving aversive racists who are anxious about appearing nonprejudiced, can contribute substantially to intergroup miscommunication and misunderstandings.

These communication obstacles and interaction problems are exacerbated by the fact that Whites and Blacks have fundamentally different perspectives on the attitudes and the actions of each other during these interactions. For example, Whites have full access to their explicit attitudes and are able to monitor and control their more overt and deliberative behaviors. They do not have such full access to their implicit attitudes or to their less monitorable behaviors. As a consequence, Whites' beliefs about how they are behaving or how Blacks perceive them would be expected to be based primarily on their explicit attitudes and their more overt behaviors, such as the verbal content of their interaction with Blacks, and not on their implicit attitudes or less deliberative (i.e., nonverbal) behaviors. In contrast to the perspective of Whites, the perspective of Black partners in these interracial interactions allows them to attend to both the spontaneous (e.g., nonverbal) and the deliberative (e.g., verbal) behaviors of Whites. To the extent that the Black partners attend to Whites' nonverbal behaviors, which may signal more negativity than their verbal behaviors, Blacks are likely to form more negative impressions of the encounter and be less satisfied with the interaction than are Whites (Shelton, 2000). Blacks tend to show heightened attentiveness and sensitivity to nonverbal cues of prejudice in interracial interactions (Richeson & Shelton, 2006; Rollman, 1978). As Vorauer and Kumhyr (2001) have demonstrated, minority group members are generally attuned to negative behaviors of majority group members that could reveal their prejudice, and detecting these behaviors makes them less comfortable and less satisfied with the interaction.

To investigate this possibility, we conducted another experiment (Dovidio, Kawakami, & Gaertner, 2002). We assessed perceptions of interracial interactions by Whites and Blacks, and we related these perceptions to White participants' explicit and implicit attitudes. We first assessed the implicit attitudes using Dovidio et al. (1997) response-latency priming technique and explicit racial attitudes using Brigham's (1993) Attitudes toward Blacks Scale. Then we arranged interracial conversations with a Black and a White dyad partner around a race-neutral topic. We videotaped the interactions and subsequently had one set of coders rate the nonverbal and verbal behaviors of White participants and another set of observers rate their global impressions of participants from a videotape recorded from their partners' perspective (i.e., recorded over the partner's shoulder and directed at the White participant).

We hypothesized that in these interracial interactions White participants would rely on their explicit, self-reported racial attitudes to shape deliberative behaviors such as their friendliness of verbal behavior toward Black relative to White partners. Explicit racial attitudes and participants' verbal behavior, in turn, were expected to predict Whites' impressions of how friendly they behaved in interactions with the Black relative to the White partner. Implicit racial attitudes, measured with response latencies, and racial bias in White participants' nonverbal behaviors, because they are not easily monitored by the participants, were not expected to predict these impressions.

We also anticipated, based on our previous research, that White participants' implicit racial attitudes would predict biases in their nonverbal friendliness. We further hypothesized that for Black and White partners and independent observers, who could monitor both the White participants' deliberative actions (verbal behaviors) and more spontaneous and subtle behaviors (nonverbal behaviors), perceptions of bias in participants' friendliness would relate significantly to perceptions of bias in participants' nonverbal behaviors and to participants' implicit attitudes. Finally, as a consequence of their different perspectives and their reliance on different cues, we also expected participants' perceptions of their own racial biases and their partners' perceptions would be only weakly related.

The results were consistent with our predictions. Implicit attitudes predicted nonverbal friendliness ($r=+0.41$) but not verbal friendliness ($r=+0.04$), based on our coders' judgments of friendliness. Less implicitly biased Whites behaved in a friendlier nonverbal manner. In contrast, the explicit, self-report measure of prejudice predicted verbal ($r=+0.40$) but not nonverbal ($r=+0.02$) friendliness. Less explicitly prejudiced Whites had more favorable verbal behaviors with the Black partner. Also as anticipated, White participants and Black partners developed very different impressions. More negative impressions of the friendliness of the White participant as judged by the partners was related to his or her nonverbal behavior, as rated by our coders ($r=+0.34$), but not to the judged friendliness of the White participants' verbal behavior ($r=-0.17$). White participants' impressions of their own friendliness was related more to their verbal behavior ($r=+0.36$) than to their nonverbal behavior ($r=-0.07$). Ultimately, the impressions of the friendliness of White participants by themselves and by their partners were essentially unrelated ($r=+0.11$). Thus, because of their very different perspectives and reliance on different information, Whites and Blacks left the same interaction with very different impressions.

Our postexperimental discussions with White participants and their Black partners separately provided vivid illustrations of the discordance. White participants typically reported that they found the interaction satisfying and expressed contentment with their contributions. Their Black partners, however, reported being relatively dissatisfied with the exchange and were uneasy about their partners' behaviors. Moreover, both dyad members, when asked, usually assumed that their partner shared the impression of the interaction that they did.

Hebl, Foster, Mannix, and Dovidio (2002) found parallel results, with more evidence of bias for subtle and spontaneous behaviors than for overt and formal actions, for another type of intergroup bias, the prejudice of potential employers toward gay men and lesbians. In this study, employers did not discriminate against confederates portrayed as gay or lesbian on formal employment behaviors, such as permission to complete a job application and callbacks for further consideration. However, bias was expressed more subtly in employers' interaction behaviors. That is, employers spent less time, used fewer words, and smiled less when interacting with the stigmatized applicants than the nonstigmatized applicants.

Moreover, similar to the results of Dovidio et al. (2002), applicants in the Hebl et al. (2002) study based their interpretations of the employers' behavior on the subtle cues. Confederates portrayed as gay perceived that employers were biased against them and anticipated discrimination from them – although no bias in actual employment actions were observed in the study. These findings further illustrate how members of majority groups and potential targets of prejudice can form different impressions of the same interaction, producing intergroup misunderstanding.

The different and potentially divergent impressions that Blacks and Whites may form during interracial interactions can have significant impact on their coordination and thus their effectiveness in task-oriented situations. Cannon-Bowers and Salas (1999) have argued that effective teamwork requires two types of skills, those associated with the technical aspects of the job and those associated with being a member of the team. For this latter factor, team competencies include the knowledge, skills, and attitudes required to work effectively with others. Besides manifesting itself in terms of different impressions and perceptions, contemporary bias can therefore also influence personal relations and group processes in ways that unintentionally but adversely affect outcomes for Blacks.

We propose that for interracial teams, both implicit and explicit racial attitudes are important for effective teamwork. To the extent that explicit attitudes are manifested overtly in less friendly and less supportive actions, interracial interactions involving more highly prejudiced Whites would be expected to be less productive. To the extent that implicit racial attitudes may also be detected, at least by a Black partner, through more subtle manifestations such as nonverbal behavior, these unconscious biases can erode the trust between group members and negatively impact group performance.

In our research on this issue (Dovidio, 2001), White college students were classified on the basis of their self-reported racial attitudes (Brigham's, 1993, Attitudes Toward Blacks Scale) and our implicit response latency measure of bias (Dovidio et al., 1997). A portion of the participants was identified as being low in prejudice on the self-report measure and unbiased on the unconscious (i.e., response latency) measure (Nonprejudiced, about 25%). Another group appeared low in prejudice on the self-report measure but had implicit racial biases (Aversive Racists, about 40%). A third group was relatively prejudiced on the self-report measure as well as biased on the implicit measure (Prejudiced, about 20%). (About 15% of the total sample could not be clearly classified into one of these three categories.) We then examined how friendly these participants felt they behaved during an interracial interaction, how friendly and trustful their Black partners perceived them, and how effectively the group performed (i.e., how quickly they could decide which items would be most valuable for am incoming student to bring to college).

The results are summarized in Table 1. As we found in our earlier research, Whites' impressions of their behavior were related primarily to their explicit attitudes, whereas Blacks impressions of Whites were related mainly to Whites' implicit attitudes. Specifically, Whites who appeared low in prejudice on the self-report measure (i.e., Nonprejudiced Whites and Aversive Racists) reported that they behaved more friendly than did those who scored high (Prejudiced Whites). Black partners perceived Whites who were unbiased on the implicit, response latency measure (Nonprejudiced Whites) to be more friendly than those who had

Table 1 Implicit and explicit prejudice and interracial perceptions and effectiveness

	Perceived friendliness of the white participant		Perceived trustworthiness of the white participant		Time to complete task
	By white participant	By black partner	By white participant	By black partner	By dyad
Nonprejudiced whites (low implicit/low explicit prejudice)	5.6	5.5	5.8	5.3	4:35
Aversive racists (high implicit/low explicit prejudice)	5.8	4.6	5.9	4.2	6:10
Prejudiced whites (high implicit/high explicit prejudice)	4.6	4.4	5.4	4.7	5:42

unconscious biases (Aversive Racists and Prejudiced Whites). Blacks were also less trustful of Prejudiced Whites and particularly of Aversive Racists and than of Nonprejudiced Whites.

Our results further revealed that Whites' racial attitudes were systematically related to the efficiency of the interracial teams. Teams with Nonprejudiced Whites solved the problem most quickly. Interracial teams involving Prejudiced Whites were next most efficient. Teams with Aversive Racists were the least efficient. Presumably, the conflicting messages displayed by Aversive Racists and the divergent impressions of the team members' interaction interfered with the task effectiveness of the team. To the extent that Blacks are in the minority in an organization and are dependent on high prejudiced Whites or aversive racists on work-related tasks, their performance is likely to be objectively poorer than the performance of Whites who predominantly interact with other Whites. Thus, even when Whites harbor unconscious and unintentional biases toward Blacks, their actions can have effects sometimes even more detrimental than those of old-fashioned racists on interracial processes and outcomes.

Implications and Conclusions

We acknowledge that blatant racism and overt discrimination still exist in the United States and strongly impact the quality of life and well-being of Black Americans. Racial hate crimes remain the most common type of hate crimes in the US today (Perry, 2002). Not all racists are aversive racists. However, we contend that aversive racism also continues to be a significant force adversely affecting the lives of Black Americans. Although aversive racism is subtle, its consequences are severe. It affects the way Whites make decisions about hiring Blacks, admitting Blacks to college, helping Blacks in both mundane and emergency need situations, and in judging guilt or innocence in the courtroom. The impact of aversive racism can be comparable to that of old-fashioned racism in restricting the opportunities for Black Americans and maintaining the social, economic, and political dominance of White Americans.

In this chapter, we have identified recent developments in research on aversive racism. Whereas the early research was aimed at identifying the operation of aversive racism and distinguishing it from old-fashioned racism, the more recent work, which was the focus of this chapter, has moved in three directions. First, we showed that, whereas overt expressions of racism have steadily declined over the past 25 years, manifestations of aversive racism appear to persist at consistent levels. We illustrated this with conceptual replications of simulated juror decisions from 1979 though 2005 (Faranda & Gaertner, 1979; Hodson et al., 2005; Johnson et al., 1995), as well as with data concerning personnel selection from exact replications in 1989 and 1999 (Dovidio & Gaertner, 2000).

We posit that because aversive racism operates in largely unrecognized ways, the personal, social, and formal forces that inhibit blatant prejudice and discrimination are not normally effective for addressing aversive racism. At the personal level, aversive racists are well intentioned; they sincerely embrace egalitarian principles and genuinely believe that they are not prejudiced. Moreover, because of the centrality of their nonprejudiced self-images, they are well practiced at denying indications of personal bias, and when they are aware that they might be discriminating, they behave in an unbiased way. Aversive racists thus have little motivation to change their racial orientations because, although they recognize that racism still exists, they do not see themselves as part of the problem.

At a societal level, aversive racism is expressed primarily when a negative decision (e.g., regarding a social policy intended to benefit Blacks) or action toward a Black person can be justified on the basis of some factor other than race. As a consequence, the role of racism in these actions is typically unacknowledged, and the social sanctions and norms that inhibit blatant racism do not operate for subtle biases. At the formal level, current legal definitions of discrimination, which emphasize the importance of personal intention and evidence that racism is the sole cause of the action, tend to make the behavioral manifestations of aversive racism immune to successful prosecution. Aversive racism operates unintentionally, and it produces discrimination primarily when the negative behavior can be justified on the basis of some factor other than race. Thus, the forces that have evolved to address blatant racism are much less effective for combating aversive racism.

A second new direction in work on aversive racism involves developments in conceptualizing and measuring unconscious negative feeling, beliefs, and attitudes, which we were previously able only to hypothesize. In particular, research in the area of implicit social cognition has provided solid evidence that people often possess attitudes and beliefs that they are not aware of and often conflict with their current conscious attitudes (Fazio & Olson, 2003). These implicit, unconscious attitudes are overlearned responses, many of which are acquired early in life (Wilson et al., 2000), or are associated with basic responses to perceived threat (Phelps et al., 2000) and are automatically activated by appropriate cues. Implicit attitudes affect behavior primarily when people are not sufficiently motivated or are not able (e.g., because of other cognitive demands) to correct their behavior to conform to their conscious attitudes (Fazio, 1990; Kawakami, Dovidio, & van Kamp, 2005).

These ideas and findings have direct application to racial attitudes, and in ways that converge with the basic premises of aversive racism. Consistent with assumptions of the aversive racism perspective, Whites in the United States typically have implicit negative attitudes and beliefs about Blacks (Blair, 2001). Moreover, implicit attitudes are largely dissociated from Whites' conscious attitudes. The correlation between implicit and explicit racial attitudes is weak ($r=0.24$; Dovidio et al., 2001). Also, whereas Whites tend to behave in accord with their conscious attitudes when they have sufficient awareness of and ability to control their responses, implicit attitudes tend to predict behaviors, such as nonverbal behaviors, that are less likely to be monitored and controlled (Dovidio et al., 1997; Fazio et al., 1995; McConnell & Leibold, 2001). Before these developments, when Whites scored high on self-report measures of prejudice, we classified them as old-fashioned racists. When they scored low on these self-report measures, we generally assumed that they were aversive racists. These new techniques permit us to distinguish between aversive racists, those who score low on explicit prejudice but have implicit biases, and Whites who are truly low prejudiced, those who show no or low prejudice on both explicit and implicit measures.

The third development in the study of aversive racism that we discuss in this chapter concerns how aversive racism subtly shapes interracial interaction, creating interracial misunderstanding and perpetuating racial tensions and biases. Building on the idea that explicit prejudice relates to overt expression of bias and racial discrimination whereas implicit prejudice relates to spontaneous behaviors, such as nonverbal behaviors, we illustrated how aversive racism contributes to miscommunication in interracial interaction. Because explicit prejudice relates to overt behaviors, aversive racist who believe that they are not prejudiced and who attempt to behave in favorable ways toward Blacks often believe that they are acting in a positive and favorable way in these interactions. And from all they can monitor – their conscious nonprejudiced attitudes and their controllable behaviors – they are expressing favorable orientations in these interracial interactions. However, the behaviors they cannot easily monitor or control, their nonverbal behaviors, undermine their actual effectiveness. Their negative implicit attitudes (Dovidio et al., 2002) and the cognitive effort and anxiety that accompany their efforts to inhibit their potential biases (Richeson & Shelton, 2003; Richeson et al., 2003) elicit nonverbal behaviors (e.g., less eye contact, less open posture) associated with negative feelings. In addition, in interracial encounters, Blacks and other minority group members, because of intergroup distrust, tend to interpret these nonverbal behaviors as reflecting the White person's "true" prejudice.

One consequence of this process is that aversive racists and their Black partners may leave their interaction with different interpretations. Aversive racists, who base their impressions on actions that they can monitor and control, tend to believe that they are friendly and effective; in contrast, their Black partners, who are particularly attuned to the nonverbal behaviors, perceive aversive racists as racially biased and, given the contrast with the apparently friendly verbal content, often as duplicitous and untrustworthy. Thus, aversive racism may contribute directly to the general distrust and suspiciousness that Blacks have of Whites in the United States (Crocker et al., 1999).

Because of these divergent perspectives, miscommunication, and mistrust, another consequence is that work teams composed of an aversive racist and a Black partner perform less effectively than do interracial work teams with a non-prejudiced White person or even a high prejudiced White person (whose implicit and explicit attitudes are consonant). Moreover, as previous research has demonstrated (Word, Zanna, & Cooper, 1974), negative nonverbal cues, controlling for verbal aspects of the interaction, can produce a self-fulfilling prophecy in which Blacks respond less positively and perform more poorly as a result. Whereas our research on hiring decisions revealed that aversive racism can adversely affects Whites' decisions to hire Blacks even when they have equivalent performance records as White candidates, this recent research demonstrates that the subtle bias associated with aversive racism may induce Black candidates to perform less well in face-to-face job interviews and actually perform less well on work-related tasks. Although it operates in subtle ways, aversive racism contributes to a reality that justifies and perpetuates racial disparities.

The three new directions in research on aversive racism that we explored in this chapter converge with our earlier evidence of the perniciousness of aversive racism. The influence of aversive racism is pervasive; it affects race relations and outcomes for Blacks in a variety of ways. And it persists because it remains largely unrecognized and thus unaddressed. However, we propose that it can be combated with new approaches and strategies that are uniquely targeted at critical components of aversive racism. For example, because aversive racists are truly motivated to be nonprejudiced, making them aware, in a nonthreatening way, of their unconscious biases can arouse motivations to change in fundamental ways, which can eventually reduce unconscious biases (Devine & Monteith, 1993; Dovidio, Kawakami, & Gaertner, 2000). Alternatively, strategies can be directed at the roots of unconscious biases, such as processes related to social categorization. We examine this approach in detail in the Gaertner and Dovidio chapter. Without sufficient recognition of the subtle nature of contemporary biases and without the appropriate tools for combating these particular biases, significant progress toward a truly just society will be difficult to achieve. Good intentions alone are not good enough.

References

Adorno, T. W., Frenkel-Brunswik, E., Levinson, D. J., & Sanford, R. N. (1950). *The authoritarian personality*. New York: Harper.

Allport, G. W. (1954). *The nature of prejudice*. New York: Addison-Wesley.

Blair, I. V. (2001). Implicit stereotypes and prejudice. In G. B. Moskowitz (Ed.), *Cognitive social psychology: The princeton symposium on the legacy and future of social cognition* (pp. 359–374). Mahwah, NJ: Erlbaum.

Blank, R. M. (2001). An overview of trends in social and economic well-being, by race. In N. J. Smelser, W. J. Wilson, & F. Mitchell, (Eds.), *Racial trends and their consequences* (Vol. 1, pp. 21–39). Washington, DC: National Academy Press.

Bobo, L. (2001). Racial attitudes and relations at the close of the twentieth century. In N. J. Smelser, W. J. Wilson, & F. Mitchell, (Eds.), *Racial trends and their consequences* (Vol. 1, pp. 264–301). Washington, DC: National Academy Press.

Brigham, J. C. (1993). College students' racial attitudes. *Journal of Applied Social Psychology, 23*, 1933–1967.

Cannon-Bowers, J. A., & Salas, E. (1999). Team performance and training in complex environments: Recent findings from applied research. *Current Directions in Psychological Science : A journal of the American Psychological Society, 7*, 83–87.

Crandall, C. S., & Stangor, C. (2005). Conformity and prejudice. In J. F. Dovidio, P. Glick, & Laurie A. Rudman (Eds.), *On the nature of prejudice: Fifty years after Allport* (pp. 295–309). Malden, MA: Blackwell.

Crocker, J., Luhtanen, R., Broadnax, S., & Blaine, B. E. (1999). Belief in U.S. government conspiracies against Blacks among Black and White college students: Powerlessness or system blame? *Personality and Social Psychology Bulletin, 25*, 941–953.

Crosby, F., Bromley, S., & Saxe, L. (1980). Recent unobtrusive studies of black and white discrimination and prejudice: A literature review. *Psychological Bulletin, 87*, 546–563.

Darley, J. M., & Latané, B. (1968). Bystander intervention in emergencies: Diffusion of responsibility. *Journal of Personality and Social Psychology, 8*, 377–383.

Devine, P. G. (1989). Stereotypes and prejudice: The automatic and controlled components. *Journal of Personality and Social Psychology, 56*, 5–18.

Devine, P. G. (2005). Breaking the prejudice habit: Allport's "inner conflict" revisited. In J. F. Dovidio, P. Glick, & Laurie A. Rudman (Eds.), *On the nature of prejudice: Fifty years after Allport* (pp. 327–342). Malden, MA: Blackwell.

Devine, P. G., Evett, S. R., & Vasquez-Suson, K. A. (1996). Exploring the interpersonal dynamics of intergroup contact. In R. M. Sorrentino & E. T. Higgins (Eds.), *Handbook of motivation and cognition* (Vol. 3, pp. 423–464). New York: Guilford.

Devine, P. G., & Monteith, M. J. (1993). The role of discrepancy-associated affect in prejudice reduction. In D. M. Mackie & D. L. Hamilton (Eds.), *Affect, cognition, and stereotyping: Interactive processes in intergroup perception* (pp. 317–344). Orlando, FL: Academic Press.

Dovidio, J. F. (2001). On the nature of contemporary prejudice: The third wave. *Journal of Social Issues, 57*, 829–849.

Dovidio, J. F., & Ellyson, S. L. (1982). Decoding visual dominance behavior: Attributions of power based on the relative percentages of looking while speaking and looking while listening. *Social Psychology Quarterly, 45*, 106–113.

Dovidio, J. F., Evans, N., & Tyler, R. B. (1986). Racial stereotypes: The contents of their cognitive representations. *Journal of Experimental Social Psychology, 22*, 22–37.

Dovidio, J. F., & Fazio, R. H. (1992). New technologies for the direct and indirect assessment of attitudes. In J. Tanur (Ed.), *Questions about survey questions: Meaning, memory, attitudes, and social interaction* (pp. 204–237). New York: Russell Sage Foundation.

Dovidio, J. F., & Gaertner, S. L. (1996). Affirmative action, unintentional racial biases, and intergroup relations. *Journal of Social Issues, 52*(4), 51–75.

Dovidio, J. F., & Gaertner, S. L. (1998). On the nature of contemporary prejudice: The causes, consequences, and challenges of aversive racism. In J. Eberhardt & S. T. Fiske (Eds.), *Confronting racism: The problem and the response* (pp. 3–32). Newbury Park, CA: Sage.

Dovidio, J. F., & Gaertner, S. L. (2000). Aversive racism and selection decisions: 1989 and 1999. *Psychological Science, 11*, 319–323.

Dovidio, J. F., & Gaertner, S. L. (2004). Aversive racism. In M. P. Zanna (Ed.), *Advances in experimental social psychology* (Vol. 36, pp. 1–51). San Diego, CA: Academic Press.

Dovidio, J. F., Gaertner, S. L., & Bachman, B. A. (2001). Racial bias in organizations: The role of group processes in its causes and cures. In M. E. Turner (Ed.), *Groups at work: Theory and research* (pp. 415–444). Mahwah, NJ: Erlbaum.

Dovidio, J. F., Gaertner, S. L., Kawakami, K., & Hodson, G. (2002). Why can't we just get along? Interpersonal biases and interracial distrust. *Cultural Diversity & Ethnic Minority Psychology, 8*, 88–102.

Dovidio, J., Kawakami, K., & Beach, K. (2001). Implicit and explicit attitudes: Examination of the relationship between measures of intergroup bias. In R. Brown & S. L. Gaertner (Eds.), *Blackwell handbook of social psychology* (Vol. 4 , pp. 175–197). Oxford, UK: Blackwell.

Dovidio, J. F., Kawakami, K., & Gaertner, S. L. (2000). Reducing contemporary prejudice: Combating explicit and implicit bias at the individual and intergroup level. In S. Oskamp (Ed.), *Reducing prejudice and discrimination* (pp. 137–163). Hillsdale, NJ: Erlbaum.

Dovidio, J. F., Kawakami, K., & Gaertner, S. L. (2002). Implicit and explicit prejudice and inter-racial interaction. *Journal of Personality and Social Psychology, 82*, 62–68.

Dovidio, J., Kawakami, K., Johnson, C., Johnson, B., & Howard, A. (1997). The nature of prejudice: Automatic and controlled processes. *Journal of Experimental Social Psychology, 33*, 510–540.

Dovidio, J. F., Pearson, A., Smith-McLallen, A., & Kawakami, K. (2005). *From the interpersonal to the intergroup: The role of nonverbal behavior in interracial interaction on intergroup relations.* Paper presented at the annual meeting of the Society of Experimental Social Psychology, San Diego, CA.

DuBois, W. E. B. (1986). *Writings.* Reprinted W. E. Burghardt (Ed.). New York: Viking Press.

Duckitt, J. (1992). *The social psychology of prejudice.* Westport, CT: Praeger.

Elvira, M. M., & Zatzick, C. D. (2002). Who's displaced first? The role of race in layoff decisions. *Industrial Relations, 41*, 329–361.

Esses, V. M., Dovidio, J. F., Jackson, L. M., & Armstrong, T. M. (2001). The immigration dilemma: The role of perceived group competition, ethnic prejudice, and national identity. *Journal of Social Issues, 57*, 389–412.

Exline, R. V. (1985). Multichannel transmission of nonverbal behavior and perceptions of power-ful men: The presidential debates of 1976. In S. L. Ellyson & J. F. Dovidio (Eds.), *Power, dominance, and nonverbal behavior* (pp. 183–206). New York: Springer-Verlag.

Fairchild, H. H., & Cowan, G. (1997). The O. J. Simpson trial: Challenges to science and society. *Journal of Social Issues, 53*(3), 583–591.

Faranda, J., & Gaertner, S. L. (1979). *The effects of inadmissible evidence introduced by the prose-cution and the defense, and the defendant's race on the verdicts by high and low authoritarians.* Paper presented at the annual meeting of the Eastern Psychological Association, New York.

Fazio, R. H. (1990). Multiple processes by which attitudes guide behavior: The MODE Model as an integrative framework. In M. P. Zanna (Ed.), *Advances in experimental social psychology* (Vol. 23, pp. 75–109). Orlando, FL: Academic Press.

Fazio, R. H., Jackson, J. R., Dunton, B. C., & Williams, C. J. (1995). Variability in automatic activation as an unobtrusive measure of racial attitudes: A bona fide pipeline? *Journal of Personality and Social Psychology, 69*, 1013–1027.

Fazio, R. H., & Olson, M. A. (2003). Implicit measures in social cognition research: Their mean-ing and uses. *Annual Review of Psychology, 54*, 297–327.

Feagin, J. R., & Sikes, M. P. (1994). *Living with racism: The Black middle-class experience.* Boston, MA: Beacon Press.

Fein, S., & Spencer, S. J. (1997). Prejudice as self-image maintenance: Affirming the self through derogating others. *Journal of Personality and Social Psychology, 73*, 31–44.

Gaertner, S. L. (1973). Helping behavior and racial discrimination among liberals and conserva-tives. *Journal of Personality and Social Psychology, 25*, 335–341.

Gaertner, S. L., & Dovidio, J. F. (1977). The subtlety of white racism, arousal, and helping behav-ior. *Journal of Personality and Social Psychology, 35*, 691–707.

Gaertner, S. L., & Dovidio, J. F. (1986). The aversive form of racism. In J. F. Dovidio & S. L. Gaertner (Eds.), *Prejudice, discrimination, and racism* (pp. 61–89). Orlando, FL: Academic Press.

Gaertner, S. L., Dovidio, J. F., Banker, B., Rust, M., Nier, J., Mottola, G., et al. C. (1997). Does racism necessarily mean anti-Blackness? Aversive racism and pro-whiteness. In M. Fine, L. Powell, L. Weis, & M. Wong (Eds.), *Off white* (pp. 167–178). London: Routledge.

Gaertner, S. L., & McLaughlin, J. P. (1983). Racial stereotypes: Associations and ascriptions of positive and negative characteristics. *Social Psychology Quarterly, 46*, 23–30.

Greenwald, A., & Banaji, M. (1995). Implicit social cognition: Attitudes, self-esteem, and stereo-types. *Psychological Review, 102*, 4–27.

Greenwald, A., McGhee, D., & Schwartz, J. (1998). Measuring individual differences in implicit cognition: The implicit association test. *Journal of Personality and Social Psychology, 74,* 1464–1480.

Hebl, M. R., Foster, J. B., Mannix, L. M., & Dovidio, J. F. (2002). Formal and interpersonal discrimination. A field study of bias toward homosexual applicants. *Personality and Social Psychology Bulletin, 28,* 815–825.

Henderson-King, E. I, & Nisbett, R. E. (1996). Anti-Black prejudice as a function of exposure to the negative behavior of a single Black person. *Journal of Personality and Social Psychology, 7,* 654–664.

Hodson, G., Hooper, H., Dovidio, J. F., & Gaertner, S. L. (2005). Aversive racism in Britain: Legal decisions and the use of inadmissible evidence. *European Journal of Social Psychology, 35,* 437–448.

Johnson, J. D., Whitestone, E., Jackson, L. A., & Gatto, L. (1995). Justice is still not colorblind: Differential racial effects of exposure to inadmissible evidence. *Personality and Social Psychology Bulletin, 21,* 893–898.

Jones, J. M. (1997). *Prejudice and racism* (2nd ed.). New York: McGraw-Hill.

Katz, I., Wackenhut, J., & Hass, R. G. (1986). Racial ambivalence, value duality, and behavior. In J. F. Dovidio & S. L. Gaertner (Eds.), *Prejudice, discrimination, and racism* (pp. 35–59). Orlando, FL: Academic Press.

Kawakami, K., Dovidio, J. F., & van Kamp, S. (2005). Kicking the habit: Effects of nonstereotypic association training and correction processes on hiring decisions. *Journal of Experimental Social Psychology, 41,* 68–75.

Kleinpenning, G., & Hagendoorn, L. (1993). Forms of racism and the cumulative dimension. *Social Psychology Quarterly, 56,* 21–36.

Knight, J. L., Guiliano, T. A., Sanchez-Ross, M. G. (2001). Famous or infamous? The influence of celebrity status and race on perceptions of responsibility for rape. *Basic and Applied Social Psychology, 23,* 183–190.

Kovel, J. (1970). *White racism: A psychohistory.* New York: Pantheon.

McConahay, J. B. (1986). Modern racism, ambivalence, and the modern racism scale. In J. F. Dovidio & S. L. Gaertner (Eds.), *Prejudice, discrimination, and racism* (pp. 91–125). Orlando, FL: Academic Press.

McConnell, A. R., & Leibold, J. M. (2001). Relations among the implicit association test, discriminatory behavior, and explicit measures of racial attitudes. *Journal of Experimental Social Psychology, 37,* 435–442.

Mehrabian, A. (1972). *Nonverbal communication.* Chicago, IL: Aldine-Atherton.

Myrdal, G. (1944). *An American dilemma: The Negro problem and modern democracy.* New York: Harper.

Nail, P. R., Harton, H. C., & Decker, B. P. (2003). Political orientation and modern versus aversive racism: Tests of Dovidio and Gaertner's (1998) integrated model. *Journal of Personality and Social Psychology, 84,* 754–770.

Otero, L., & Dovidio, J. F. (2005). Unpublished data. Department of Psychology, University of Connecticut, Storrs, CT.

Perry, B. (2002). Defending the color line: Racially and ethnically motivated hate crime. *The American Behavioral Scientist, 46,* 72–92.

Pettigrew, T. F., & Meertens, R. W. (1995). Subtle and blatant prejudice in Western Europe. *European Journal of Social Psychology, 25,* 57–76.

Phelps, E. A., O'Connor, K. J., Cunningham, W. A., Funayama, E. S., Gatenby, J. C., Gore, J. C., et al. (2000). Performance on indirect measures of race evaluation predicts amygdala activation. *Journal of Cognitive Neuroscience, 12,* 729–738.

Plant, E. A., & Devine, P. G. (1998). Internal and external motivation to respond without prejudice. *Journal of Personality and Social Psychology, 75,* 811–832.

Richeson, J. A., Baird, A. A., Gordon, H. L., Heatherton, T. F., Wyland, C. L., Trawalter, S., et al. (2003). An fMRI investigation of the impact of interracial contact on executive function. *Nature Neuroscience, 6,* 1323–1328.

Robinson, P. H., & Darley, J. M. (1995). *Justice, liability, and blame.* Boulder, CO: Westview Press.

Richeson, J., & Shelton, J. N. (2003). When prejudice does not pay: Effects of interracial contact on executive function. *Psychological Science, 14*, 287–290.

Rollman, S. A. (1978). The sensitivity of Black and White Americans to nonverbal cues of prejudice. *Journal of Social Psychology, 105*, 73–77.

Saucier, D. A., Miller, C. T., & Doucet, N. (2005). Differences in helping Whites and Blacks: A meta-analysis. *Personality and Social Psychology Review, 9*, 2–16.

Schuman, H., Steeh, C., Bobo, L., & Krysan, M. (1997). *Racial attitudes in America: Trends and interpretations.* Cambridge, MA: Harvard University Press.

Sears, D. O., Henry, P. J., & Kosterman, R. (2000). Egalitarian values and contemporary racial politics. In D. O. Sears, J. Sidanius, & L. Bobo (Eds.), *Racialized politics: The debate about racism in America* (pp. 75–117). Chicago, IL: University of Chicago Press.

Shelton, J. N. (2000). A reconceptualization of how we study issues of racial prejudice. *Personality and Social Psychology Review, 4*, 374–390.

Shelton, J. N. (2003). Interpersonal concerns in social encounters between majority and minority group members. *Group Processes and Intergroup Relations, 6*, 171–185.

Shelton, J. N., & Richeson, J. A. (2006). Interracial interactions: A relational approach. In M. P. Zanna (Ed.), *Advances in experimental social psychology* (Vol. 38, pp. 121–181). New York: Academic Press.

Shiffrin, R., & Schneider, W. (1977). Controlled and automatic human information processing: Perceptual learning, automatic attending, and a general theory. *Psychological Review, 84*, 127–190.

Sidanius, J., Levin, S., & Pratto, F. (1998). Hierarchical group relations. Institutional terror, and the dynamics of the criminal justice system. In J. Eberhardt & S. T. Fiske (Eds.), *Confronting racism: The problem and the response* (pp. 136–165). Newbury Park, CA: Sage.

Sidanius, J., & Pratto, F. (1999). *Social dominance: An intergroup theory of social hierarchy and oppression.* New York: Cambridge University Press.

Smedley, B. D., Stith, A. Y., & Nelson, A. R. (Eds.). (2003). *Unequal treatment: Confronting racial and ethnic disparities in health care.* Washington, DC: National Academy Press.

Sommers, S. R., & Ellsworth, P. C. (2000). Race in the courtroom: Perceptions of guilt and dispositional attributions. *Personality and Social Psychology Bulletin, 26*, 1367–1379.

Sommers, S. R., & Ellsworth, P. C. (2001). White juror bias: An investigation of prejudice against Black defendants in the American courtroom. *Psychology, Public Policy, and Law, 7*, 201–229.

Vorauer, J. D., & Kumhyr, S. M. (2001). Is this about you or me? Self- versus other-directed judgments and feelings in response to intergroup interaction. *Personality and Social Psychology Bulletin, 27*, 706–719.

Vorauer, J. D., & Turpie, C. (2004). Disruptive effects of vigilance on dominant group members' treatment of outgroup members: Choking versus shining under pressure. *Journal of Personality and Social Psychology, 27*, 706–709.

Wilson, T. D., Lindsey, S., & Schooler, T. Y. (2000). A model of dual attitudes. *Psychological Review, 107*, 101–126.

Wittenbrink, B., Judd, C., & Park, B. (1997). Evidence for racial prejudice at the implicit level and its relationship with questionnaire measures. *Journal of Personality and Social Psychology, 72*, 262–274.

Word, C. O., Zanna, M. P., & Cooper, J. (1974). The nonverbal mediation of self-fulfilling prophecies in interracial interaction. *Journal of Experimental Social Psychology, 10*, 109–120.

4

The Role of Race and Racial Prejudice in Recognizing Other People

John C. Brigham

Harmonious interactions between individuals and between groups of people depend upon, among other things, the ability to recognize individuals, distinguish them from each other, and treat each individual appropriately. If one is unable to distinguish members of a particular group from each other, then it is difficult to treat each person with the individuality that he or she deserves. Failing to treat a person as a unique individual is often seen as a central characteristic of stereotyping and prejudice.

Many things can interfere with one's motivation or ability to treat others as individuals. Group membership is one such factor. Researchers have identified the *outgroup homogeneity effect*, the finding that people in outgroups are seen as more homogeneous, more similar to each other, than are members of one's own group. The outgroup homogeneity effect stems from the idea that because they are classified as a group, the members of the group must be alike (Judd, Ryan, & Park, 1991). People tend to see their own group as a heterogeneous set of unique individuals, while outgroups are seen as homogeneous sets of similar persons. A meta-analysis by Mullen and Hu (1989) found a small but significant effect that they labeled *relative heterogeneity*. On average, outgroups were seen as more homogeneous than the scale midpoint, whereas ingroups were seen as somewhat less homogeneous than the midpoint. This effect was stronger when the ingroup and outgroups were real, enduring groups, and weaker when they were artificial, laboratory-created groups. The effect also was stronger as the relative size of the ingroup increased.

While most of this research has focused upon group members' assumptions about attitudes and about perceived personality characteristics, the outgroup homogeneity effect is also visible in the area of perception, particularly race perception. What I am referring to has been variously called the "cross-race effect," the "own-race bias," or the "other-race effect" in face recognition. These terms describe the tendency of people to recognize the faces of members of their own racial group more easily and with less error than the faces of members of other racial groups. An awareness of the difficulty of recognizing other-race people is often illustrated by the comment, "They all look alike to me."

The cross-race effect (CRE) has been investigated by cognitive psychologists for its relevance to general theories of memory, and by psycholegal scholars concerned about its impact on the justice system. But it seems to me that it also has

68

C. Willis-Esqueda (ed.), *Motivational Aspects of Prejudice and Racism.*
© Springer 2008

important relevance to the study of prejudice and intergroup relations. The CRE can make intergroup interactions more difficult and unrewarding, since it increases the likelihood of mistakes in recognizing individual members of the other group, or of confusing them with one another. In addition, a person's fear of making such a mistake can lead to feelings of intergroup anxiety and may also cause the person to be more cautious in the interaction, thereby making the individual appear to be unfriendly. Taken together, these factors increase the chances that an interaction will have a negative outcome, thus likely increasing the levels of stereotyping and prejudice felt toward members of the other group. I will discuss these possibilities in some detail, after first reviewing the research findings on the CRE.

The Cross-Race Effect in Face Recognition

Characteristics of the Cross-Race Effect

During the past 35 years, a host of studies have investigated the CRE as it applies to adults' face recognition. In a review, Chance and Goldstein (1996, p. 171) observed that, "The number of studies that have replicated the other-race effect is impressive. Few psychological findings are so easy to duplicate." Several meta-analyses have evaluated the findings (Anthony, Copper, & Mullen, 1992; Bothwell, Brigham, & Malpass, 1989). In the largest and most recent of these, Meissner and Brigham (2001) analyzed responses from 39 studies involving almost 5,000 participants. Their analysis found a significant CRE that accounted for 15% of the variance across studies. Overall, own-race faces were 1.40 times more likely to be correctly identified than were other-race faces, and other-race faces were 1.56 times more likely to be falsely identified than were own-race faces. Interestingly, the CRE had significantly decreased in more recent years (studies ranged in date from 1969 to 2000) for overall accuracy measures (A', d') and for proportion of "hits," but had significantly increased in recent years when measured as proportion of "false alarms," that is, incorrect responses that a face had been seen before, when it had not been.

The CRE has been found in members of majority groups and minority groups alike, but the Meissner and Brigham (2001) meta-analysis found that the effect was, on average, stronger for White perceivers than for Black perceivers. Surveys of research "experts" in this area, published in 1989 and 2001, have found that most of them endorsed the importance and reliability of the CRE (Kassin, Ellsworth, & Smith, 1989; Kassin, Tubb, Hosch, & Memon, 2001). In the most recent survey of expert eyewitness researchers, over 90% of them responded that evidence for the CRE was "reliable enough" to justify delivering expert testimony in court on this issue (Kassin, Tubb, et al., 2001).

The meta-analysis also found a significant CRE for response criterion. People generally showed a more liberal response criterion (the tendency to respond that a face has been seen before) for other-race faces than for own-race faces. This difference is directly related to the greater number of false alarm responses usually made to other-race faces.

While a vast majority (85%) of the studies analyzed in the Meissner and Brigham (2001) meta-analysis were of Blacks and Whites, most of them in the US and Canada, there have been a few studies of other groups that indicate that the CRE in recognition accuracy is not limited to these two groups or to North America. Research with Black and White participants in parts of Africa and the United Kingdom has found evidence of a CRE (see Chiroro & Valentine, 1995; Wright, Boyd, & Tredoux, 2001, 2003), and a study of Turks and Germans found that Germans exhibited the CRE, but Turks shown the same stimuli did not (Sporer, 2001).

Other racial and ethnic groups have also been studied. Platz and Hosch (1988) found a significant CRE for Mexican-American, Black, and White convenience store workers in identifying customers who had interacted with them earlier in the day. Clerks in each of the three groups recognized persons of their own group better than those from either of the other two groups. Teitelbaum and Gieselman (1997) studied Whites, Blacks, Hispanics, and Asians. They found that Hispanic partici-pants performed no differently than White participants on White faces, but did significantly more poorly on Black faces. Finally, MacLin, MacLin, and Malpass (2001) studied Hispanics' recognition of Hispanic and Black faces and found that across two experiments, Hispanics showed better recognition for Hispanic faces than for Black faces. Studies with Asian participants have also found evidence of a CRE (Luce, 1974; Ng & Lindsay, 1994).

The Developmental Course of the Cross-Race Effect

Are There Face-Specific "Modules" in the Brain?

There are two major theoretical perspectives about how face recognition develops through childhood (Brigham, 2002). The *modularity hypothesis* takes the position that face recognition is "special," a unique perceptual/cognitive process that is mediated by a separate face-specific "module" in the brain that is biologically endowed and relatively unaffected by experience. A module has been defined as a mandatory, domain-specific, hardwired input system that performs innately deter-mined operations (Fodor, 1983). There are two ways in which modularity can be conceived: as the existence of a specific part of the brain (a processing system) that processes faces in a way similar to other systems (*specificity*), or in terms of a proc-ess of recognizing faces that is qualitatively different than recognizing other stimuli (*uniqueness*) (Hay & Young, 1982). These concepts are theoretically independent of one another, and both have been invoked as evidence for modularity (Tanaka & Gauthier, 1997).

At a conceptual level, it has been asserted that because recognizing others is of vital importance to people, "it makes sense to postulate a selective evolutionary pressure to evolve neural mechanisms specifically for the recognition of faces"

(Nachson, 1995, p. 257). The possibility that there can be cortical cells that respond specifically to faces has been supported by the discovery of neurons in the monkey's visual cortex that respond predominantly to faces. These neurons respond to human faces as well as to monkey faces, and to facial photographs as well as live faces (Brigham, 2002; Rolls, 1992; Rolls, Baylis, & Leonard, 1989).

Research findings on the effects of facial inversion have been seen as supporting the modularity position. Generally, faces are recognized more easily than any other class of stimuli that are as similar to one another in their configuration as faces are. But turn them upside down (invert them), and faces become harder to distinguish than other classes of inverted stimuli such as airplanes, stick figures, and houses. This effect was first reported in a series of studies by Yin (1969, 1970, 1978). Yin argued that the unique impact of reversal on recognition accuracy for faces, from best upright to worst inverted, indicated face recognition was the product of a system different from that for recognizing other types of visual stimuli. Yin suggested that neural specialization had evolved to support a process that was specific to (upright) human faces.

Subsequent research, however, has questioned Yin's explanation for these findings. It appears that the strong inversion effect found for faces is not unique to faces but rather is apparently due to *expertise* with the stimulus materials. In several experiments, Diamond and Carey (1986) showed that when people are highly experienced in perceiving stimuli, inverting those stimuli causes a major disruption in encoding. They found that expert dog breeders showed the same inversion effect for dog faces (of the breed for which each was an expert) that people show for human faces. Diamond and Carey argued that experts, who are accustomed to discriminating between highly similar objects from the same class (e.g., human faces, or dog faces from a single breed for dog breeders), rely on a *holistic* strategy of encoding (also called configural encoding), wherein the stimulus is processed as a whole, rather than as a collection of individual features. In contrast, a strategy that looks at distinctive features of the stimulus object is known as *featural* encoding. While a holistic strategy generally results in better memory than does a featural strategy, a holistic strategy works poorly for inverted objects; holistic encoding is more disrupted by inversion than is featural encoding. Therefore, what first seemed to be a face-specific effect may instead be an expertise-specific effect (Cohen-Levine, 1989; Nachson, 1995).

It is also true, however, that face recognition appears "special" in the sense that it involves more holistic processing than does the recognition of other objects (Tanaka & Farah, 1993). A possible extension of the modularity position could posit that such modules may be *race-specific*, just as they are species-specific. From this perspective, the CRE could be seen as a natural product of a race-specific face-recognition module that is present throughout life. As far as I am aware, however, none of the theorists in this area have addressed this possibility.

In contrast, the *skill* or *expertise* hypothesis asserts that the recognition of faces is not a unique process but rather occurs in the same way as recognition of other objects. Researchers have asserted that facial processing represents an area of skilled memory in which individuals gradually acquire knowledge and expertise in discriminating particular members from a class of stimuli. Certain strategies may be developed that allow individuals to manage and catalog the vast number of faces seen each day. One such strategy involves the "chunking" of individual features of the face into a holistic pattern (Fallshore & Schooler, 1995; Tanaka & Farah, 1993). The mechanism of chunking has been demonstrated to produce significant increases in memory for stimuli in a wide range of skilled areas (Chase & Ericsson, 1982).

It is not immediately clear what either hypothesis would predict about the developmental course of the CRE. If it represents an innate module, is the effect constant through life, or is it affected by maturation or by subsequent events? If the CRE results from learning and experience, is it absent in infancy and very early childhood? Should it be stronger in early childhood when the child's preschool experiences may be largely limited to same-race persons (family, family friends), or should it be stronger later in childhood when the child has a longer history of experiences with same-race people?

How Early in Life is the Cross-Race Effect Visible?

Recent studies indicate that individuals may be aware of racial differences in appearance very early in life, even at 3 months of age. Sangrigoli and de Schonen (2004a) studied White infants in France, who presumably had had no contact with Asians. Each infant was habituated to a photo of a single White or Asian face (with the hair covered by a shower cap). Following habituation, the infants were shown a pair of faces, the previously seen face paired with a novel, not-seen-before face in the same front view, and their eye movements were videotaped. Each infant underwent two experimental habituation-test sessions, one with White faces and one with Asian faces, order counterbalanced across participants. Their videotaped eye movements were encoded frame by frame. The infants showed a significant "novelty preference" when viewing a pair of White faces, looking longer at the never-seen-before, novel White face than the face seen previously, suggesting that they recognized the previously seen face and focused their attention on the new one. They did not do this for the Asian faces, indicating that they did not recognize that they had seen one of the Asian faces before. Other research has also shown a novelty preference effect at the age of 3 months, but no such effect at 1 month of age (De Haan, Johnson, Maurer, & Perrett, 2001).

In a related experiment, Sangrigoli and de Schonen (2004a) found that a novelty effect could be obtained with photos of Asians as well, but only when White infants had been given three earlier trials with Asian faces, in order to give them some familiarity with Asian faces before the test trials began. The researchers suggested that by the age of 3 months, the face-recognition system is biased toward the predominant race of the faces seen in the environment, that is, the system is "tuned" very early by experience.

The question of changes in the CRE was addressed in a recent study that compared face recognition performance of adult Koreans who were born in Korea and had been adopted between ages 3 and 9 by Caucasian families in Europe, to that of adult Koreans who had been raised in Korea, and to adult Caucasians in Europe. Sangrigoli, Pallier, Argenti, Ventureyra, and de Schonen (2005) found that both Caucasians and the adopted Korean participants were better at recognizing Caucasian faces than Asian faces. In contrast, the nonadopted Koreans were better at recognizing Asian faces. Sangrigoli and her coworkers asserted that since research suggests that the CRE may be evident before age 3, their findings indicate that the CRE can be modified "drastically" by experience. The CRE does not seem to be permanent, they proposed, because it can be modified by early experience, as indicated by their studies. The CRE develops along with face processing skills during the first 3 months, they asserted, and is therefore not a long-term result of acquisition experiences.

While it has been shown that people use holistic processing more for faces (as well as other stimuli for which they are experts), the origin of this tendency remains an intriguing issue. As noted earlier, some researchers (e.g., Slater & Quinn, 2001) have proposed that a face-processing module is present at birth. Others have asserted that perceptual experience, very early in life, is necessary for the proper development of holistic face-processing. Consistent with this view, researchers found that children who suffered from early visual deprivation showed impaired holistic processing later in life. LeGrand, Mondloch, Maurer, and Brent (2004) studied children born with bilateral congenital cataracts; these children were born essentially blind, and their vision was corrected to an "almost normal" level by surgery 3–6 months later. When studied at age 8 or older, the children showed less ability to process objects holistically than did other children. The researchers concluded that, "early visual experience is necessary to set up or maintain the neural substrate that leads to holistic processing of faces" (LeGrand et al., p. 762).

Studies indicate that children have the ability to recognize racial differences at a very young age. But does this ability translate into meaningful behavioral differences or preferences? Many people have assumed that children come in to the world with their minds a "blank slate" when it comes to making racial distinctions. However, research by Katz (2002, 2003) and others indicates that a preverbal awareness of racial and gender differences is present very early in life. For example, in a study of children from 6 months to 6 years of age, Katz and Downey (2002) found that children had preverbal concepts of both race and gender at the age of 6 months. At 6 months, Black children were generally more responsive to race cues than to gender cues, while White children were more responsive to gender cues. Preference for same-race peers increased from ages 3 to 6 for White children, but decreased over this same period for Black children. Overall, according to Katz (2003, p. 905), "at no point in the study did the children exhibit the Rousseau type of color-blindness that most adults expect." The salience of racial cues is further illustrated by a study in which 5- and 6-year-old children were given a set of photos of people varying in race and gender, and asked to sort them into two piles: 68% of the children sorted them by race, as opposed to 16% who sorted by gender, and another 16% who sorted according to some other criterion (Katz, 2003). This issue of "color blindness" in children, or rather the lack of it, is illustrated in another recent study of American children and adults, Blacks and Whites. Bigler

(1999) found that most adults of each race did not endorse blatantly prejudicial statements characteristic of "old-fashioned racism" (a concept discussed a bit later in this chapter), but many children did. The researcher concluded that, "It is clear …that racial stereotyping is pervasive among children and is resistant to change" (Bigler, p. 701).

Turning our attention back to recognition memory, it has been well established that children's ability to recognize faces of unfamiliar people improves with age (e. g., Carey & Diamond, 1977; Chance, Turner, & Goldstein, 1982; Ellis & Flin, 1990). Recognition accuracy has also been shown to increase with age when adolescents have been compared to adults (e.g., Ellis, Shepherd, & Bruce, 1973; Saltz & Sigel, 1967). As noted earlier, this could be attributable to the maturation of a face-specific module, to the development of a skill through extensive experience with faces, or to an interaction between a face-recognition system and very early visual experiences. Forensically, these various possibilities have different implications for children's accuracy in recognizing faces, such as when they make an identification from a lineup. If face recognition is an innate skill, then perhaps the experiences of any particular child are not relevant to the likelihood that the child can make an accurate identification decision. In contrast, if face recognition is a learned skill, then the amount of contact the child has with members of a group should affect recognition ability, with more experience and more contact leading to better recognition. Forensically, the amount of experience that the child has had in recognizing faces of strangers could be seen as important for determining how much confidence one should have in the accuracy of the child's identification decision.

Studies of the Cross-Race Effect in Children

Until the last 5 years or so, most of the studies that had looked at face memory in children were published in the 1970s or early 1980s, and their results were quite inconsistent. This lack of research attention in the later 1980s and 1990s is particularly surprising when compared with the amount of attention devoted in those years to other aspects of children's memory and testimony, such as their suggestibility, memory for traumatic events, and the effects of questioning style (e.g., see Ceci & Bruck, 1995; Dent & Flin, 1992; Doris, 1991; Poole & Lamb, 1998). Because children are increasingly likely to be called to testify as identification witnesses in the courtroom in recent years, knowledge about the developmental course of the CRE, and its malleability, is of considerable applied importance, as well as of theoretical interest.

In the first published examination of the CRE in children, Cross, Cross, and Daly (1971) examined the effect in 7-, 12-, and 17-year-olds, half of whom were Black and half of whom were White. An overall CRE occurred for correct recognition, but unfortunately, no data were presented on the relationship between age of participant, race of participant, and race of stimulus photograph. Therefore, it cannot be determined *when* the CRE appeared, whether it was present at all ages, or whether it increased or decreased with age. Feinman and Entwisle (1976) examined first-, second-, third-, and sixth-graders. They found that recognition accuracy (hits and correct rejections) increased with age, with the increase from first to third grade smaller than the increase from third to sixth grade. In addition, a significant CRE was found, which was greatest among the White children.

Predicting that the CRE would be stronger in older children than in younger children, Goldstein and Chance (1980) first tested their assumptions on White children in first through sixth grades, with pictures of White and Japanese faces as stimuli. Accuracy, as measured by d', increased with age from 6 to 12 for both White and Japanese faces, but there was no evidence of a CRE. In a later study, Chance et al. (1982) studied the ability of White children in grades 1–2, 5–6, and 7–8, and White undergraduates to recognize White and Japanese adult faces. Evidence of a CRE was found at every age level except for the first and second graders. The magnitude of the CRE was larger for older participants than for younger participants.

The recognition ability of 5–6, 9–10, and 12–13 year olds and undergraduates for Asian American, White, and Black faces was studied by Lee and Goodman (2000). The children were Asian Americans and Whites, and the adults (undergraduates) were Asian Americans, Whites, and Blacks. Preliminary analyses yielded a marginally significant three-way interaction between age, race of participant, and race of face, indicating a CRE that differed for different ages and races. In brief, the youngest children (5–6 year olds) and the adults recognized all faces equally well. However, a CRE was observed for the middle groups of children (9– 10-year-old Whites and 12–13-year-old Whites and Asian Americans). It is unclear why the CRE should appear at age 9 and then disappear in adulthood, but the authors suggested that a cohort effect may be to blame. The authors speculated that the absence of a CRE in their adult sample was due to the increasingly multicultural society to which their participants had been exposed, as their study was conducted in California, a culturally diverse state.

In contrast to these results, several other studies have found a CRE in 3- to 5-year-old children. Pezdek, Blandon-Gitlin, and Moore (2003) found a significant CRE in 5-year-old children, when they showed White and Black children a video of a White man and a Black man working at a bakery, and then later asked them to identify the men from two videotaped lineups. They studied kindergarteners, third graders, and college undergraduates, and found that face-recognition accuracy increased with age. A CRE occurred, but, the magnitude of the CRE was roughly the same in all three age groups. Sangrigoli and de Schonen (2004b) found a CRE in 3-year-old children. A recent study of Whites and Blacks in the Southeast by Bennett and Brigham (2005) found evidence of a CRE in Whites at each of four grade levels (grades 2, 6, 10, and college), but not in Black respondents at any of the 4 grade levels.

To summarize these diverse research outcomes, most, but not all, of the studies have found a CRE in children. While this result is relatively consistent and well documented, little is yet known about the development of the CRE within childhood. One study (Chance et al., 1982) found the CRE to be greatest among older children, while another (Lee & Goodman, 2000) found that it was strongest among the middle age range of children (9–13 years old), and other studies (Bennett & Brigham, 2005; Pezdek et al., 2003) found it to be equally strong at each age level. Clearly, there is more to be learned here.

Brain-Imaging Studies of the Cross-Race Effect

Brain-imaging studies are a promising new avenue for investigating how faces are perceived and processed by the brain. Work is just beginning on how the race of a face may stimulate different areas of the brain when it is viewed. For example, Cunningham, Johnson, et al. (2004) used *fMRI* analyses to investigate the brain regions that were most active when Whites viewed faces of Blacks. When the Whites viewed a Black face at a speed that precluded conscious recognition (30 ms), a brain area associated with emotional responses, the amygdala, was activated. The activation was stronger in people who had shown stronger racial prejudice on an indirect behavioral measure of prejudice. In contrast, when a Black face was shown at a speed that allowed conscious recognition (525 ms), activation occurred in two regions of the brain that are associated with the suppression of emotional responses, the dorsolateral PFC and the anterior cingulate. The researchers suggested that this pattern of brain activity is associated with attempts to control unwanted prejudicial responses to Black faces.

The "default option" of the amygdala is the important task of assessing threat and potential dangers in one's environment (see meta-analyses by Murphy, Nimmo-Smith, & Lawrence, 2003; Phan, Taylor, & Liberzon, 2002). The Cunningham, Johnson, et al. (2004) study found that this brain area was activated more strongly to Black faces than to White faces, even when the exposure was so brief that the person could not consciously recognize the race of the face that they had briefly seen. Other research has found that Whites who were more prejudiced, according to other measures, showed higher levels of amygdala activity to Black faces than did less-prejudiced Whites (Phelps et al., 2000). Another measure of brain activity, event-related evoked potentials (ERPs), has also been found to respond differently according to the race of the face viewed, again at a very early stage in cognitive processing – within 120 ms (Ito & Urland, 2003). Taken together, these studies indicate that individuals categorize others by race (as well as by gender) very quickly, well before they become consciously aware of the categorization.

The recent studies of brain functioning and the perception of race might seem to paint a bleak picture for future intergroup relations, given that Whites appear to show a very rapid, apparently unlearned, negative response to Black faces, as contrasted to White faces. (It remains to be seen how brain functions in other groups react when perceiving own and other-group faces.) But all may not be lost. Other recent research indicates that these quick responses may not be as automatic and immutable as first assumed. For example, Wheeler and Fiske (2005) showed that when people were given a nonsocial visual search task (finding a dot in each facial photo), they showed the same degree of activation in the amygdala (as measured by fMRI) to White faces and to Black faces. Other work has found a good deal of individual differences in amygdala activation; although most Whites show the pattern of greater activation to Black faces, some do not (Phelps et al., 2001). Further, those who did not show this pattern of activation also evinced less evidence of prejudice on an indirect behavioral measure.

Cognitive, Perceptual, and Motivational Processes Involved in the Cross-Race Effect

There are at least five major positions regarding the cognitive, perceptual, and motivational processes that may be involved in the CRE (1) differences in attention paid to own and other-race faces; (2) differences in the type of information attended to; (3) differential encoding strategies when own- or other-race faces are perceived; (4) differences in the way that own- and other-race faces are represented in memory; and (5) encoding race as a pre-eminent feature. I will address each of these in turn.

Attentional Differences

Many observers have noted that ingroup members may behave as if outgroup members are "invisible" to them. Rodin (1987) proposed that people conserve their cognitive resources by using what she labeled a *cognitive disregard strategy*, whereby some strangers (e.g., some outgroup members) are recognized and categorized only at a superficial level and no individual or individuating information is sought or stored (Sporer, 2001). In the case of race, adopting a cognitive disregard strategy for other-race faces, which could lead to a CRE in recognition memory, would seem efficient if the amount of other-race contact was minimal, but such a strategy would become more problematic as the amount of other-race contact increased.

Differences in the Type of Information Attended to

Another possibility is that people may pay attention to facial features that are useful and informative for faces of their own race but are relatively uninformative for distinguishing among persons of another race. Whites who learn to focus on hair color, or African Americans who focus on skin tone when differentiating between members of their own race, might find this orientation counterproductive when viewing other-race faces. If certain facial characteristics are particularly useful in helping one to discriminate among members of one's own race, one might continue to focus on those same features when evaluating other-race faces, even if a different set of features might be more informative. Thus, Ellis, Deregowski, and Shepherd (1975) found that British Whites and African Blacks tended to focus on somewhat different characteristics when describing facial pictures.

Different Encoding Strategies

A third general possibility is that different encoding strategies may be employed, depending on the age of the perceiver and/or the race of the perceiver and of the target person. Some researchers have asserted that, before age 10 or so, children are less likely to encode and recognize faces via the holistic encoding strategy than are older children and adults (Carey, 1981; Carey, Diamond, & Woods, 1980; Chung & Thomson, 1995; Thomson, 1986, 1989). Older children, in contrast, utilize holistic information about the global appearance of a face, taking into consideration the relationship between various facial features. Some studies have found a temporary dip in face-recognition accuracy, as well as other types of memory, around the ages of 11–14 (Carey et al.; Flin, 1980, 1985; Mann, Diamond, & Carey, 1979; Somerville & Wellman, 1979). It has been suggested that this dip results from the difficulty of switching from a featural encoding strategy to a holistic strategy during this time. However, it should be noted that the research evidence is not entirely consistent. Other researchers have argued that there is *not* an age-related strategy shift, but rather that older children and adults are simply able to encode more information of all types than are younger children (Baenninger, 1994; Chung & Thomson; Flin, 1985; Flin & Dziurawiec, 1989; Thomson, 1986).

As far as I am aware, no one has yet attempted to assess how frequently children of different ages use these two encoding processes with own vs. other-race faces. But one possibility is that children, and perhaps adults as well, may be more likely to use featural encoding for other-race faces and holistic encoding for own-race faces.

Different Representational Systems

A fourth general possibility is that people *encode* same-race faces in a different way than they do other-race faces. Valentine's (1991) "multidimensional face space model" assumes that specific faces are stored as category (i.e., racial) exemplars. Valentine and Endo (1992) argued that faces are encoded as locations (points, nodes) in a multidimensional space. Familiar individual faces are represented as points (nodes) and face categories (such as race) are represented as different clusters or "clouds" of points (Levin, 1996). When trying to decide whether or not one has seen a particular face before, one will compare the face to the exemplars encoded in memory. The nearest, and therefore most active, node will be chosen as the appropriate one for that face. Because "the dimensions of the space are based on experience with faces of predominantly one race, the feature dimensions underlying the multidimensional space will be those that are appropriate for discriminating one particular race of faces" (Valentine, p. 190). Representations of other-race faces are more densely clustered in the multidimensional space, because the dimensions of the space are most appropriate for own-race faces (e.g., eye color for White faces or skin tone for Black faces), not for other-race faces. In other words, this "similarity-based" model of face recognition asserts that other-race faces are more "psychologically similar" as a group than are same-race faces, and are therefore more confusable (Levin, 2000). Because the dimensions are optimal for recognizing own-race faces, exemplars of own-race faces are distributed around the intersection of any two central dimensions. Exemplars of other-race faces, in contrast, are more tightly clustered because (it is assumed) the dimensions of the face space are not a good match with the characteristics that differentiate other-race faces from one another. For example, a White person might use eye color and hair color as two dimensions on which to encode other people. While there is considerable range in these characteristics among White people, there is much less perceived variance among Blacks, who are likely to have dark hair and eyes. Therefore, as depicted in Fig. 1, exemplars of Blacks are clustered tightly together in the upper left quadrant (dark hair, dark eyes), while exemplars of Whites are more widely distributed. It should therefore be easier to tell whether a White face has been seen before (i.e., whether it matches one of the exemplars) than whether a particular Black face has been seen before.

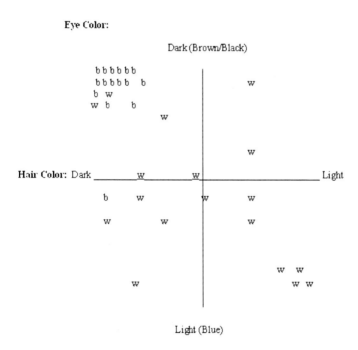

b = Encoded representations of Black people.

w = Encoded representations of White people.

Fig. 1 Possible locations of representations of Blacks and Whites as encoded in the "face space" of a White perceiver's brain, using the dimensions of hair color and eye color (based on Valentine's multidimensional face-space model)

Other research (Johnston & Ellis, 1995a, 1995b) indicates that children appear to have fewer facial prototypes in memory, likely due to their limited exposure to faces. Hence, the child's "face space" likely has fewer dimensions than an adult's. While there is some early support for the validity of this model (e.g., Chiroro & Valentine, 1995), the jury is still out regarding its overall applicability and accuracy.

Encoding Race as a Pre-Eminent Feature

Another encoding possibility is that people may encode race as a pre-eminent feature of other-race people, thereby hampering their ability to later distinguish between other-race persons. Levin (1996, 2000) asserted that people use a "facilitated classification process" for other-race faces, an automated classification process in which race-specific encoding is performed without regard for other individuating information, which is largely ignored. This encoding by race alone is insufficient to facilitate later discrimination between other-race faces, Levin suggested, leading to a tendency to respond "seen before" during test, producing the high rate of false alarms for other-race faces that was identified in the Meissner and Brigham (2001) meta-analysis.

In a series of experiments, Levin (2000) found that Whites who are poor at recognizing Black faces were, paradoxically, quick to detect them when asked to categorize faces by race. Levin's findings suggest that other-race persons are encoded using more category-related information (for example, stereotypes that apply to an entire group) and less individuating information, than are same-race persons. For faces, race-specifying information is more likely to be encoded as a visual feature in other-race faces than in same-race faces (MacLin & Malpass, 2001). The contrast between other-race and same-race faces is encoded as a *feature-present/feature-absent* manner. Encoding race as a feature (of an other-race face) leaves less room for encoding truly individuating information (Levin, 1996). Therefore, at recognition there is less individuating information available for other-race faces and, as a consequence, recognition accuracy is poorer. Levin (1996, 2000) and MacLin and Malpass (2001, 2003) have suggested that this automatic inclination to categorize other-race faces by race may distract from the encoding of individuating information, and thereby lead to poorer performance when recognizing other-race faces. Attention directed toward the encoding of race as a facial feature may divert cognitive resources that would otherwise be used to seek out individuating information.

As an example of how this process might operate, I can offer my own experience. In a college class of 50 students, I may notice early on that there appears to be a single student in a particular race/gender category (e.g., Asian woman). The day of the first exam I am surprised to see two Asian women present. Has one of them never come to class before, or has each of them come to class occasionally, just never on the same day? Much to my embarrassment, I may have no idea. I believe that what I have done, unwittingly, is to encode each of them in a feature-present manner (as Asian/woman) and, because this appeared sufficient to differentiate her from her classmates, I failed to encode to encode any truly individuating information.

Regarding the effects of contact, Levin (2000) asserted that the hypothesis that greater contact with other-race persons improves ability to recognize them, "at some level...*has* to be true unless one posits an innate inability to accurately code CR [other-race] faces." (As noted earlier, a race-specific face-recognition module would be one possible innate mechanism.) Perhaps, as Levin and others (e.g., Shepherd, 1981; Valentine, Chiroro, & Dixon, 1995) have suggested, motivation is a key element: recognition of other-race faces will be improved only by contact that involves processing other-race faces with the *goal* of individuation. Further, it can be hypothesized that people with more experience with other-race persons (from greater or more personalized, individuating contact) would be less likely to generate the race-feature response to other-race persons, but would instead seek out more individuating information, or check for the race-based feature most important for that culture, which would facilitate later recognition. I will return to the issue of contact effects later.

Levin (1996) pointed out that the race-feature effect should only operate when the other race is in the numerical minority (e.g., Blacks in the US), where categorization by race and one or two additional features would usually be sufficient for later recognition (of Blacks by Whites). Our meta-analysis provided some support for this prediction, as the magnitude of the CRE, as measured by false alarms or by a composite accuracy measure, was found to be significantly greater for White perceivers than for Black perceivers. However, there was no racial difference in the magnitude of the CRE when hit scores were the recognition measure (Meissner & Brigham, 2001).

Remembering vs. "Just Knowing"

Dual-process theories of memory assert that memory can stem from either of two processes: fluid, perceptually based information that is encoded in a nonconscious automatic manner that is associated with feelings of *familiarity* or of just "knowing," vs. conscious-level conceptual information that is elaborately encoded and is associated with *recollection* and remembering (e.g., see Gardiner & Richardson-Klavehn, 2000; Jacoby, 1991; Kelley & Jacoby, 2000). Chase and Simon (1973) and others have theorized that skilled memory operations are associated with this latter type of encoding. Researchers have demonstrated the independence of these processes in their influence on memory. For example, manipulations that influence encoding (such as divided attention and length of study time) have generally been shown to alter processes of recollection, whereas the unconscious effects of priming tend to influence processes of familiarity (Meissner, Brigham, & Butz, 2005).

We attempted to contrast these two approaches with respect to the CRE by investigating the way that Blacks and Whites rated a series of faces of both races on five dimensions that have been isolated by previous researchers: likability, attractiveness, memorability, typicality, and familiarity (Meissner et al., 2005). Four separate factor analyses (both samples, both races of face) yielded the same two factors: memorability (memorability and typicality) and familiarity (familiarity, attractiveness, and likability). This provides the first evidence that Blacks and Whites in the US use the same general standards in evaluating faces of either race. In a second study, participants of both races underwent a typical face recognition study, except that after each "seen before" response they checked whether their response was based more on remembering, on "just knowing", or was a guess. When we analyzed those items for which participants gave a "remember" (recollection) response, we found a significant CRE for both races. However, when we analyzed those items for which they gave a "know" (familiarity) response, a CRE did not occur. Taken together, these results indicate that the CRE stems from recollection-based responding, a feeling of memory. We concluded that the CRE appears to be due to superior encoding of own-race faces that triggers episodic recollections, rather than vague feelings of familiarity ("knowing"). People encode more useful information when looking at own-race faces, information that is particularly diagnostic for subsequent recognition situations. A further indicator that the CRE is an encoding-level phenomenon comes from our meta-analysis, which found that study time, an encoding-level factor, was a significant moderator of the CRE. The CRE was stronger, largely due to higher false alarm rates, in conditions that employed shorter study times (Meissner & Brigham, 2001).

We also found that, at the perceptual level, own-race faces were perceived differently than other-race faces. Although all participants rated the same set of faces and yielded the same factor structure in their ratings, participants of each race rated faces of their own race as significantly more familiar, memorable, distinctive, attractive, and likable, than the other-race faces.

Another way to study processing is by analyzing eye movements as people view and encode faces. It has been suggested that Blacks and Whites may attend to different aspects of the face, aspects that are most diagnostic for differentiating between persons of their own race, such as hair color for Whites and skin tone for Blacks. If so, this could produce different patterns of eye movements. Meissner, Brigham, and Bennett (2007) studied US college students of both races as they viewed projected faces of both races and later took a recognition memory test. An eye-tracking machine assessed the number of eye fixations per second and the distance between successive fixations. We hypothesized that participants would encode same-race faces with greater efficiency, thereby being able to achieve more fixations per second and permitting greater distance between successive fixations, when compared with performance on other-race faces. We predicted the same differences would occur during the later recognition test. The results indicated that, as predicted, own-race faces were encoded more efficiency by both Whites and Blacks. When viewing own-race faces and attempting to remember them, participants made more and faster fixations, and had greater distances between fixations, than for other-race faces. At recognition, participants generated a recognition response more quickly for own-race faces, yet at a greater fixation rate, indicating more efficient scanning and retrieval of details from memory for own-race faces. We also assessed self-reported amount of other-race contact in the past and during present everyday interactions. The contact scores were significantly correlated with fixation rate at encoding and also were related to recognition accuracy for other-race faces during the recognition test. A path analysis indicated that the amount of self-reported other-race contact significantly predicted both

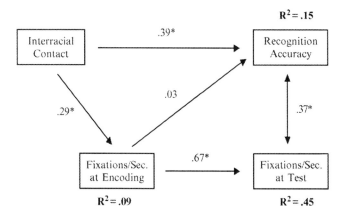

Fig. 2 Path analysis of accuracy in recognizing other-race faces as related to eye movements while viewing faces and to self-reported amount of interracial contact (Meissner et al., 2007)

fixations at encoding ($r=.29$) and accuracy in the recognition test ($r=.39$) for other-race faces (Fig. 2). The results of these two studies are consistent in indicating that the CRE appears to be based on recollection-based processes that are part of the encoding process.

Legal Consequences of Errors in Recognition Memory

The Scope of the Problem

In my view, there are two areas where the CRE can have an effect of major importance at an applied level – in the criminal justice system, and in the origin and maintenance of intergroup prejudice. Looking first at the legal arena, for many years some legal scholars have been particularly concerned with the possible impact of recognition memory errors in the context of the justice system, where false alarms made by eyewitness can translate into erroneous identifications of innocent suspects. In a 1932 book entitled *Convicting the Innocent*, Borchard described the problem of erroneous identifications of innocent suspects. Thereafter, the problematic nature of eyewitness evidence was explicitly acknowledged by the US Supreme Court in its 1967 *United States v. Wade* decision. In *Wade*, Justice Brennan noted that, "The vagaries of eyewitness identification are well-known; the annals of criminal law are rife with instances of mistaken identification." Additionally, the justices cited a well-known legal text by Wall (1965), who had written that many judges and lawyers agreed with the assertion that, "Mistaken identifications have been responsible for more miscarriages of justice than any other factor – more so, perhaps, than all other factors combined (p. 26)."

The prevalence of identification errors made by adult eyewitnesses has received wide research attention in recent years (e.g., Brigham, Wasserman, & Meissner, 1999; Cutler & Penrod, 1995; Sporer, Malpass, & Koehnken, 1996; Technical Working Group for Eyewitness Evidence, 1999). Huff, Rattner, and Sagarin (1996) made an exhaustive search for cases in the US since 1900 in which clear instances of erroneous convictions had occurred, wherein indisputable evidence of the person's innocence came to light after the conviction, by way of new forensic evidence or confessions by others. They identified 205 such cases and categorized each of them by the type of error that led most directly to the conviction (e.g., perjury, forensic errors, negligence by criminal justice officials, coerced confessions, and so forth). In over half of these cases (52.3%), the primary causal factor leading to conviction was an incorrect eyewitness identification.

In the early days of DNA testing, the National Institute of Justice, under the auspices of the US Department of Justice, made a study of wrongful convictions that had later been shown by DNA evidence to be erroneous. The 1996 report identified 28 cases in which the convicted person was later exonerated by DNA tests that showed that this person could not have been the perpetrator (Conners, Lundregan, Miller, & McEwan, 1996). All of these cases involved sexual assault, though many involved other additional offenses. More importantly, all of these cases involved eyewitness identifications, and in the vast majority of them (86%) erroneous eyewitness identification was the primary evidence that had led to the conviction. In all 28 cases, DNA evidence had not been available at trial and the triers of fact had to rely on eyewitness testimony, which turned out to be inaccurate. The number of convictions reversed due to DNA evidence, spearheaded by The Innocence Project (see Scheck, Neufeld, & Dwyer, 2001), grew to more than 200 by 2007, and eyewitness mistakes were by far the most prevalent reason for the original wrongful conviction.

While the exact prevalence of mistaken convictions is impossible to specify, Huff and his coworkers (1996) described survey responses from several areas of the US that seemed to indicate that a good guess might be that the wrong person is convicted in perhaps 0.5% of felony cases (1 in 200). While that proportion may seem miniscule, the impression changes dramatically when the actual numbers are plugged in. In 2000, there were over 2.2 million felony arrests in the US. The conviction rate was about 70%, meaning about 1.5 million convictions. Given our estimate of 0.5% wrongful convictions, that comes out to almost 8,000 a year. If over half of those are due to eyewitness errors, then over 4,000 innocent persons are convicted each year on the basis of mistaken eyewitness memory.

The Cross-Race Effect and the Construction of Lineups

Race may play a role in the *construction* of lineups, as well as in identifications from lineups. A "fair" lineup is generally defined as one in which the suspect is not *distinctive* in any way, that is, he does not fit the criminal's description more closely than the other lineup members do, and he or his photograph are not distinctive in any other noticeable way (Brigham & Brandt, 1992; Brigham & Pfeifer, 1994). When creating a photo lineup, the law enforcement officer attempts to find five foils that match the general characteristics of the suspect or the description of the perpetrator, either from a stack of available photos or from a computer file. If the officer is of a different race from the suspect, might this hamper the officer's ability to find five foils that are genuinely similar in appearance to the suspect since, in his or her eyes, they all may look more similar to each other than they really are?

To investigate this possibility we (Brigham & Ready, 1985) presented college students with a single male target facial photo and a stack of 80 other male facial photos of the same race. Their task was to go through the stack, one by one, until they had found five photos that were "similar in appearance" to the target photo. The students, Blacks and Whites, did this once with photos of Blacks, and once with photos of Whites. As we had suspected, when looking at photos of their own race, students of each race looked through significantly *more* photos before they found five that they thought were "similar" in appearance to the target photo. That is, they used a stricter response criterion when evaluating the own-race photos – they made finer distinctions between the own-race photos and hence needed to view a greater number in order to find five that seemed sufficiently similar to the target photo. Applying this finding to the police station, these findings suggest that an officer will be more likely to create a "fair" lineup, one in which the five foils are quite similar in appearance to the suspect (who is analogous to the target photo in the above study), when the officer is of the same race as the suspect. Since fairer lineups have been shown to produce fewer eyewitness errors (Brigham, Meissner, & Wasserman, 1999; Brigham & Pfeifer, 1994), this issue is of considerable applied significance.

Possible Safeguards and Remedies

In response to concerns about possible problems with eyewitness memory, the justice system has struggled to ensure that adequate safeguards are in place to protect the accused during the investigatory stage and at trial. In response to concerns about how eyewitness evidence is gathered, the US Department of Justice (DOJ) created a commission to establish national guidelines for eyewitness evidence (Technical Working Group for Eyewitness Evidence, 1999). The commission agreed on four central standards (1) All of the foils in a lineup should fit the eyewitness's description of the perpetrator; (2) Instructions to the witness should stress that the perpetrator may or may not be in the lineup; (3) Only one suspect should be in a lineup; and (4) Investigators should ask open-ended questions and avoid leading questions. Several other standards were suggested by the researchers in the Technical Working Group, but were not adopted.

At about the same time, the American Psychology-Law Society (Division 41 of the American Psychological Society) published its first "Scientific Review Paper," which was entitled, "Eyewitness Identification Procedures: Recommendations for Lineups and Photospreads" (Wells et al., 1998). The panel of leading researchers made four recommendations, which are complementary to those made by the DOJ Technical Working Group. The procedures recommended by the AP-LS panel were (1) Distracters (foils) for a lineup should be selected based on their similarity to the eyewitness's verbal description of the perpetrator; (2) A "double-blind" procedure should be used for showing the lineup to the eyewitness, in which the person administering the lineup to the witness is unaware ("blind") of which lineup member is the suspect. This would prevent the administrator from giving any cues to the witness, intentionally or unintentionally, about who to pick. (3) A witness's confidence in his/her lineup choice should be carefully assessed and recorded at the time of the identification; and (4) A sequential lineup (where the foils are viewed one by one) is preferable to the usual simultaneous lineup. Research has indicated that sequential lineups produce significantly greater overall accuracy in judgments: fewer false identifications, while the number of correct identifications may be reduced a little, but not as much. In a companion article, Kassin (1998) suggested a fifth "rule": all identification procedures should be videotaped.

Turning to the trial phase, several "remedies" have been suggested, as presented below. (In contrast, other legal scholars have argued that no additional safeguards or remedies are necessary, because it is the jury's job to evaluate the credibility of any witness.)

"Skillful" Cross-Examination

Traditionally, it has been proposed that the most effective safeguard against a mistaken eyewitness misleading the jury is skillful cross-examination of the witness which, it has been argued, can be an effective tool in casting doubt upon the eyewitness's identification of the defendant. The problem is, of course, that cross-examination, no matter how skillfully done, cannot establish whether or not a witness is correct in his or her identification. Witnesses who are honestly mistaken will respond no differently than witnesses who are correct. Illustrating this point, studies by Wells, Lindsay, and their colleagues have shown that mock jurors who view eyewitnesses being cross-examined by experienced lawyers cannot distinguish accurate from inaccurate eyewitnesses (Lindsay, Wells, & Rumpel, 1981; Wells, Lindsay, & Ferguson, 1979).

Cautionary Jury Instructions

A second traditional safeguard is to have the judge give cautionary instructions to jurors before they begin deliberating. Probably the most widely utilized instructions about eyewitness memory are those adopted in 1972 by the US Court of Appeals for the District of Columbia in *United States v. Telfaire*. Unfortunately, however, the *Telfaire* instructions were developed from legal precedents and were not based on scientific research findings. Hence, they do not address most of the areas that research has shown to be problematic, including cross-race identifications.

Recently, however, in *New Jersey v. Cromedy* (1999), the New Jersey Supreme Court ruled that in some cases witnesses should be given special jury instructions that point out the possible importance of race. A White college student who had been raped by a Black man failed to identify the perpetrator in several sets of photographs she was shown shortly thereafter. Almost 8 months later, she saw McKinley Cromedy walking down the street and believed that he was the rapist. She rushed home and called the police and, within 15 min she viewed him in a one-person "showup" from behind a one-way mirror. She identified him as the man who had raped her and who she had just seen on the street. Interestingly, his photo had been among those that the victim had been shown in the days after the rape, when she was unable to identify anyone. There was no other evidence tying him to the rape. At trial, the defense asked the judge to read the following instructions to the jury:

> When a witness who is a member of one race identifies a member who is of another race we say that there has been a cross-racial identification. You may consider, if you think it is appropriate to do so, whether the cross-racial nature of the identification has affected the accuracy of the witness's original perception and/or accuracy of a subsequent identification.

The trial judge refused to use this jury charge and Cromedy was convicted. Seven years later the New Jersey Supreme Court reversed the conviction, saying that in some cases where there is a cross-race identification and no other evidence points to the suspect, the jury should be given a charge such as the one proposed during the trial. Hence, in New Jersey, when there is a cross-race identification in the absence of any other compelling evidence, judges must now give this special instruction to jurors.

Educational Expert Testimony

Another possible safeguard is to allow expert testimony by researchers that is designed to educate jurors about the CRE and other troublesome areas of eyewitness memory. The importance of race in identification was pointed out by Feingold back in 1914, who wrote that it is "well known that, all other things being equal, individuals of a given race are distinguishable from each other in proportion to our familiarity, to our contact with the race as a whole (Feingold, 1914, p. 50)." Although expert testimony about eyewitness memory has been offered in courtrooms throughout the US, Canada, and Great Britain (Fulero, 1993), in many jurisdictions trial judges routinely refuse to allow it. The reasons judges give for not allowing the testimony include that it is not "relevant" to that particular case, or would not be "helpful" to jurors. Alternately, some judges have decided that an awareness of the fallibility of eyewitness memory is already "within the common knowledge" of jurors and expert testimony is thus unnecessary. However, contrary to this judicial assumption, research indicates that such knowledge is *not* within the common knowledge of most jurors (e.g., see Brigham & Bothwell, 1983; Brigham, Wasserman, & Meissner, 1999). In still other cases, judges have ruled that the testimony should not be admitted for fear it would instigate a so-called "battle of experts," as has happened in some other areas of expertise. Judges seem unaware that such battles would be unlikely in this area, where empirical research findings are presented, in contrast to more subjective areas, such as some types of clinical evaluations of individuals. The previously discussed surveys of memory researchers have shown that there is great consensus among researchers about the central findings of eyewitness memory research, including the CRE (Kassin et al., 1989, 2001). (For further discussions of the legal and criminal-justice issues involved, see Brigham, Bennett, Meissner, & Mitchell, 2007; Brigham & Hyme, 2001; Brigham, Wasserman, & Messiner, 1999; Chance & Goldstein, 1996; Cutler & Penrod, 1995; Fulero; Huff et al., 1996; Lindsay, Brigham, Brimacombe, & Wells, 2002).

The Role of the Cross-Race Effect in Prejudice and Intergroup Interactions

Belief in Outgroup Homogeneity of Appearance

The consequences of mistaken recognition are not limited to police lineups or to the courtroom. It seems to me that the everyday consequences of race-related errors in recognition memory can have a significant impact on intergroup interactions and prejudice. At the most basic level, there are two types of face-recognition errors that could interfere with social interactions: false alarms and misses. A *false alarm* response occurs when you mistakenly believe that a stranger is someone you have seen before; a *miss* occurs when you fail to recognize a person that you have seen before. All of us have made such errors and, at a minimum, either type of error can make a social interaction awkward and uncomfortable. If the interaction is an interracial one, the target person may see such a mistake as insulting, or demeaning, or as the result of prejudice or racism. Further, persons who are aware that they may make this kind of error in an interracial situation might be particularly nervous and wary in interracial situations, or might try to avoid such interactions entirely. Later I will suggest that this may increase feelings of threat and anxiety that are causal factors in intergroup prejudice.

A belief that other-race people "all look alike" appears to be associated with prejudice. Brigham (1993) developed two 20-item measures of racial attitudes: *Attitude toward Blacks* (ATB) and *Attitude toward Whites* (ATW), based on extensive factor analytic work on hundreds of possible questions, involving several samples of Black college students and White college students. One of the 20 items that made the final cut for the ATB reads as follows: I think black people look more similar to each other than white people do. Similarly, a parallel item ended up on the ATW: I think that white people look more similar to each other than black people do. Participants responded on labeled seven-point Likert scales. White students' ($N = 262$) endorsement of this item correlated .50 with their responses to the other 19 ATB items, while Black students' ($N = 81$) responses to the parallel item correlated .41 with their responses to the other 19 ATW items. Hence, a belief in other-race similarity of appearance is a significant component of prejudice in Blacks and in Whites, at least as measured by the ATW and the ATB. [For comparison purposes, in the same sample of Whites, total ATB scores correlated .70 with their scores on the *Modern Racism Scale* developed by McConahay, Hardee, and Batts (1981), and .45 with scores on the *Symbolic Racism Scale* developed by Kinder and Sears (1981).] It seems likely that people who believe in outgroup homogeneity of appearance will be more likely to feel uncomfortable in intergroup contact, perhaps fearing that they will make a mistake in mistaking one outgroup member for another, or they may avoid such contact situations altogether.

Conceptualizations of Prejudice and Racism

> The human mind must think with the aid of categories...once formed, categories are the basis for normal prejudgments. We cannot possibly avoid this process. Orderly learning depends upon it. (Allport, 1954, p. 19)

Conceptualizations and definitions of prejudice are varied. In his classic 1954 work, *The Nature of Prejudice,* Gordon Allport defined prejudice as, "an antipathy based upon a faulty and inflexible generalization" (Allport, 1954, p. 9). Elsewhere, I have suggested that prejudice be defined as, "A negative attitude that is considered unjustified by an observer" (Brigham, 1991, p. 459). I feel that it is an observer who labels a negative attitude as "prejudicial," according to the observer's value judgment. It seems to me that not all negative intergroup attitudes are the same, that there are some situations in which a negative attitude toward a group would be appropriate, such as when one's group suffers an unprovoked attack from another group, or is unjustly exploited by another group. Nevertheless, the most common approach in psychology today seems to be to define prejudice simply as a negative attitude toward a group or its members, without worrying about the justifiability of that negativity.

In recent years many investigators have asserted that new types of subtle prejudice and racism have emerged, largely replacing so-called "old-fashioned racism" in adults that is exemplified by undisguised hostility and bigotry. (As noted earlier, however, Katz (2003) pointed out that many young children still show the more direct form of prejudice.) The newer varieties of racism include modern racism (e. g., McConahay, 1986), symbolic racism (e.g., Kinder, 1986; Sears, 1988), aversive racism (e.g., Gaertner & Dovidio, 1986), and ambivalent racism (e.g., Katz & Hass, 1988). What these theoretical approaches have in common is the notion that a hostile attitude or discriminatory behaviors toward outgroup members may not be recognized by the actor or, if recognized, the actor may try to disguise or justify them.

Much recent work has focused on *conflicts* that a prejudiced person may feel. These may be the conflict between egalitarian values and negative feelings toward outgroups (aversive racism theory), conflict between contrasting emotions (ambivalent racism theory), conflict between symbolic values and perceived outgroup characteristics seen as threatening these values (symbolic racism theory), or conflict between a desire to appear unprejudiced toward outgroups and negative feelings toward those groups (modern racism theory).

According to social identity theory people, especially those high in prejudice, will work to maximize the perceived distinction between their ingroup and outgroups, in order to avoid "contaminating" the ingroup (Brigham, 1971). As an example, highly prejudiced people were found to be more careful than were less prejudiced people, when asked to categorize a series of racially-ambiguous faces as Black or as White. Prejudiced people appear to be more highly motivated to make accurate judgments of racial categorizations, being more cautious and taking longer at the task. They seem very concerned that they not make the mistake of including an outgroup member in the ingroup category (Blascovich, Wyer, Swart, & Kibler, 1997).

Another important issue is the distinction between *explicit attitudes*, which can be measured by traditional self-report measures, and *implicit attitudes*, evaluations that are activated by the mere presence (actual or symbolic) of the attitude object, and typically function in a more "automatic" manner, outside of a person's awareness and control (Greenwald & Banaji, 1995). Many studies have demonstrated that intergroup biases can occur automatically or with little intent or conscious awareness (e.g., Ashburn-Nardo, Voils, & Monteith, 2001; Greenwald & Banaji, 1995). Researchers have been concerned that traditional, explicit measures of prejudice, such as self-report attitude questionnaires, may not always be accurate – either because an individual may answer untruthfully in order to present a socially desirable image (e.g., to appear tolerant and unprejudiced), or because the respondent is consciously unaware of his/her underlying negative feelings. Implicit attitudes can be seen as unconscious analogues to self-reported (conscious) attitudes (DeSteno, Dasgupta, Bartlett, & Cajdric, 2004).

The potential conflict between these automatic involuntary reactions and other, more easily controlled behaviors, has stimulated a plethora of research in recent years (e.g., Dovidio, Kawakami, & Gaertner, 2002; Fazio, Jackson, Dunton, & Williams, 1995; Greenwald & Banaji, 1995). It has been shown repeatedly that significant biases against outgroups can be identified in situations in which traditional questionnaires would not indicate bias (e.g., see Blair & Banaji, 1996; Dovidio, Kawakami, Johnson, Johnson, & Howard, 1997; Fazio et al., 1995).

Probably the most widely used technique for accessing implicit attitudes is the *Implicit Associations Test* (IAT) developed by Greenwald and his coworkers (Greenwald, McGhee, & Schwartz, 1998). The IAT is based on the premise that if an attitude object evokes a particular emotion, it will facilitate responses to stimuli that are evaluatively congruent with that emotion, as opposed to neutral or incongruent. When assessing racial prejudice via the IAT, a negative implicit attitude in a White respondent would be indicated if the respondent responded more efficiently (shorter response latency, fewer errors) when instructed to respond in terms of prejudice-congruent associations than when responding to prejudice-incongruent associations. For example, in the prejudice-congruent association condition, the respondent might be asked to push one button whenever a White face or a positive word appears, and to press another button whenever a Black face or a negative word appears. In the prejudice-incongruent condition, in contrast, one button would be pushed for White faces or for negative words, while the other button would be for Black faces or positive words. For the prejudiced person, the theory goes, the prejudice-congruent condition is "easier" (leading to faster, more accurate responding) because it fits his/her way of categorizing things. So an individual's level of racial prejudice is indexed by subtracting the efficiency of prejudice-incongruent associations from prejudice-congruent associations (e.g., see DeSteno et al., 2004; Lowery, Hardin, & Sinclair, 2001; Vanman, Saltz, Nathan, & Warren, 2004).

A related issue concerns peoples' efforts to control their prejudiced reactions and to respond without prejudice. Devine and her coworkers (e.g., Devine, 1989; Devine & Monteith, 1993; Devine, Monteith, Zuwerink, & Elliot, 1991; Plant & Devine, 1998) have proposed that it is virtually impossible for a majority-group member to grow up in our society without being exposed to stereotypes and ethnic slurs against minority group members, creating automatic, implicit negative attitudes. Even if the person does not endorse such views, they are "psychologically available" and may surface in times of stress. Devine (1989) likened prejudice to a "bad habit" that one may acquire unintentionally and must work hard to eliminate. The majority group member who wishes to behave without prejudice must make a conscious and determined effort to suppress and eliminate these views, just as if trying to unlearn a bad habit.

Research by Devine, Plant, and their coworkers identified two very different motives for trying to learn to respond without prejudice. Those with an internal motivation to respond without prejudice are motivated by a desire to respond consistently with their nonprejudiced beliefs and values. In contrast, those with an external motivation are concerned with making a good impression and avoiding negative reactions from others (Devine, Plant, Amodio, Harmon-Jones, & Vance, 2002). Plant and Devine (1998) developed the *Internal* and *External Motivation to Respond Without Prejudice Scales* (the IMS and EMS, respectively) to assess these motivations. Scores on the two scales are only slightly related (average $r = -.14$). While IMS scores are strongly related to traditional measures of prejudice such as the *Attitudes Toward Blacks* (ATB) scale (Brigham, 1993) and the *Modern Racism Scale* (McConahay, 1986), EMS scores are only modestly related to these measures (Plant & Devine). IMS and EMS scores apparently do not covary with one implicit attitude measure, facial EMG scores (Cunningham, Nezlek, & Banaji, 2004), but one combination of scores – high IMS scores and low EMS scores – is associated with low prejudice responses on the IAT. This pattern is also associated with high scores on a measure of self-determination, as conceptualized by Ryan and Connell (1989). Those who were low in internal standards but high in external, in contrast, were especially low in self-determination (Devine et al., 2002).

We would expect explicit and implicit attitudes to differ most in situations where social norms are in the direction counter to one's private feelings. In the current context, this could be when one has negative feelings about a culturally disadvantaged group in a culture that explicitly endorses egalitarian goals, such as, perhaps, relations between ethnic groups in the US (Cunningham, Nezlek, & Banaji, 2004). In contrast, in other contexts we might expect explicit and implicit attitudes to be congruent with each other. As an example, Nosek, Banaji, and Greenwald (2001) found that individuals' explicit and implicit (IAT) attitudes toward political candidates were quite closely related. Further, situations that cause changes in explicit attitudes have been shown to affect implicit attitudes as well. Thus, students who were enrolled in a prejudice and conflict seminar showed less explicit prejudice (stereotyping) and also less implicit prejudice (IAT scores) after taking the course (Rudman, Ashmore, & Gary, 2001). In a similar vein, another study found that individuals who were led to engage in counterstereotypic mental imagery not only showed less explicit stereotyping, but also had less negative implicit attitudes, as assessed by the IAT (Blair, Ma, & Lenton, 2001).

While it is clear from public opinion poll data that the level of "old-fashioned racism" expressed by White adults in the US has decreased markedly since the 1950s, it is not clear whether this represents a drop in overall prejudice and racism, or whether old-fashioned racism has simply "mutated" into more subtle, implicit forms. As Jones (2002, p. 64) indicated in a recent book on prejudice, "... whether there is indeed a 'new racism' (i.e., more covert, more disguised) is debatable."

Is the Cross-Race Effect Related to Prejudice?

It has been suggested that prejudicial racial attitudes could cause or contribute to the CRE (Brigham & Malpass, 1985). One could speculate that negative attitudes toward another race could lead people to cease processing a face, once it has been categorized as belonging to a member of the disliked group, as in Rodin's (1987) concept of cognitive disregard. Further, one could speculate that negative intergroup attitudes could motivate one to avoid contact with members of the disliked group, or to limit contact to very superficial interactions, thereby constraining the opportunity to develop expertise in distinguishing between other-race faces (Chance & Goldstein, 1996).

Conversely, however, one could hypothesize that prejudice might motivate some people to be highly *vigilant* when encountering other-race persons, as a prejudiced shop owner might keep a close eye on other-race customers, fearing they may be shoplifters. Recall the finding that highly prejudiced people were more careful than were less-prejudiced people, when asked to categorize racially ambiguous faces by race (Blascovich et al., 1997). Such increased vigilance over time might produce greater skill in recognizing faces of other-race persons. It is my guess that several conflicting associations may come into play and cancel each other out because, for whatever reason, research to date has failed to find *any* substantial relationship between facial recognition accuracy and attitudes toward the group whose faces are identified (e.g., Brigham & Barkowitz, 1978; Platz & Hosch, 1988; Slone, Brigham, & Meissner, 2000). Racial attitudes did not show a significant relationship to the CRE across 14 studies analyzed in the Meissner and Brigham (2001) meta-analysis.

Racial attitudes are, however, related to the amount of intergroup contact that one reports, at least for Whites. The role of intergroup contact has long been studied as an important factor in causing or ameliorating prejudice and racism (e.g., Allport, 1954; Amir, 1969; Brewer & Miller, 1984; Cook, 1970; Devine, Evett, & Vasquez-Suson, 1996; Pettigrew, 1998). The impact of intergroup contact on racial attitudes has been captured in a wide-ranging meta-analysis conducted by Pettigrew and Tropp (2000). They analyzed results from 203 studies and 313 independent samples including 90,000 participants from 23 nations (73% of the studies were from the US). In almost all (94%) of the studies, there was an inverse relationship between contact and prejudice, and the magnitude of the overall effect size was considerable, $d = .42$. They concluded that, "overall, face-to-face interaction between members of distinguishable groups is importantly related to reduced prejudice" (p. 109).

We have assessed the relationship between self-reported amount of interracial contact and racial attitude as assessed by the ATB for White respondents and the ATW for Black respondents in our lab in a half-dozen studies over a 15-year period (e.g., Brigham, 1993; Slone et al., 2000). For White respondents, the relationship has consistently been positive and significant, with a mean correlation of about .55. For Black respondents, the relationship has been small to moderate and more variable, with a mean correlation of about .25–.30. The Meissner and Brigham (2001) meta-analysis evaluated ten studies that had assessed self-reported interracial contact and racial attitude, and found a small but significant positive relationship. They did not analyze this relationship separately for Black perceivers and White perceivers, however.

Threat and Intergroup Anxiety

In recent years, several theorists have asserted that anxiety and perceived threat may be critical aspects of intergroup prejudice. Indeed, James Jones (1997, p. 317) stated that, "Prejudice is a problem with intergroup anxiety," and elsewhere he noted that. "… much inter*personal* anxiety may be affected by inter*group* anxiety" (Jones, 1997, p. 234, italics in original). In their integrated threat theory, Stephan and Stephan (1985, 2000) proposed that there are four types of threat associated with intergroup interactions (1) realistic threat, as from conflict and competition, (2) symbolic threat, stemming from perceived differences in morals values, standards, and beliefs, (3) threat based on negative stereotypes; and (4) threat due *to* intergroup anxiety. Intergroup anxiety originates from concerns about anticipated negative outcomes, such as being embarrassed rejected, exploited, or ridiculed. Intergroup anxiety can be a major complicating factor in intergroup interactions, in part because it can cause a reliance on oversimplified cognitive heuristics and it amplifies emotional reactions.

Several studies have found intergroup anxiety to be associated with negative attitudes and evaluations (e.g., Britt, Boneicki, Vescio, Biernat, & Brown, 1996; Islam & Hewstone, 1993). For example, Stephan, Ybarra, and Bachman (1999) investigated self-reported intergroup anxiety and ethnic attitudes in three settings: Florida residents' feelings toward Cuban immigrants, New Mexico residents' feelings about Mexican immigrants, and Hawaii residents' attitudes toward Asian immigrants. Intergroup anxiety was assessed by a modified version of the scale developed by Stephan and Stephan (1985), which assessed reactions to 12 terms relevant to the respondents' feelings when interacting with the target group: apprehensive, uncertain, worried, awkward, anxious, threatened, comfortable, trusting, friendly, confident, safe, and at ease. In all three settings, intergroup anxiety correlated significantly with negative attitudes (correlations from .58 to .66).

According to the Stephans' theory, anxiety increases the likelihood of negative consequences which, in turn, increase the likelihood of avoidance behaviors, stereotyping, generally heightened arousal, and prejudice. Bearers of stigma can cause perceivers to feel a sense of uncertainty, discomfort, anxiety, or even danger during social interactions (Crocker, Major, & Steele, 1998). Further, people who interact with stigmatized others show poor performance and cardiovascular reactivity that is consistent with feelings of threat (Blascovich, Mendes, Hunter, Lickel, & Kowai-Bell, 2001). People who are strongly identified with their ingroup are likely to react to threat with feelings of prejudice toward an outgroup. On the other hand, intergroup contact may have a moderating influence by reducing novelty or unfamiliarity, thereby producing less threat and less anxiety (Blascovich et al., 2001; Plant & Devine, 2003). It seems possible that such contact might also reduce the likelihood of the CRE.

Can the Cross-Race Effect be Lessened or Eliminated?

I have suggested that the CRE can have deleterious consequences in two general arenas. The first is the criminal justice system, where the CRE increases the odds that an innocent other-race suspect may be wrongly identified due to a "false alarm" response by an eyewitness. The second area is in everyday intergroup interactions. People are more likely to make errors by misrecognizing or failing to recognize individuals if those individuals belong to a different racial group. Furthermore, many people are likely to feel social anxiety due to fear of making such errors, which can poison their interaction and hinder effective communication. I will discuss several aspects of this issue (1) The effects of intergroup contact on the CRE; (2) The effectiveness of attempts to eliminate the CRE in others via training; (3) The effects of incentives for accuracy in recognizing other-race faces; and (4) Trying to reduce the CRE in oneself, as when one is motivated to control a (potentially) prejudiced response.

The Impact of Intergroup Contact on the Cross-Race Effect

As noted earlier, one way of conceptualizing the CRE is as a skill deficit in the ability to cognitively process, categorize, encode, and remember other-race faces. If this is the case, then it follows that this skill should be improved by practice in distinguishing other-race faces from each other. One could predict that high levels of contact would play a role in decreasing the magnitude of the CRE, since those individuals who have had a great deal of interracial contact will presumably have had a lot of practice in identifying and distinguishing between other-race persons. This assumption that one's degree of experience with other-race persons can affect the likelihood that the CRE will occur has been around for almost a century (Feingold, 1914). Many contemporary researchers have also endorsed this race-specific perceptual expertise hypothesis (e.g., Brigham & Malpass, 1985; Chance & Goldstein, 1996; Ng & Lindsay, 1994). (This approach implies that the contact is of a positive or neutral nature. If the contact was largely negative, in contrast, the resulting increase in hostility, cognitive disregard, and future avoidance might have a different impact on the CRE.)

We know little about the cognitive mechanisms through which a reduction in CRE due to positive or neutral intergroup contact might occur. At a very general level, it could be hypothesized that increased contact leads to more experience in processing other-group faces, thereby increasing one's expertise in making such discriminations. One could also speculate that increased contact might reduce the perceived complexity of previously unfamiliar classes of stimuli, that is, other-race faces (Goldstein & Chance, 1971), or that it might convince people that stereotypi-cal responses to other-race faces are not useful and thus instigate the search for more individuating characteristics (Shepherd, 1981). Alternatively, one could pre-dict that increased levels of contact make it more likely that one's social rewards and punishments are dependent on correctly distinguishing among other-race persons with whom one has contact, presumably increasing one's motivation to remember faces of other-race persons accurately (Malpass, 1990). Contact might also serve to reduce the social anxiety that people may otherwise feel in intergroup relations.

As logical as these processes may sound, studies with adults that have attempted to identify the role of contact in the CRE have had only limited success. The meta-analysis of 29 studies that measured self-reported interracial contact found that amount of contact accounted for a small but reliable amount of variability in the CRE, approximately 2% (Meissner & Brigham, 2001). The results from individual studies have varied considerably. Several investigations found no relationship between an experience measure and recognition of Black and White faces (Brigham & Barkowitz, 1978; Malpass & Kravitz, 1969; Ng & Lindsay, 1994; Swope, 1994). Several other studies found that self-reported interracial contact, friendships, and experiences were predictive of ability to recognize persons of another race (Brigham, Maass, Snyder, & Spaulding, 1982; Carroo, 1986, 1987; Lavrakas, Buri, & Mayzner, 1976). Still others have found mixed results within the same study

(Chiroro & Valentine, 1995; Platz & Hosch, 1988). It seems likely that either the theoretical grounds for predicting a relationship between contact/experience and face recognition accuracy are not adequately specified, or that our methods for empirically assessing the quantity and/or quality of contact or experience with other-race persons are not adequate (Brigham & Malpass, 1985; Shepherd, 1981; Slone et al., 2000). I have the feeling that if we can develop a valid measure of the *quality* of interracial contact, contact that involves individuating situations and meaningful consequences for correct or incorrect recognition of others, it will relate more strongly to the CRE.

Training/Practice in Recognizing Other-Race Faces

The issue of improving performance in cross-race face recognition can be approached from at least two directions (a) increasing expertise via training or practice and (b) increasing perceivers' motivation to do well. The possibility of training adults to better recognize other-race faces received some empirical attention in the 1970s and early 1980s, with mixed results. Elliott, Wills, and Goldstein (1973) found that Whites trained on a paired associates task with White and Japanese faces showed improved performance on Japanese faces immediately after training. Goldstein and Chance (1985) used a similar training technique and found that improved performance for Japanese faces persisted up to 5 months after the training. Other training studies, however, found that training had no effect on memory for other-race faces (Malpass, 1981; Woodhead, Baddeley, & Simmonds, 1979), or found that the effects of training were inconsistent and temporary (Lavrakas et al., 1976; Malpass, Lavigueur, & Weldon, 1973). Hence, it is unclear at this juncture whether or not systematic training can reduce or eliminate the CRE, and the temporal nature of any change that occurs is also unclear. Indeed, it appears that investigators in the past two decades have not even found this to be an interesting empirical question.

There are a number of mechanisms by which training or experience could improve memory performance, relating to improving cognitive strategies or acquiring relevant knowledge (Kuhn, 1992). More specifically, these include: improving processing efficiency, improving encoding and representation, improving strategy selection and regulation, improving the execution of strategies, improving processing capacity, and increasing domain-specific knowledge (Klahr, 1992; Poole & Lamb, 1998).

Given that there have been no published studies of training with children, we (Brigham, Bennett, & Butz, 2005) developed a series of studies designed to provide participants with experience in distinguishing between other-race faces in a game-like situation, with the goal of improving their ability to make cross-race identifications and thereby reducing or eliminating the CRE. We developed a "memory game" in which participants viewed a 4 × 5 grid of 20 face-down cards on a computer screen, with a head-and-shoulders photo of an adult on the other side of each. The participant turned over any two cards by mouse clicks; if there was a match, they disappeared from the board. Otherwise, they were turned face-down again. The participant's task was to remove all the cards in as few trials as possible. Each participant played the game six times, either with sets of same-race faces, or other-race faces, or a control game that did not involve face memory (pinball). After a short distracter task, all responded to a standard face recognition memory task with different faces.

Prior to using this new paradigm with children, we conducted two initial studies with college students, Blacks and Whites. As predicted, in both studies we found a significant three-way interaction [race of participant by race of face (indicative of the CRE) by training condition] on both mean accuracy scores (A', false alarms) and on a measure of response criterion. However, examination of the means indicated that it was *not* the cross-race training that accounted for the effect. Rather, the *own-race* training produced a more liberal response criterion (i.e., responding "seen before" in the recognition task) for own-race faces, similar to what is typically seen for other-race faces, leading to more false alarms (and hence poorer recognition scores) for own-race faces. Because of this, the CRE was not present for those in the own-race training conditions in either study, but it was still present for those in the other-race training condition, as well as those in the control condition. Figure 3 illustrates that false alarms rates in the recognition task were much larger for other-race faces than for own-race faces for those who had had practice with other-race faces (left panel). However, for those given practice with own-race faces, false alarm rates in the recognition test did not differ according to race of face (right panel).

One possible explanation for these counterintuitive results is that the nature of the task encouraged our participants to adopt a featural encoding style. This might have had no impact on those in the other-race condition, because research suggests that people already use featural encoding on objects that they do not have expertise with, such as other-race faces. However, those in the own-race condition, in

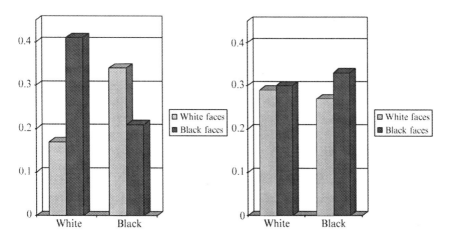

Fig. 3 False alarms in face recognition: After training with other-race faces (*left panel*), and with own-race faces (*right panel*) (Brigham et al., 2005)

contrast, who might ordinarily use a holistic encoding process (since people are experts with own-race faces), perhaps decided that they could do best in the memory game by focusing on specific facial features, and this featural orientation could have carried over into the recognition phase, making their recognition of own-race faces just as poor as recognition of other-race faces. These findings clearly indicate that the *type* of training or practice can have a dramatic impact on its effectiveness in influencing the recognition of own- and other-race faces.

Increasing Motivation to Remember Other-Race Faces Accurately

A third possible route is to increase *motivation to do well* in recognizing other-race faces. There is evidence that incentives can enhance accuracy in memory tasks under some conditions (e.g., Koriat & Goldsmith, 1994, 1996; Liberman & Tversky, 1993). It should be noted, however, that encouraging people to do a "good job" on a memory task does not always produce better performance. In a study of description memory, my colleagues and I (Meissner, Brigham, & Kelley, 2001) had participants describe a person they had seen. Some were encouraged to give as full and complete a description as possible (such instructions are often given to witnesses to crimes), while others were not. Those given the encouragement gave significantly less inaccurate descriptions and also were less able to identify the target person from a lineup. They generated a great deal of misinformation (bad guesses) in attempting to provide as much information as possible, and apparently that self-generated misinformation hampered their later ability to recognize the target person.

If the CRE is due to insufficient encoding because less attention is paid to other-race faces, for example, then providing an incentive for accuracy might increase attention that is given to these faces and thereby improve performance. Individuals who are victims or witnesses to serious crimes often say that they tried very hard to remember the face of the perpetrator (e.g., Loftus, 1979). Does this high motivation improve the quality of the memory, increasing the likelihood of an accurate identification? In a crime situation, one could have high motivation to remember during any or all of the three phases of memory: the encoding phase (during the crime), the retention interval (the time between the crime and the identification), and the retrieval phase (while viewing a lineup). If the CRE is due largely to *poorer ability* to encode or to retrieve other-race faces, then enhanced motivation should have little effect. In contrast, if the CRE bias is due largely to *greater difficulty* in processing or accessing other-race faces, then enhanced motivation might be expected to lessen or eradicate the CRE, as highly motivated participants would be willing to work harder on the difficult-to-process other-race faces, thereby improving their memory performance.

Experimentally, one could attempt to manipulate participants' motivation at each of the three phases to see how motivation effects memory performance; a couple of facial-memory studies have taken this approach. Barkowitz and Brigham (1982) told half their respondents in a face recognition paradigm that they could win tickets toward a small lottery (from $5 to $35); the better their recognition performance, the more lottery tickets they could win. The other participants were told nothing about any monetary reward. We found no significant effect for incentive on overall performance or on the magnitude of the CRE. However, because the level of incentive used in this study was quite small, the null results do not rule out the possibility that raising motivation can affect performance.

Years later we decided to take another shot at the issue of motivation, by offering incentives to do well at three different points during the recognition memory process (Buck, Dore, & Brigham, 2005). Forty Black and 40 White college students saw a series of faces and then attempted to identify those faces from a larger group of faces 2 days later. In three conditions, participants were offered an incentive for accurate performance – they were told that the top half of the performers would receive money orders of up to $50, depending on the accuracy level of their performance. It was explained that accuracy would be measured by hits minus false alarms. In one condition, they were given this information before they viewed the original pictures (encoding motivation), in a second condition they were told immediately after they had viewed the pictures (rehearsal motivation), while others were given the information two days later, immediately before the recognition test (retrieval motivation). A control group was given no incentive instructions. A significant CRE was visible in all four conditions, but it did not differ in magnitude across conditions. These findings suggest that increasing motivation does not seem to lead to better memory performance in face recognition.

Trying to Reduce the Cross-Race Effect in Oneself

Devine and her coworkers have questioned what they see as a basic assumption of symbolic racism, modern racism, and aversive racism: in each of those models, if discriminatory responses persist despite self-reported changes in attitudes, this is taken as evidence of continuing prejudice. This assumption is "somewhat troubling," Devine and her coworkers asserted, because a person can indeed adopt less prejudiced attitudes but still be unable to express these attitudes behaviorally (Devine et al., 1996, p. 428). It seems to me that the same issue could arise regarding the CRE. If one is aware that he or she is susceptible to this effect, perhaps from personal experiences of making identification mistakes in interactions with outgroup members, can the individual overcome this tendency?

There is abundant evidence that many people in contemporary American society are concerned with not acting or appearing prejudiced (Ickes, 1984; Plant & Devine, 1998). Furthermore, if an individual unwittingly behaves in a way that could be interpreted as prejudicial in an intergroup interaction, it seems likely that the individual's intergroup anxiety will be heightened in any subsequent interactions. As one example, I have experienced extreme embarrassment and discomfort when I unwittingly confused one minority-group student with another in an after-class interaction. (Later discussions with several colleagues indicated that they had made similar mistakes, much to their chagrin.) As a consequence, in subsequent interactions with minority-group students, I worried about making another similar mistake. Did this anxiety have an impact on my behavior in the interactions? It certainly seems possible.

Although Devine's work has not explicitly dealt with face recognition issues, it seems to me that the central principles still apply. Overcoming one's prejudice is a difficult process, she proposed, because one must overcome years of exposure to biased and stereotypical information (Devine, 1989; Devine et al., 2002). According to Devine and her coworkers this involves a multistep process: first, the person must consciously decide to stop responding in a prejudiced way toward the group. Second, nonprejudiced standards must be internalized and integrated into one's self-concept. Third, the person must learn to behave in line with the nonprejudiced personal standards. This is particularly difficult to do with subtle, difficult-to-control responses, such as those assessed by the IAT (Devine et al., 2002).

Prejudice reduction thus involves both motivation and ability components. As in the breaking of any habit, the first step (motive) is to resolve to overcome the bad habit. But motivation alone is not sufficient overcome this learned tendency to make a prejudicial response. The second task is to develop the skills (ability) to overcome it. Low prejudice people are highly motivated to respond without prejudice, but they may lack, or fear that they lack, the skills to act in accordance with their nonprejudiced standards. And if they fail in this effort, they are likely to feel guilty or engage in self-criticism (Devine et al., 1991). Those higher in prejudice, in contrast, have a different reaction if they fail to make the desired nonprejudiced impression. They are likely to feel negative affect toward others, most often toward minority group members (Devine et al., 1996; Monteith, Devine, & Zuwerink, 1993).

From this perspective, a person's reaction to a possible intergroup interaction will be determined by motivation to respond without prejudice and perceived ability to respond consistently with nonprejudiced standards. A person who is worried about failing to behave in a nonprejudiced way or to convey a nonprejudiced image is likely to feel *social anxiety*, as well as the intergroup anxiety that may be inherent in any interactions with members of a group that is often the target of prejudice. As described by Leary and Atherton (1986), social anxiety is likely in social situations, real or imagined, under conditions of potentially negative personal evaluation, when one has low expectations about the effectiveness of their behavior or about the outcome of the interaction (e.g., they may receive a negative reaction from others). It seems to me that a person's fear of confusing one outgroup member with another, a feeling that "they really do all look alike to me," could be an important source of social anxiety in intergroup interactions.

If a person is feeling social anxiety during an interaction with members of another group, and is making self-regulatory efforts to control his/her behavior, the resulting interaction is likely to be, at best, awkward and strained. Research has shown that people who are making conscious efforts to monitor their nonverbal behavior (such as eye contact) act nervous (hesitant speech, fidgeting, stuttering) and show disaffiliative tendencies, such as decreased eye contact and increased social distance (DePaulo, 1992; Poskocil, 1977). Unfortunately, these nervous and disaffiliative behaviors are exactly the same behaviors that often are seen as indicators of prejudice (Devine et al., 1996).

To summarize this position, the reactions of low prejudiced people in intergroup interactions are likely to be the product of their motivation to respond without prejudice and their ability to respond consistently with their nonprejudiced standards. While some nonprejudiced people may be at ease in such interactions, others may face a difficult quandary. They may feel social anxiety resulting from their concern about being seen as prejudiced and, ironically, this anxiety can produce nervousness and avoidant nonverbal behaviors that may be perceived as indicators of prejudice.

Devine and her coworkers have argued, therefore, that while reducing prejudicial attitudes is a laudable goal, more attention should also be paid to ways of helping people learn *how* to express their less prejudiced attitudes and to behave consistently with those attitudes. As noted earlier, there are two very different reasons why people may chose to monitor their behavior and try to behave in a nonprejudicial manner (Plant & Devine, 1998). Those with internal motivation to behave in a nonprejudicial, nondiscriminatory manner (high-IMS) act for personal reasons, because it is personally important for them to behave in accordance with their nonprejudicial standards. In contrast, those with external motivation (high-EMS) monitor their behavior in order to *appear* nonprejudiced, largely to make a good impression and avoid negative reactions from others. Working with two alternative measures of implicit bias, the IAT with race-stereotypical names, and the IAT with Black faces and White faces, Plant and Devine found that externally motivated people could control responses when they were easy to control (e.g., self-reported attitudes on the ATB), but were unable to control the more subtle reactions assessed by the IAT. It seems likely that high-IMS people and high-EMS people may both be motivated to avoid the cross-race error in intergroup interactions, the former so as not to *behave* in a prejudiced way, the latter so as not to *appear* prejudiced to others. Given the overall finding that the CRE is apparently not easy to control, as evidenced by studies showing that neither training nor high incentives for accuracy can ameliorate the CRE, future efforts in training should perhaps focus their efforts on high-IMS/low-EMS individuals. A first step would be to see whether the magnitude of the CRE differs according to IMS and EMS scores, in members of various ethnic groups.

Where Do We Go From Here?

We have learned a great deal about intergroup prejudice and racism in the half-century since Allport's (1954) seminal work was published. Much progress has been made in identifying and measuring different varieties of intergroup antipathy that may occur between an individual and the groups that he/she considers to be outgroups. We know now that antipathy can manifest itself in many different ways, some explicit and direct, but many, perhaps most, implicit or indirect. We know that even when majority-group members feel that they are not prejudiced, or strive mightily to behave in a nonracist, egalitarian manner, this can be a very difficult undertaking. We know further that even those persons with the best of intentions will have a hard time not being influenced, at a conscious or an unconscious level, by the plethora of anti-outgroup information that surrounds them as they grow up in the modern world.

It seems to me that, although the CRE is a phenomenon that has been studied as a cognitive/perceptual phenomenon in the lab by cognitive and social psychologists for the last three decades, its relevance to everyday living has been largely ignored by researchers. To wit, people who are unable to distinguish easily between members of an outgroup, or fear that they will not be able to do so, are likely to approach any interaction with outgroup members with reluctance. In the interaction itself, they may be perceived as unfriendly, distant, or perhaps even racist. If they do misidentify an outgroup member, or confuse one with another, they may be seen as careless, or thoughtless, or practicing "cognitive disregard," or even, once again, as racist.

In my judgment, it seems that we can benefit greatly from research findings that tell us how the CRE develops through childhood, adolescence, and into adulthood, in both majority members and minority group members, in various cultures. As perhaps with most areas of prejudice, research to date has paid more attention to majority-group members' perceptions and behaviors, than to those of minority group members. I am not aware of any studies that have looked directly at how outgroup members feel (and react) as a consequence of feeling that a majority-group person thinks that "they all look alike," but attention to this issue seems warranted.

The issue of surmounting the CRE and overcoming it is a complex one. Early research results, including those from my own lab, have yet to yield particularly promising results. It appears difficult to change the intergroup perceptions of others in any meaningful way. And we know from the work of Devine, Plant, and others, that it is very difficult to change one's *own* behavior in intergroup interactions. Merely attempting to monitor and control one's behavior may make the interaction more difficult and awkward from the start. Nevertheless, it seems that information on how one can learn to be less susceptible to the CRE would be very valuable, particularly for people who interact with members of another group on a regular basis and might be susceptible to manifesting the CRE.

Another interesting question is this: if a person was able to overcome the perceptual tendency to view outgroup members as all looking alike, would that person also show a lesser tendency to manifest other aspects of the outgroup homogeneity assumption? That is, would the individual also be less likely to believe that all outgroup members think alike or behave similarly? Further, would the person be less likely to engage in stereotypic thinking, or to hold prejudicial attitudes, or to behave in a discriminatory manner toward outgroup members? The answers to these questions must await further research scrutiny.

References

Allport, G. W. (1954). *The nature of prejudice*. Reading, MA: Addison-Wesley.

Amir, Y. (1969). Contact hypothesis in ethnic relations. *Psychological Bulletin, 41*, 753–767.

Anthony, T., Copper, C., & Mullen, B. (1992). Cross-racial facial identification: A social cognitive integration. *Personality and Social Psychology Bulletin, 18*, 296–301.

Ashburn-Nardo, L., Voils, C. I., & Monteith, M. J. (2001). Implicit associations as the seeds of intergroup bias: How easily do they take root? *Journal of Personality and Social Psychology, 81*, 789–799.

Baenninger, M. A. (1994). The development of face recognition: Featural or configural processing? *Journal of Experimental Child Psychology, 57*, 377–396.

Barkowitz, P., & Brigham, J. C. (1982). Recognition of faces: Own-race bias, incentive, and time delay. *Journal of Applied Social Psychology, 12*, 255–268.

Bennett, L. B., & Brigham, J. C. (2005). *The development of the "cross-race effect" in children's face recognition memory*. Unpublished manuscript. Florida State University.

Bigler, R. S. (1999). The use of multicultural curricula and materials to counter racism in children. *Journal of Social Issues, 55*(4), 687–705.

Blair, I., & Banaji, M. (1996). Automatic and controlled processes in stereotype priming. *Journal of Personality and Social Psychology, 70*, 1142–1163.

Blair, I. V., Ma, J. E., & Lenton, A. P. (2001). Imaging stereotypes away: The moderation of implicit stereotypes through mental imagery. *Journal of Personality and Social Psychology, 81*, 828–841.

Blascovich, J., Mendes, W. B., Hunter, S. B., Lickel, B., & Kowai-Bell, N. (2001). Perceived threat in social interactions with stigmatized others. *Journal of Personality and Social Psychology, 80*, 253–267.

Blascovich, J., Wyer, N. A., Swart, L. A., & Kibler, J. L. (1997). Racism and racial categorization. *Journal of Personality and Social Psychology, 72*, 1364–1372.

Borchard, E. M. (1932). *Convicting the innocent; Sixty-five actual errors of criminal justice*. New Haven, CT: Yale University Press.

Bothwell, R. K., Brigham, J. C., & Malpass, R. S. (1989). Cross-racial identification. *Personality and Social Psychology Bulletin, 15*, 19–25.

Brewer, M. B., & Miller, N. (1984). Beyond the contact hypothesis. In N. Miller, & M. B. Brewer (Eds.), *Groups in contact* (pp. 281–302). New York: Academic Press.

Brigham, J. C. (1971). Ethnic stereotypes. *Psychological Bulletin, 76*, 15–38.

Brigham, J. C. (1991). *Social psychology* (2nd ed.). New York: HarperCollins.

Brigham, J. C. (1993). Racial attitudes of college students. *Journal of Applied Social Psychology, 23*, 1933–1967.

Brigham, J. C. (2002). Face identification: Basic processes and developmental changes. In M. L. Eisen, J. A. Quas, & G. S. Goodman (Eds.), *Memory and suggestibility in the forensic interview* (pp. 115–140). Mahwah, NJ: Lawrence Erlbaum.

Brigham, J. C., & Barkowitz, P. (1978). Do "they all look alike"? The effect of race, sex, experience, and attitudes on the ability to recognize faces. *Journal of Applied Social Psychology, 8*, 306–318.

Brigham, J. C., Bennett, L. B., & Butz, D. (2005). *The effect of training in face recognition: When practice does not make perfect*. Symposium presentation. La Jolla, CA: American Psychology-Law Society.

Brigham, J. C., Bennett, L. B., Meissner, C. A., & Mitchell, T. A. (2007). The influence of race on eyewitness memory. In R. C. L. Lindsay, D. F. Ross, J. D. Read, & M. P. Toglia (Eds.), *Handbook of eyewitness psychology. Volume II: Memory for people* (pp. 257–281). Hillsdale, NJ: Lawrence Erlbaum.

Brigham, J. C., & Bothwell, R. K. (1983). The ability of prospective jurors to estimate the accuracy of eyewitness identifications. *Law and Human Behavior, 7*, 19–30.

104 J. C. Brigham

Brigham, J. C., & Brandt, C. C. (1992). Measuring lineup fairness: Mock witness responses vs. direct evaluations of lineups. *Law and Human Behavior, 16,* 475–489.

Brigham, J. C., & Hyme, H. S. (2001). Dealing with fallible eyewitness evidence: How scientific research and expert testimony can help, Part I. *The Trial Lawyer, 24,* 301–307.

Brigham, J. C., Maass, A., Snyder, L. D., & Spaulding, K. (1982). The accuracy of eyewitness identifications in a field setting. *Journal of Personality and Social Psychology, 42,* 673–681.

Brigham, J. C., & Malpass, R. S. (1985). Differential recognition for faces of own- and other-race persons: What is the role of experience and contact? *Journal of Social Issues, 41*(3), 139–155.

Brigham, J. C., Meissner, C. A., & Wasserman, A. W. (1999). Applied issues in the construction and expert assessment of photo lineups. *Applied Cognitive Psychology, 13,* S73–S92.

Brigham, J. C., & Pfeifer, J. E. (1994). Evaluating the fairness of lineups. In D. F. Ross, J. D. Read, & M. P. Toglia (Eds.), *Adult eyewitness testimony: Current trends and developments* (pp. 201–222). Cambridge, UK: Cambridge University Press.

Brigham, J. C., & Ready, D. R. (1985). Own-race bias in lineup construction. *Law and Human Behavior, 9,* 415–424.

Brigham, J. C., Wasserman, A. W., & Meissner, C. A. (1999). Disputed eyewitness identification evidence: Important legal and scientific issues. *Court Review, 36*(2), 12–25.

Britt, T. W., Boniecki, K. A., Vescio, T. K., Biernat, M. R., & Brown, L. M. (1996). Intergroup anxiety: A person X situation approach. *Personality and Social Psychology Bulletin, 22,* 1177–1188.

Buck, J., Dore, H., & Brigham, J. C. (2005). *Does trying harder matter? Can incentives reduce the cross-race effect in face recognition?* Unpublished manuscript. Florida State University.

Carey, S. (1981). The development of face perception. In G. Davies, H. Ellis, & J. Shepherd (Eds.), *Perceiving and remembering faces* (pp. 9–38). New York: Academic Press.

Carey, S., & Diamond, R. (1977). From piecemeal to configural representation of faces. *Science, 195,* 312–314.

Carey, S., Diamond, R., & Woods, B. (1980). The development of face recognition – A maturational component? *Developmental Psychology, 16,* 257–269.

Carroo, A. W. (1986). Other race recognition: A comparison of Black American and African subjects. *Perceptual and Motor Skills, 62,* 135–138.

Carroo, A. W. (1987). Recognition of faces as a function of race, attitudes, and reported cross-racial friendships. *Perceptual and Motor Skills, 64,* 319–325.

Ceci, S. J., & Bruck, M. (1995). *Jeopardy in the courtroom: A scientific analysis of children's testimony.* Washington, DC: American Psychological Association.

Chance, J. E., & Goldstein, A. G. (1996). The other-race effect and eyewitness identification. In S. L. Sporer, R. S. Malpass, & G. Koehnken (Eds.), *Psychological issues in eyewitness identification* (pp. 153–176). Mahwah, NJ: Lawrence Erlbaum.

Chance, J. E., Turner, A. L., & Goldstein, A. G. (1982). Development of face recognition for own- and other-race faces. *Journal of Psychology, 112,* 29–37.

Chase, W. G., & Ericsson, K. A. (1982). Skill and working memory. In G. H. Bower (Ed.), *Psychology of learning and motivation* (Vol. 16, pp. 1–58). New York: Academic Press.

Chase, W. G., & Simon, H. A. (1973). Perception in chess. *Cognitive Psychology, 4,* 55–81.

Chiroro, P., & Valentine, T. (1995). An investigation of the contact hypothesis of the own-race bias in face recognition. *Quarterly Journal of Experimental Psychology, 48A,* 879–894.

Chung, M. S., & Thomson, D. (1995). Development of face recognition. *British Journal of Psychology, 86,* 55–87.

Cohen-Levine, S. (1989). The question of faces: Special is in the brain of the beholder. In A. W. Young, & H. D. Ellis (Eds.), *Handbook of research on face processing* (pp. 37–48). Amsterdam: Elsevier.

Conners, E., Lundregan, T., Miller, N., & McEwan, T. (1996). *Convicted by juries, exonerated by science. Case studies in the use of DNA evidence to establish innocence after trial.* Washington, DC: National Institute of Justice.

Cook, S. W. (1970). Motives in a conceptual analysis of attitude-related behavior. In W. J. Arnold, & D. Levine (Eds.), *Nebraska symposium on motivation, 1969.* Lincoln, NE: University of Nebraska Press.

Crocker, J., Major, B., & Steele, C. (1998). Social stigma. In D. Gilbert, S. T. Fiske, & G. Lindsey (Eds.), *The handbook of social psychology* (Vol. 2, 4th ed., pp. 504–553). New York: McGraw-Hill.

Cross, J. F., Cross, J., & Daly, J. (1971). Sex, race, age, and beauty as factors in recognition of faces. *Perception and Psychophysics, 10*, 393–396.

Cunningham, W. A., Johnson, M. K., Raye, C. L., Gatenby, J. C., Gore, J. C., & Banaji, M. R. (2004). Separable neural components in the processing of Black and White faces. *Psychological Science, 15*, 806–813.

Cunningham, W. A., Nezlek, J. B., & Banaji, M. R. (2004). Implicit and explicit ethnocentrism: Revisiting the ideologies of prejudice. *Personality and Social Psychology Bulletin, 30*, 1332–1346.

Cutler, B. L., & Penrod, S. D. (1995). *Mistaken identification: The eyewitness, psychology, and the law.* Cambridge, UK: Cambridge University Press.

De Haan, M., Johnson, M. H., Maurer, D., & Perrett, D. I. (2001). Recognition of individual faces and average face prototype by 1- and 3-month-old infants. *Cognitive Development, 16*, 1–20.

Dent, H., & Flin, R. (1992). *Children as witnesses.* New York: Wiley.

DePaulo, B. M. (1992). Nonverbal behavior and self-presentation. *Psychological Bulletin, 111*, 203–243.

DeSteno, D., Dasgupta, N., Bartlett, M., & Cajdric, A. (2004). Prejudice from thin air: The effect of emotion on automatic intergroup attitudes. *Psychological Science, 15*, 319–324.

Devine, P. G. (1989). Stereotypes and prejudice: Their automatic and controlled components. *Journal of Personality and Social Psychology, 56*, 5–18.

Devine, P. G., Evett, S. R., & Vasquez-Suson, K. A. (1996). Exploring the interpersonal dynamics of intergroup contact. In R. M. Sorrentino, & E. T. Higgins (Eds.), *Handbook of motivation and cognition* (Vol. 3, pp. 423–465). New York: Guilford.

Devine, P. G., & Monteith, J. J. (1993). The role of discrepancy associated affect in prejudice reduction. In D. M. Mackie, & D. L. Hamilton (Eds.), *Affect, cognition, and stereotyping: Interactive processes in intergroup perception* (pp. 317–344). San Diego, CA: Academic Press.

Devine, P. G., Monteith, J. J., Zuwerink, J. R., & Elliot, A. J. (1991). Prejudice with and without compunction. *Journal of Personality and Social Psychology, 60*, 817–830.

Devine, P. G., Plant, E. A., Amodio, D. M., Harmon-Jones, E., & Vance, S. L. (2002). The regulation of explicit and implicit race bias: The role of motivations to respond without prejudice. *Journal of Personality and Social Psychology, 82*, 835–848.

Diamond, R., & Carey, S. (1986). Why faces and are not special: An effect of expertise. *Journal of Experimental Psychology. General, 115*, 107–117.

Doris, J. L. (Ed.). (1991). *The suggestibility of children's recollections.* Washington, DC: American Psychological Association.

Dovidio, J. F., Kawakami, K., & Gaertner, S. L. (2002). Implicit and explicit prejudice and interracial interaction. *Journal of Personality and Social Psychology, 82*, 62–68.

Dovidio, J. F., Kawakami, K., Johnson, C., Johnson, B., & Howard, A. (1997). The nature of prejudice: Automatic and controlled processes. *Journal of Experimental Social Psychology, 33*, 510–540.

Elliott, E. S., Wills, E. J., & Goldstein, A. G. (1973). The effects of discrimination training on the recognition of white and oriental faces. *Bulletin of the Psychonomic Society, 2*, 71–73.

Ellis, H. D., Deregowski, J. B., & Shepherd, J. W. (1975). Descriptions of white and black faces by white and black subjects. *International Journal of Psychology, 10*, 119–123.

Ellis, H. D., & Flin, R. H. (1990). Encoding and storage effects in 7 year olds' and 10 year olds' memory for faces. *British Journal of Developmental Psychology, 8*, 77–92.

Ellis, H. D., Shepherd, J., & Bruce, A. (1973). The effects of age and sex upon adolescents' recognition of faces. *Journal of Genetic Psychology, 123*, 173–174.

Fallshore, M. F., & Schooler, J. W. (1995). The verbal vulnerability of perceptual expertise. *Journal of Experimental Psychology. Learning, Memory, and Cognition, 21*, 628–634.

Fazio, R. H., Jackson, J. R., Dunton, B. C., & Williams, C. J. (1995). Variability in automatic activation as an unobtrusive measure of racial attitudes: A bona fide pipeline? *Journal of Personality and Social Psychology, 69*, 1013–1027.

Feingold, G. A. (1914). The influence of environment on the identification of persons and things. *Journal of Criminal Law and Political Science, 5*, 39–51.

Feinman, S., & Entwisle, D. R. (1976). Children's ability to recognize other children's faces. *Child Development, 47*, 506–510.

Flin, R. H. (1980). Age effects in children's memory for unfamiliar faces. *Developmental Psychology, 16*, 373–374.

Flin, R. H. (1985). Development of face recognition: An encoding switch? *British Journal of Psychology, 76*, 123–134.

Flin, R. H., & Dziurawiec, S. (1989). Developmental factors. In A. Young, & H. D. Ellis (Eds.), *Handbook of research on face processing* (pp. 335–378). Amsterdam: North Holland.

Fodor, J. (1983). *The modularity of the mind.* Cambridge, UK: MIT Press.

Fulero, S. M. (1993). *Eyewitness expert testimony: An overview and annotated bibliography,* Unpublished manuscript. Sinclair (Ohio) College.

Gaertner, S. L., & Dovidio, J. (1986). The aversive form of racism. In J. Dovidio, & S. L. Gaertner (Eds.), *Prejudice, discrimination and racism* (pp. 61–89). New York: Academic Press.

Gardiner, J. M., & Richardson-Klavehn, A. (2000). Remembering and knowing. In E. Tulving, F. Craik, & I. M. Fergus (Eds.), *The Oxford handbook of memory* (pp. 229–244). London: Oxford University Press.

Goldstein, A. G., & Chance, J. E. (1971). Visual recognition of complex configurations. *Perception and Psychophysics, 9*, 237–241.

Goldstein, A. G., & Chance, J. E. (1980). Memory for faces and schema theory. *Journal of Psychology, 105*, 47–59.

Goldstein, A. G., & Chance, J. E. (1985). Effects of training on Japanese faces recognition: Reduction of the other-race effect. *Bulletin of the Psychonomic Society, 23*, 211–214.

Greenwald, A. G., & Banaji, M. R. (1995) Implicit social cognition: Attitudes, self-esteem, and stereotypes. *Psychological Review, 102*, 4–27.

Greenwald, A. G., McGhee, D. E., & Schwartz, J. L. K. (1998). Measuring individual differences in implicit cognition: The implicit association test. *Journal of Personality and Social Psychology, 74*, 1464–1480.

Hay, D. C., & Young, A. W. (1982). The human face. In A. W. Ellis (Ed.), *Normality and pathology in cognitive functions* (pp. 173–202). New York: Academic Press.

Huff, R., Rattner, A., & Saragin, E. (1996). *Convicted but innocent: Wrongful conviction and public policy.* Thousand Oaks, CA: Sage.

Ickes, W. (1984). Black and white interaction. *Journal of Personality and Social Psychology, 47*, 330–341.

Islam, R. M., & Hewstone, M. (1993). Dimensions of contact as predictors of intergroup anxiety, perceived out-group variability, and out-group attitude: An integrative model. *Personality and Social Psychology Bulletin, 19*, 700–710.

Ito, T. A., & Urland, G. O. (2003). Race and gender in the brain: Electrocortical measures of attention to the race and gender of multiply categorizable individuals. *Journal of Personality and Social Psychology, 85*, 616–626.

Jacoby, L. L. (1991). A process dissociation framework: Separating automatic from intentional uses of memory. *Journal of Memory and Language, 30*, 513–541.

Johnston, R. A., & Ellis, H. D. (1995a). Age effects in the processing of typical and distinctive faces. *Quarterly Journal of Experimental Psychology, 48A*, 447–465.

Johnston, R. A., & Ellis, H. D. (1995b). The development of face recognition. In T. Valentine (Ed.), *Cognitive and computational aspects of face recognition: Explorations in face space* (pp. 1–23). London: Routledge.

Jones, J. M. (1997). *Prejudice and racism* (2nd ed.). New York: McGraw-Hill.

Jones, M. (2002). *Social psychology of prejudice.* Upper Saddle River, NJ: Prentice-Hall.

Judd, C. M., Ryan, C. S., & Park, B. (1991). Accuracy in the judgment of in-group and out-group variability. *Journal of Personality and Social Psychology, 61*, 366–379.

Kassin, S. M. (1998). Eyewitness identification procedures: The fifth rule. *Law and Human Behavior, 22*, 649–653.

Kassin, S. M., Ellsworth, P. C., & Smith, V. L. (1989). The "general acceptance" of psychological research on eyewitness testimony: A survey of the experts. *American Psychologist, 44*, 1089–1098.

Kassin, S. M., Tubb, V. A., Hosch, H. M., & Memon, A. (2001). On the general acceptance of eyewitness testimony research. *American Psychologist, 56*, 405–416.

Katz, P. A. (2002). *Development of gender and race stereotypes*. Unpublished manuscript. Boulder, CO: Institute for Research on Social Problems.

Katz, P. A. (2003). Racists or tolerant multiculturalists? How do they begin? *American Psychologist, 58*, 897–909.

Katz, P. A., & Downey, E. P. (2002). *Infant categorization of race and gender cues*. Unpublished manuscript. Boulder, CO: Institute for Research on Social Problems.

Katz, I., & Hass, R. G., (1988). Racial ambivalence and American value conflict: Correlational and priming studies of dual cognitive structures. *Journal of Personality and Social Psychology, 55*, 893–905.

Kelley, C. M., & Jacoby, L. L. (2000). Recollection and familiarity: Process-dissociation. In E. Tulving, F. Craik, & I. M. Fergus (Eds.), *The Oxford handbook of memory* (pp. 215–228). London: Oxford University Press.

Kinder, D. R. (1986) The continuing American dilemma: White resistance to racial change 40 years after Myrdal. *Journal of Social Issues, 42*, 151–172.

Kinder, D. R., & Sears, D. O. (1981). Prejudice and politics: Symbolic racism versus racial threats to the good life. *Journal of Personality and Social Psychology, 40*, 414–431.

Klahr, D. (1992). Information-processing approaches to cognitive development. In M. H. Bornstein, & M. E. Lamb (Eds.), *Developmental psychology: An advanced textbook* (3rd ed., pp. 273–336). Hillsdale, NJ: Lawrence Erlbaum.

Koriat, A., & Goldsmith, M. (1994). Memory in naturalistic and laboratory contexts: Distinguishing the accuracy-oriented and quantity-oriented approaches to memory assessment. *Journal of Experimental Psychology. General, 123*, 297–315.

Koriat, A., & Goldsmith, M. (1996). Monitoring and control processes in the strategic regulation of memory accuracy. *Psychological Review, 103*, 490–517.

Kuhn, D. (1992). Cognitive development. In M. H. Bornstein, & M. E. Lamb (Eds.), *Developmental psychology: An advanced textbook* (3rd ed., pp. 211–272). Hillsdale, NJ: Lawrence Erlbaum.

Lavrakas, P. J., Buri, J. R., & Mayzner, M. S. (1976). A perspective on the recognition of other-race faces. *Perception and Psychophysics, 20*, 475–481.

Leary, M. R., & Atherton, S. C. (1986). Self-efficacy, social anxiety, and inhibition in interpersonal encounters. *Journal of Social and Clinical Psychology, 4*, 256–267.

Lee, J. S., & Goodman, G. (2000). *The development of memory for own- and other- racial/ethnic faces*. Unpublished manuscript. University of California at Davis.

LeGrand, R. L., Mondloch, C. J., Maurer, D., & Brent, H. P. (2004). Impairment in holistic face processing following early visual deprivation. *Psychological Science, 15*, 762–768.

Levin, D. T. (1996). Classifying faces by race: The structure of face categories. *Journal of Experimental Psychology. Learning, Memory, and Cognition, 22*, 1364–1382.

Levin, D. T. (2000). Race as a visual feature: Using visual search and perceptual discrimination tasks to understand face categories and the cross race recognition deficit. *Journal of Experimental Psychology. General, 129*, 559–574.

Liberman, A., & Tversky, A. (1993). On the evaluation of probability judgments: Calibration, resolution, and monotonicity. *Psychological Bulletin, 114*, 162–173.

Lindsay, R. C. L., Brigham, J. C., Brimacombe, C. A. E., & Wells, G. L. (2002). Eyewitness research. In J. R. P. Ogloff (Ed.), *Taking psychology and law into the twenty-first century* (pp. 199–223). New York: Kluwer Academic/Plenum Press.

Lindsay, R. C. L., Wells, G. L., & Rumpel, C. M. (1981). Can people detect eyewitness identification accuracy within and across situations? *Journal of Applied Psychology, 66*, 79–89.

Loftus, E. F. (1979). *Eyewitness testimony*. Cambridge, MA: Harvard University Press.

Lowery, B. S., Hardin, C. D., & Sinclair, S. (2001). Social influence effects in automatic racial prejudice. *Journal of Personality and Social Psychology, 81*, 842–855.

Luce, T. S. (1974). The role of experience in inter-racial recognition. *Personality and Social Psychology Bulletin, 1*, 39–41.

MacLin, O. H., MacLin, M. K., & Malpass, R. S. (2001). Race, arousal, attention, exposure and delay: An examination of factors moderating face recognition. *Psychology, Public Policy, and Law, 7*, 134–152.

MacLin, O. H., & Malpass, R. S. (2001). Racial categorization of faces: The ambiguous race face effect. *Psychology, Public Policy, and Law, 7*, 98–118.

MacLin, O. H., & Malpass, R. S. (2003). The ambiguous race face illusion. *Perception, 32*, 249–252.

Malpass, R. S. (1981). Training in face recognition. In G. Davies, H. Ellis, & J. Shepherd (Eds.), *Perceiving and remembering faces* (pp. 271–285). London: Academic Press.

Malpass, R. S. (1990). An excursion into utilitarian analyses, with side trips. *Behavioral Science Research, 24*, 1–15.

Malpass, R. S., & Kravitz, J. (1969). Recognition of faces of own and other race. *Journal of Personality and Social Psychology, 13*, 330–334.

Malpass, R. S., Lavigueur, H., & Weldon, D. E. (1973). Verbal and visual training in face recognition. *Perception and Psychophysics, 14*, 285–292.

Mann, V. A., Diamond, R., & Carey, S. (1979). Development of voice recognition: Parallels with face recognition. *Journal of Experimental Psychology, 27*, 153–165.

McConahay, J. B. (1986). Modern racism, ambivalence and the modern racism scale. In J. F. Dovidio, & S. L. Gaertner (Eds.), *Prejudice, discrimination and racism* (pp. 91–125). Orlando, FL: Academic Press.

McConahay, J. B., Hardee, B. B., & Batts, V. (1981). Has racism declined in America? It depends on who is asking and what is asked. *Journal of Conflict Resolution, 25*, 563–579.

Meissner, C. A., & Brigham, J. C. (2001). Thirty years of investigating the own-race bias in memory for faces: A meta-analytic review. *Psychology, Public Policy, and Law, 7*, 3–35.

Meissner, C. A., Brigham, J. C., & Bennett, L. B. (2007). *Eye-tracking and the cross-race effect: A skilled memory perspective.* Unpublished manuscript. University of Texas at El Paso.

Meissner, C. A., Brigham, J. C., & Butz, D. (2005). Memory for own- and other-race faces: A dual process approach. *Applied Cognitive Psychology, 19*, 545–567.

Meissner, C. A., Brigham, J. C., & Kelley, C. M. (2001). The influence of retrieval processes in verbal overshadowing. *Memory and Cognition, 29*, 176–186.

Monteith, M. J., Devine, P. G., & Zuwerink, J. R. (1993). Self-directed vs. other-directed affect as a consequence of prejudice-related discrepancies. *Journal of Personality and Social Psychology, 64*, 198–210.

Mullen, B., & Hu, L. (1989). Perceptions of ingroup and outgroup variability: A meta-analytic integration. *Basic and Applied Psychology, 10*, 233–252.

Murphy, F. C., Nimmo-Smith, I., & Lawrence, A. D. (2003). Functional neuroanatomy of emotions: A meta-analysis. *Cognitive, Affective, and Behavioral Neuroscience, 3*, 207–233.

Nachson, I. (1995). On the modularity of face recognition: The riddle of domain specificity. *Journal of Clinical and Experimental Neuropsychology, 17*, 256–275.

New Jersey v. Cromedy, 727 A.2d. (N.J. 1999).

Ng, W., & Lindsay, R. C. L. (1994). Cross-race facial recognition: Failure of the contact hypothesis. *Journal of Cross-Cultural Psychology, 25*, 217–232.

Nosek, B. A., Banaji, M. R., & Greenwald, A. G. (2002). Harvesting implicit group attitudes and beliefs from a demonstration Web site. *Group Dynamics, 6*, 101–115.

Pettigrew, T. F. (1998). Intergroup contact theory. *Annual Review of Psychology, 49*, 65–85. Palo Alto, CA: Annual Reviews, Inc.

Pettigrew, T. F., & Tropp, L. A. (2000). Does intergroup contact reduce prejudice? Recent meta-analytic findings. In S. Oskamp (Ed.), *Reducing prejudice and discrimination* (pp. 93–114). Mahwah, NJ: Lawrence Erlbaum.

Pezdek, K., Blandon-Gitlin, I., & Moore, C. (2003). Children's face recognition memory: More evidence for the cross-race effect. *Journal of Applied Psychology, 88*, 760–763.

Phan, K. L., Wager, T., Taylor, S. F., & Liberzon, I. (2002). Functional neuroanatomy of emotions: A meta-analysis of emotion activation studies in PET and fMRI. *NeuroImage, 16*, 331–348.

Phelps, E. A., O'Connor, K. J., Cunningham, W. A., Funayama, E. S., Gatenby, J. C., Gore, J. C., et al. (2000). Performance on indirect measures of race evaluation predicts amygdale activation. *Journal of Cognitive Neuroscience, 12*, 729–738.

Phelps, E. A., O'Connor, K. J., Gatenby, J. C., Gore, J. C., Grillon, C., & Davis, M. (2001). Activation of the left amygdale to a cognitive representation of fear. *Nature Neuroscience, 4*, 437–441.

Plant, E. A., & Devine, P. G. (1998). Internal and external motivation to respond without prejudice. *Journal of Personality and Social Psychology, 75*, 811–832.

Plant, E. A., & Devine, P. G., (2003). Antecedents and implications of intergroup anxiety. *Personality and Social Psychology Bulletin, 29*, 790–801.

Platz, S. J., & Hosch, H. M. (1988). Cross-racial/ethnic eyewitness identification: A field study. *Journal of Applied Social Psychology, 18*, 972–984.

Poole, D. A., & Lamb, M. E. (1998). *Investigative interviews of children.* Washington, DC: American Psychological Association.

Poskocil, A. (1977). Encounters between blacks and liberals: The collision of stereotypes. *Social Forces, 55*, 715–727.

Rodin, M. J. (1987). Who is memorable to whom? A study of cognitive disregard. *Social Cognition, 5*, 144–165.

Rolls, E. T. (1992). The processing of face information in the primate temporal lobe. In V. Bruce, & M. Burton (Eds.), *Processing images of faces* (pp. 41–68). Norwood, NJ: Abley.

Rolls, E. T., Baylis, G. C., & Leonard, C. M. (1989). Role of low and high spatial frequencies in the face-selective responses of neurons in the cortex in the superior temporal sulcus. *Vision Research, 25*, 1021–1035.

Rudman, L. A., Ashmore, R. D., & Gary, M. L. (2001). "Unlearning" automatic biases: The malleability of implicit prejudice and stereotypes. *Journal of Personality and Social Psychology, 81*, 856–868.

Ryan, R. M., & Connell, T. P. (1989). Perceived locus of causality and internalization: Examining reasons for acting in two domains. *Journal of Personality and Social Psychology, 57*, 749–761.

Saltz, E., & Sigel, I. E. (1967). Concept overdiscrimation in children. *Journal of Experimental Psychology, 73*, 1–18.

Sangrigoli, S., & de Schonen, S. (2004a). Recognition of own-race and other-race faces by three-month-old infants. *Journal of Child Psychology and Psychiatry, 45*, 1219–1227.

Sangrigoli, S., & de Schonen, S. (2004b). Effect of visual experience on face processing: A developmental study of inversion and non-native effects. *Perception, 31*, 1109–1121.

Sangrigoli, S., Pallier, C., Argenti, A. M., Ventureyra, V. A. G., & de Schonen, S. (2005). Reversibility of the other-race effect in face recognition during childhood. *Psychological Science, 16*, 440–444.

Scheck, B., Neufeld, P., & Dwyer, J. (2001). *Actual innocence: When justice goes wrong and how to make it right.* New York: Signet.

Sears, D. O. (1988). Symbolic racism. In P. A. Katz, & D. A. Taylor (Eds), *Eliminating racism: Profiles in controversy* (pp. 53–84). New York: Plenum Press.

Shepherd, J. (1981). Social factors in face recognition. In G. Davies, H. Ellis, & J. Shepherd (Eds.), *Perceiving and remembering faces* (pp. 55–79). San Diego, CA: Academic Press.

Slater, A., & Quinn, P. C. (2001). Face recognition in the newborn infant. *Infant and Child Development, 10*, 21–24.

Slone, A., Brigham, J. C., & Meissner, C. A. (2000). Social and cognitive factors affecting the own-race bias in whites. *Basic and Applied Social Psychology, 22*, 71–84.

Somerville, S. C., & Wellman, H. M. (1979). The development of understanding as an indirect memory strategy. *Journal of Experimental Child Psychology, 27*, 71–86.

Sporer, S. L. (2001). Recognizing faces of other ethnic groups: An integration of theories. *Psychology, Public Policy, and Law, 7*, 36–97.

Sporer, S. L., Malpass, R. S., & Koehnken, G. (1996). *Psychological issues in eyewitness identification.* Mahwah, NJ: Lawrence Erlbaum.

Stephan, W. G., & Stephan, C. W. (1985). Intergroup anxiety. *Journal of Social Issues, 41*, 151–175.

Stephan, W. G., & Stephan, C. W. (2000). An integrated threat theory of prejudice. In S. Oskamp (Ed.), *Reducing prejudice and discrimination* (pp. 23–45). Mahwah, NJ: Lawrence Erlbaum.

Stephan, W. G., Ybarra, O., & Bachman, G. (1999). Prejudice toward immigrants, *Journal of Applied Social Psychology, 11*, 2221–2237.

Swope, T. M. (1994). *Social experience, illusory correlation, and facial recognition ability.* Unpublished masters thesis. Florida State University.

Tanaka, J. W., & Farah, M. J. (1993). Parts and wholes in face recognition. *Quarterly Journal of Experimental Psychology, 46*, 225–245.

Tanaka, J., & Gauthier, I. (1997). Expertise in object and face recognition. *Psychology of Learning, 36*, 83–125.

Technical Working Group for Eyewitness Evidence (1999). *Eyewitness evidence: A guide for law enforcement.* Washington, DC: US Department of Justice, Office of Justice Programs.

Teitelbaum, S., & Geiselman, R. E. (1997). Observer mood and cross-racial recognition of faces. *Journal of Cross-Cultural Psychology, 28*, 93–106.

Thomson, D. M. (1986). Face recognition: More than a feeling of familiarity? In H. D. Ellis, M. A. Jeeves, F. Newcombe, & A. Young (Eds.), *Aspects of face processing* (pp. 391–399). Amsterdam: Elsevier.

Thomson, D. M. (1989). Issues posed by developmental research. In A. W. Young, & H. D. Ellis (Eds.), *Handbook of research on face processing* (pp. 391–399). Amsterdam: Elsevier.

United States v. Telfaire, 469 F. 2d. 552, 558–559. (D. C. Cir., 1972).

United States v. Wade, 388 U. S. 218. (1967).

Valentine, T. (1991). A unified account of the effects of distinctiveness, inversion and race in face recognition. *The Quarterly Journal of Experimental Psychology, 43A*, 161–204.

Valentine, T., Chiroro, P., & Dixon, R. (1995). An account of the other-race effect and the contact hypothesis based on a 'face space' model of face recognition. In T. Valentine (Ed.), *Cognitive and computational aspects of face recognition: Exploration of face space* (pp. 69–94). London: Routledge.

Valentine, T., & Endo, M. (1992). Towards an exemplar model of face processing: The effects of race and distinctiveness. *The Quarterly Journal of Experimental Psychology, 44A*, 671–703.

Vanman, E. J., Saltz, J. L., Nathan, L. R., & Warren, J. A. (2004). Racial discrimination by low-prejudice Whites: Facial movements as implicit measures of attitudes related to behavior. *Psychological Science, 15*, 711–714.

Wall, P. (1965). *Eyewitness identification in criminal cases.* Springfield, IL: Charles C. Thomas.

Wells, G. L., Lindsay, R. C. L., & Ferguson, T. J. (1979). Accuracy, confidence and juror perceptions in eyewitness identifications. *Journal of Applied Psychology, 64*, 440–448.

Wells, G. L., Small, M., Penrod, S., Malpass, R. S., Fulero, S. M., & Brimacombe, C. A. E. (1998). Eyewitness identification procedures: Recommendations for lineups and photospreads. *Law and Human Behavior, 22*, 603–647.

Wheeler, M. E., & Fiske, S. T. (2005). Controlling racial prejudice: Social-cognitive goals affect amygdala and stereotype activation. *Psychological Science, 16*, 56–63.

Woodhead, M. M., Baddeley, A. D., & Simmonds, D. C. (1979). On training people to recognize faces. *Ergonomics, 22*, 333–343.

Wright, D. B., Boyd, C. E., & Tredoux, C. G. (2001). A field study of own-race bias in South Africa and England. *Psychology, Public Policy, and Law, 7*, 119–133.

Wright, D. B., Boyd, C. E., & Tredoux, C. G. (2003). Inter-racial contact and the own-race bias for face recognition in South Africa and England. *Applied Cognitive Psychology, 17*, 365–373.

Yin, R. K. (1969). Looking at upside-down faces. *Journal of Experimental Psychology, 81*, 141–145.

Yin, R. K. (1970). Face recognition by brain-injured patients: A dissociable ability? *Neuropsychologia, 8*, 395–402.

Yin, R. K. (1978). Face perception: A review of experiments with infants, normal adults, and brain-injured persons. In R. Held, H. W. Leibovitz, & H. L. Tueber (Eds.), *Handbook of sensory physiology. Vol. VIII: Perception* (pp. 593–608). New York: Springer-Verlag.

5
Addressing Contemporary Racism: The Common Ingroup Identity Model

Samuel L. Gaertner and John F. Dovidio

Addressing Contemporary Racism: The Common Ingroup Identity Model

In the preceding chapter in this volume, we described our research on the dynamics of an unintentional, very subtle, yet pernicious form of racism, that is, aversive racism. In the current chapter, we describe our attempts to examine a strategy intended to motivate people to reduce this form of prejudice: the common ingroup identity model.

When we described our findings on aversive racism formally, in papers and presentations, and informally, a common question arose, "What can we do about subtle biases, particularly when we do not know for sure whether we have them?" Like a virus that has mutated, racism may have evolved into different forms that are more difficult not only to recognize but also to combat. Because of its pervasiveness, subtlety, and complexity, the traditional techniques for eliminating bias that emphasized the immorality of prejudice and illegality of discrimination are not effective for combating aversive racism. Aversive racists recognize that prejudice is bad, but they do not recognize that *they* are prejudiced.

One basic argument we have made in our research on aversive racism is that the negative feelings that develop toward other groups may be rooted, in part, in fundamental, normal psychological processes. One such process, identified in the classic work of Tajfel, Allport, and others, is the categorization of people into ingroups and outgroups, "we's" and "they's." People respond systematically more favorably to others whom they perceive to belong to their group than to different groups. Thus, if bias is linked to fundamental, normal psychological processes, such as social categorization, then attempts to ameliorate bias should be directed not at eliminating these processes entirely, which are functional in many ways, but rather at redirecting the forces of ingroup bias to produce more harmonious intergroup relations. By shifting the basis of categorization from race to an alternative dimension, shared by Blacks and Whites who may be interacting, we can potentially alter who is a "we" and who is a "they," undermining a potentially contributing force to aversive racism.

As these ideas were developing, we also began to consider the possibility that the discrimination we were observing in our studies of aversive racism may have

111

C. Willis-Esqueda (ed.), *Motivational Aspects of Prejudice and Racism.*
© Springer 2008

reflected discrimination not only *against* Blacks but also discrimination *in favor of* Whites. That is, we began to view aversive racism as a problem that, in part, involved Whites having a more generous, helpful, and forgiving orientation toward Whites than toward Blacks. Even though this pro-White form of racism can be as pernicious as anti-Black bias, it does not assume an underlying motivation to be hurtful – either consciously or unconsciously. Rather, for aversive racists, part of the problem may be that there is no emotional connection to Blacks and other minorities and they do not regard them as part of their circle of inclusion for sharing and caring as readily as they accept Whites. Racially dissimilar others, then, do not ordinarily have the same capacity as fellow Whites to elicit empathic, prosocial reactions. But, what if Whites perceived Blacks and other minorities, even temporarily, as members of their own group – as ingroup members – rather than as members of different groups? Would behavior toward them become more favorable? And how specifically can intergroup contact be structured to reduce bias and conflict?

In this chapter, we first explore the influence of social categorization on how people feel about, think about, and behave toward others. We then consider ways of reducing intergroup bias by affecting the process of social categorization. The third section elaborates on the process of recategorization, describing the common ingroup identity model and support for it. Finally, we identify promising directions for studying how different forms of recategorization, including a dual identity, can reduce prejudice and other forms of bias.

Social Categorization and Orientations Toward Others

One universal facet of human thinking essential for efficient functioning is the ability to sort the many different objects, events and people encountered quickly and effectively into a smaller number of meaningful categories (Hamilton & Sherman, 1994; Hamilton & Trolier, 1986). Categorization enables decisions to be made quickly about incoming information because the instant an object is categorized, it is assigned the properties shared by other category members. Time-consuming consideration of each new experience is forfeited because it is usually wasteful and unnecessary. Categorization often occurs spontaneously on the basis of physical similarity, proximity, or shared fate (Campbell, 1958). In this respect, people may be characterized as "cognitive misers" who compromise total accuracy for efficiency when confronted with the often overwhelming complexity of their social world (Fiske & Taylor, 1991; Macrae, Milne, & Bodenhausen, 1994).

When people or objects are categorized into groups, actual differences between members of the same category tend to be perceptually minimized (Tajfel, 1969) and often ignored in making decisions or forming impressions. Members of the same category seem to be more similar than they actually are, and more similar than they were before they were categorized together. In addition, although members of a social category may be different in some ways from members of other categories, these differences tend to become exaggerated and overgeneralized. Thus, categorization enhances perceptions of similarities within groups and differences between groups, emphasizing social difference and group distinctiveness. For social categorization, this process becomes more ominous because these within- and between-group distortions have a tendency to generalize to additional dimensions (e.g., character traits) beyond those that differentiated the categories originally (Allport, 1954). Furthermore, as the salience of the categorization increases, the magnitude of these distortions also increases (Abrams, 1985; Brewer, 1979, Brewer & Miller, 1984; Deschamps & Doise, 1978; Dion, 1974; Doise, 1978; Skinner & Stephenson, 1981; Turner, 1981, 1985).

Moreover, in the process of categorizing people into groups, people typically classify themselves *into* one of the social categories (and *out of* the others). The insertion of the self into the social categorization process increases the emotional significance of group differences and thus leads to further perceptual distortion and to evaluative biases that reflect favorably on the ingroup (Sumner, 1906), and consequently on the self (Tajfel & Turner, 1979). In social identity theory, Tajfel and Turner (1979) proposed that a person's need for positive self-identity may be satisfied by membership in prestigious social groups. This need for positive distinctiveness motivates social comparisons that favorably differentiate ingroup from outgroup members. In addition, individuals frequently derive material benefit, receive valuable information, and experience a sense of belonging and security from the ingroup (Correll & Park, 2005). Perhaps one reason why ethnocentrism is so prevalent is because these biases operate even when the basis for the categorization is quite trivial, such as when group identity is assigned randomly (Billig & Tajfel, 1973).

This perspective also proposes that a person defines or categorizes the self along a continuum that ranges at one extreme from the self as the embodiment of a social collective or group to the self as a separate individual with personal motives, goals, and achievements. At the individual level, one's personal welfare and goals are most salient and important. At the group level, the goals and achievements of the group are merged with one's own (see Brown & Turner, 1981), and the group's welfare is paramount. At each extreme, self-interest fully is represented by the pronouns "I" and "we," respectively. Intergroup relations begin when people think about themselves as a group member rather than as a distinct individual.

Upon social categorization of people as members of the ingroup and of outgroups, people favor ingroup members in reward allocations (Tajfel, Billig, Bundy, & Flament, 1971), in esteem (Rabbie, 1982), and in the evaluation of the products of their labor (Ferguson & Kelley, 1964). Also, ingroup membership decreases psychological distance and facilitates the arousal of promotive tension or empathy (Hornstein, 1976). Moreover, empathy has a more significant impact for helping ingroup than outgroup members (Stürmer, Snyder, & Omoto, 2005). Relatedly, prosocial behavior is offered more readily to ingroup than to outgroup members (Piliavin, Dovidio, Gaertner, & Clark, 1981). In addition people are more likely to be cooperative and exercise more personal restraint when using endangered common resources when these are shared with ingroup members than with others (Kramer & Brewer, 1984).

In terms of information processing, people retain more information in a more detailed fashion for ingroup members than for outgroup members (Park & Rothbart, 1982), have better memory for information about ways ingroup members are similar and outgroup members are dissimilar to the self (Wilder, 1981), and remember less positive information about outgroup members (Howard & Rothbart, 1980). In addition, people are more generous and forgiving in their explanations for the behaviors of ingroup relative to outgroup members. Positive behaviors and successful outcomes are more likely to be attributed to internal, stable characteristics (the personality) of ingroup than outgroup members, whereas negative outcomes are more likely to be ascribed to the personalities of outgroup members than of ingroup members (Hewstone, 1990; Pettigrew, 1979). Relatedly, observed behaviors of ingroup and outgroup members are encoded in memory at different levels of abstraction (Maass, Salvi, Arcuri, & Semin, 1989). Undesirable actions of outgroup members are encoded at more abstract levels that presume intentionality and dispositional origin (e.g., she is hostile) than identical behaviors of ingroup members (e.g., she slapped the girl). Desirable actions of outgroup members, however, are encoded at more concrete levels (e.g., she walked across the street holding the old man's hand) relative to the same behaviors of ingroup members (e.g., she is helpful).

These cognitive biases help to perpetuate social biases and stereotypes even in the face of countervailing evidence. For example, because positive behaviors of outgroup members are encoded at relatively concrete levels, it becomes less likely that counter-stereotypic positive behaviors would generalize across situations or other outgroup members (see also Karpinski & von Hippel, 1996). People do not remember that an outgroup member was "helpful," but only the very concrete descriptive actions. Thus, outgroup stereotypes containing information pertaining to traits, dispositions or intentions are not likely to be influenced by observing counter-stereotypic outgroup behaviors.

Language plays another role in intergroup bias through associations with collective pronouns. Collective pronouns such as "we" or "they" that are used to define people's ingroup or outgroup status are frequently paired with stimuli having strong affective connotations. As a consequence, these pronouns may acquire powerful evaluative properties of their own. These words (we, they) can potentially increase the availability of positive or negative associations and thereby influence beliefs about, evaluations of and behaviors toward other people, often automatically and unconsciously (Perdue, Dovidio, Gurtman, & Tyler, 1990).

Whereas social categorization can initiate intergroup biases, the type of bias due largely to categorization primarily represents a pro-ingroup orientation (i.e., preference for ingroup members) rather than an anti-outgroup orientation usually associated with hostility or aggression. Nevertheless, disadvantaged status due to preferential treatment of one group over another can be as pernicious as discrimination based on anti-outgroup orientations (Murrell, Dietz-Uhler, Dovidio, Gaertner, & Drout, 1994). Pro-ingroup biases can also provide a foundation for generating hostility and conflict that can result from intergroup competition for economic resources and political power.

Because categorization is a basic process that is also fundamental to intergroup bias, social psychologists have targeted this process as a place to begin to improve intergroup relations. In the next section, we explore how the forces of categorization can be harnessed and redirected toward the elimination of intergroup bias.

Reducing Intergroup Bias by Targeting Social Categorization

The process of social categorization is not completely uncontrollable and unalterable. Categories are hierarchically organized, and higher level categories (e.g., animals) are more inclusive of lower level ones (e.g., cats and dogs). By modifying a perceiver's goals, motives, past experiences, expectations, as well as factors within the perceptual field and the situational context more broadly, there is opportunity to alter the level of category inclusiveness that will be primary in a given situation. That is, it may be possible to encourage *recategorization* such that people from different groups conceive of themselves as common members of a more inclusive group, and thus see themselves, at least temporarily, as all ingroup members.

Although perceiving people in terms of a social category is easiest and most typical in forming impressions, appropriate goals, motivation, and effort can produce more individuated, *decategorized* impressions of others (Brewer, 1988; Fiske, Lin, & Neuberg, 1999). That is, it may be possible to induce people to identify themselves as distinct individuals rather than as group members on the continuum proposed by Tajfel and Turner (1979, see also Brewer, 1988; Brewer & Miller, 1984; Fiske et al.; Wilder, 1978). This malleability of the level at which impressions are formed—from broad to more specific categories to individuated responses—is important because of its implications for altering the way people think about members of other groups, and consequently about the nature of intergroup relations.

From these perspectives, it is possible to engineer a *decategorization* or recategorization of perceived group boundaries in ways that reduce the original intergroup bias and conflict (see Wilder, 1986). In each case, reducing the salience of the original group boundaries is expected to decrease intergroup bias. In terms of decategorization, if the memberships of two groups come to conceive of themselves or others as separate individuals (Wilder, 1981) bias will be reduced because original ingroup members no longer benefit from the pro-ingroup biases associated with social categorization. In addition, if decategorization occurs through personalized interactions, in which information about each other's unique qualities is exchanged, intergroup bias will be further reduced by undermining the validity of the outgroup (Brewer & Miller, 1984; Miller, 2002; Miller, Brewer, & Edwards, 1985). With recategorization as proposed by the common ingroup identity model (Gaertner, Dovidio, Anastasio, Bachman, & Rust, 1993), if members of different groups are induced to conceive of themselves as a single more inclusive, superordinate group, rather than just as two completely separate groups, attitudes toward former outgroup members would be expected to become more positive through processes involving pro-ingroup bias.

Theoretically, the rationale for these changes in intergroup bias rests on two related conclusions from Brewer's (1979) analysis that fit nicely with social identity theory (Tajfel & Turner, 1979; Turner, 1975) and self-categorization theory (Turner, 1985). First, intergroup bias often takes the form of ingroup enhancement rather than outgroup devaluation. Second, the formation of a group brings ingroup members closer to the self, whereas the distance between the self and noningroup members remains relatively unchanged. Thus, upon ingroup formation or when an individual assumes a group level identification, the egocentric biases that favor the self are transferred to other ingroup members. Increasing the inclusiveness of group boundaries enables some of those cognitive and motivational processes that contributed initially to intergroup bias to be redirected or transferred to former outgroup members. Alternatively, if ingroup and outgroup members are induced to conceive of themselves as separate individuals rather than as group members, former ingroup members would no longer benefit from the egocentric biases transferred to the group upon self-identification as a group member.

The recategorization and decategorization strategies and their respective means of reducing bias were directly examined in a laboratory study (Gaertner, Mann, Murrell, & Dovidio, 1989). In this experiment members of two separate laboratory-formed groups were induced through various structural interventions (e.g., seating arrangement) either to recategorize themselves as one superordinate group or to decategorize themselves and to conceive of themselves as separate individuals. Supportive of the value of altering the level of category inclusiveness, these changes in the perceptions of intergroup boundaries reduced bias. Furthermore, as expected, these strategies reduced bias in different ways. Recategorizing ingroup and outgroup members as members of a more inclusive group reduced bias by increasing the attractiveness of the former outgroup members. Decategorizing members of the two groups by inducing conceptions of themselves as separate individuals decreased bias by decreasing the attractiveness of former ingroup members. Consistent with Turner's (1985) self-categorization theory, "the attractiveness of an individual is not constant, but varies with the ingroup membership" (p. 60).

These ideas about recategorization and decategorization have also provided explanations for how the apparently loosely connected diverse features specified by the contact hypothesis may operate psychologically to reduce bias. Allport's (1954) revised contact hypothesis proposed that for contact between groups to be successful, certain prerequisite features must be present (see Dovidio, Gaertner, & Kawakami, 2003). These include equal status between the groups, cooperative (rather than competitive) intergroup interaction, opportunities for self-revealing personal acquaintance between the members, especially with those whose personal characteristics do not support stereotypic expectations, and supportive norms by authorities within and outside of the contact situation. Whereas this prescription has been easier to write than to implement, there is evidence to support the efficacy of this formula when these conditions are present particularly for changing attitudes toward those people actually in the contact setting (Cook, 1984; Johnson, Johnson, & Maruyama, 1983). In the next two parts of the section we examine two perspectives on how intergroup contact can reduce bias by altering the nature of social categorization processes.

Decategorization and Personalization

Brewer and Miller (1984) offered a conceptually unifying theoretical framework that proposed that the features specified by the contact hypothesis (e.g., equal status, cooperative interaction, self-revealing interaction, and supportive norms) share the capacity to *decategorize* group boundaries and to promote more differentiated and personalized conceptions, particularly of outgroup members. With a more differentiated representation of outgroup members, there is the recognition that there are different types of outgroup members (e.g., sensitive as well as tough professional hockey players) thereby weakening the effects of categorization and the tendency to perceptually minimize and ignore differences between category members. When personalized interactions occur, ingroup and outgroup members slide even further toward the individual side of the self as individual-group member continuum. Members "attend to information that replaces category identity as the most useful basis for classifying each other" (Brewer & Miller, 1984: 288).

During personalization, members focus on information about an outgroup member that is relevant to the self (as an individual rather than self as a group member). Repeated personalized interactions with a variety of outgroup members should over time undermine the value of the category stereotype as a source of information about members of that group. Thus, the effects of personalization would be expected to generalize to new situations as well as to heretofore unfamiliar outgroup members. For the benefits of personalization to generalize, however, it is of course necessary for outgroup members' group identities to be salient, although not primary, during the interaction to enable the group stereotype to be weakened.

A number of experimental studies provide evidence supporting this theoretical perspective (Bettencourt, Brewer, Croak, & Miller, 1992; Marcus-Newhall, Holtz, & Brewer, 1993; Miller et al., 1985). In Miller et al., for example, contact that permitted more personalized interactions (e.g., when interaction was person-focused rather than task focused) resulted not only in more positive attitudes toward those outgroup members present, but to other outgroup members viewed on video. Thus, these conditions of intergroup contact reduced bias in both an immediate and generalizable fashion.

Although there are similarities between perceiving ingroup and outgroup members as "separate individuals" and having "personalized interactions" with outgroup members, these are related but theoretically distinct concepts. Personalization involves receiving self-relevant, more intimate information about members of the outgroup, such that each can be differentiated from the others in relation to comparisons with the self. In contrast, perceiving either outgroup members (see Wilder, 1986) or both memberships structurally as "separate individuals" denotes perceiving them as individuals, not as groups. It does not necessarily imply that this perception is based on information exchange. For example, strangers waiting for a bus may regard themselves as separate individuals, as opposed to a group. Thus, increasing the perception that outgroup members are "separate individuals" by revealing variability in their opinions or having outgroup members respond as individuals rather than as a group, renders each member more distinctive and thus potentially blurs the prior categorization scheme (Wilder, 1978). Another decategorization strategy of repeatedly crisscrossing category memberships by forming new subgroups each composed of members from former subgroups changes the pattern of who's "in" and who's "out" (Brewer, Ho, Lee, & Miller, 1987; Commins & Lockwood, 1978; Deschamps & Doise, 1978; Vanbeselaere, 1987) and can also render the earlier categorization less salient (Brown & Turner, 1979).

Whereas personalization and crossed-categorization strategies are designed to degrade group boundaries, another approach acknowledges the difficulty of eliminating perceptions of group identities and instead focuses on changing perceptions of the relationship between the groups.

Mutual Intergroup Differentiation

Brown and Hewstone (2005; see also Hewstone & Brown, 1986) posit that intergroup relations will be harmonious when group identities remain strong, rather than threatened by extinction, but maintained in the context of cooperative intergroup interaction. From the perspective of social identity theory, threats to group distinctiveness associated with high degrees of similarly between groups or attempts to degrade intergroup boundaries motivates members to reestablish positive group distinctiveness, a goal that is achieved by regarding one's ingroup as better than the other group. Thus, relative to the personalization or the purely one-group strategies, this Mutual Intergroup Differentiation perspective proposes that maintaining group distinctiveness within a cooperative intergroup relationship would be associated with low levels of intergroup threat and, consequently, with lower levels of intergroup bias. In addition, the salience of intergroup boundaries provides an associative mechanism through which changes in outgroup attitudes that occur during intergroup contact can generalize to the outgroup as a whole.

Although these different models suggest divergent intervention strategies, they may also be viewed as complementary approaches. Conceptually, for example, the common ingroup identity model acknowledges the effectiveness of personalization. Moreover, Gaertner and Dovidio (2000) posited that developing a common ingroup identity between people formerly viewed in terms of different group memberships can facilitate personalized interactions, which further reduces prejudice and stereotyping. In addition, developing a common ingroup identity does not require people to abandon previous group identities entirely.

In addition to *decategorization*, and *mutual differentiation* we propose that the features specified by the contact hypothesis also reduce bias through *recategorization* that increases rather than decreases the level of category inclusiveness (Gaertner & Dovidio, 2000; Gaertner et al., 1993; Gaertner, Rust, Dovidio, Bachman, & Anastasio, 1994, 1996). That is, these contact conditions facilitate a reduction in bias, in part, because they share the capacity to transform members' representations of the memberships from separate groups to more inclusive social entity. We do not necessarily, however, regard the *decategorization* and *recategorization* frameworks to be completely mutually exclusive theoretically; we believe them to be capable of working in parallel and complementary ways. Given the complexity of intergroup attitudes, it is plausible that these features of contact operate through several related as well as different pathways. In the next section, we will present support for the common ingroup identity model and the effects of *recategorization*. In addition, we will discuss the value of a "dual identity" in which original group identities are maintained, but within the context of a superordinate identity.

The Common Ingroup Identity Model

In contrast to the decategorization approaches described above, recategorization is not designed to reduce or eliminate categorization but rather to structure a definition of group categorization at a higher level of category inclusiveness in ways that reduce intergroup bias and conflict. Specifically, we hypothesize that if members of different groups are induced to conceive of themselves within single group rather than as completely separate groups, attitudes toward former outgroup members will become more positive through processes involving pro-ingroup bias (Gaertner & Dovidio, 2000; Gaertner et al., 1993).

This model identifies potential antecedents and outcomes of recategorization, as well as mediating processes. Figure 1 summarizes the general framework and specifies the causes and consequences of a common ingroup identity. Specifically, it is hypothesized that the different types of intergroup interdependence and cognitive, perceptual, linguistic, affective, and environmental factors can either independently or in concert alter individuals' cognitive representations of the aggregate. These resulting cognitive representations (i.e., one group, two-subgroups with one group, two groups, or separate individuals) are then proposed to result in the specific cognitive, affective and overt behavioral consequences (listed on the right). Thus, the causal factors listed on the left (that include features specified by the contact hypothesis) are proposed to influence members' cognitive representations of the memberships (center) that in turn mediate the relationship, at least in part, between the causal factors (left) and the cognitive, affective and behavioral consequences (on the right). In addition, we proposed that common ingroup identity may be achieved by increasing the salience of existing common superordinate memberships (e.g., a school, a company, a nation) or by introducing factors (e.g., common goals or fate) that are perceived to be shared by the memberships.

Once outgroup members are perceived as ingroup members, it is hypothesized that they would be accorded the benefits of ingroup status heuristically and in

The Common Ingroup Identity Model

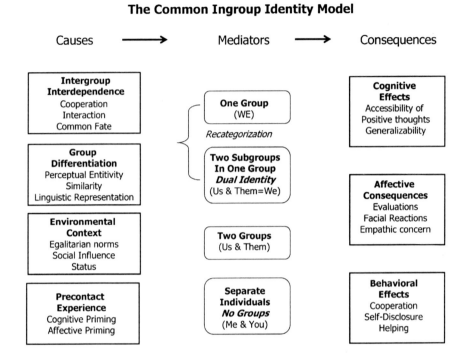

Fig. 1 The Common Ingroup Identity Model

stereotyped fashion. There would likely be more positive thoughts, feelings and behaviors (listed on the right) toward these former outgroup members by virtue of categorizing them now as ingroup members. These more favorable impressions of outgroup members are not likely to be finely differentiated, at least initially (see Mullen & Hu, 1989). Rather, we suggest that these more elaborated, personalized impressions can soon develop within the context of a common identity because the newly formed positivity bias is likely to encourage more open communication and greater self-disclosing interaction between former outgroup members. Thus, over time a common identity is proposed to encourage personalization of outgroup members and thereby initiate a second route to achieving reduced bias.

The development of a common ingroup identity does not necessarily require each group to forsake its less inclusive group identity completely. Social identities are complex; every individual belongs to multiple groups simultaneously (Brewer, 2000). Thus, depending on their degree of identification with different categories and contextual factors that make particular identities more salient, individuals may activate one or more of these identities simultaneously (Roccas & Brewer, 2002) as well as sequentially (Turner, 1985). As depicted by the "subgroups within one group" (i.e., a dual identity) representation, we believe that it is possible for members to conceive of two groups (for example, parents and children) as distinct units within the context of a superordinate (i.e., family) identity.

When group identities and the associated cultural values are central to members' functioning or when they are associated with high status or highly visible cues to group membership, it would be undesirable or impossible for people to relinquish these group identities or, as perceivers, to be "color-blind." Indeed, demands to forsake these group identities or to adopt a "color-blind" ideology would likely arouse strong reactance and result in especially poor intergroup relations (see Schofield, 1986). If, however, people continued to regard themselves as members of different groups but all playing on the same team or as part of the same superordinate entity, intergroup relations between these "subgroups" would be more positive than if members only considered themselves as "separate groups" (see Brewer & Schneider, 1990). In the next section, we examine empirical tests of the common ingroup identity model.

Common Identity and the Reduction of, Intergroup Bias

Among the antecedent factors proposed by the common ingroup identity model (listed on the left) are the features of contact situations (Allport, 1954) that are necessary for intergroup contact to be successful (e.g., interdependence between groups, equal status, equalitarian norms). From this perspective, cooperative interaction, for example, enhances positive evaluations of outgroup members (an affective consequence listed on the right), at least in part, because cooperation transforms members' representations of the memberships from separate groups to one group.

From this recategorization perspective, cooperation among Sherif and Sherif's (1969) groups of summer campers increased positive attitudes toward outgroup members because it changed members' perceptions of one another from "us" and "them" to a more inclusive "we." To test this hypothesis directly, we conducted a laboratory experiment (Gaertner, Mann, Dovidio, Murrell, & Pomare, 1990) that brought two 3-person laboratory groups together under conditions designed to vary independently the members' representations of the aggregate as one group or two groups (by varying factors such as seating arrangement) and the presence or absence of intergroup cooperation interaction. In the absence of cooperative interaction, participants induced to feel like one group relative to those whose separate group identities were reinforced reported that the aggregate did feel more like one group. They also had lower degrees of intergroup bias in their evaluations (likable, cooperative, honest, and trustworthy) of ingroup and outgroup members. We regard this as an important preliminary finding because it helps to establish the causal relation between the induction of a one-group representation and reduced bias, even in the absence of intergroup cooperation.

Supportive of the hypothesis concerning how cooperation reduces bias, among participants induced to feel like two groups, the introduction of cooperative interaction increased their perceptions of one group and also reduced their bias in evaluative ratings relative to those who did not cooperate during the contact period. Also supportive of the common ingroup identity model, reduced bias associated with

introducing cooperation was due to enhanced favorable evaluations of outgroup members. Consistent with Brewer's (1979) analysis, cooperation appeared to move the new ingroup members closer to the self.

Consistent with our mediation hypothesis, cooperation induced group formation among members of the two groups and also reduced bias. In addition, more direct support for the mediation hypothesis was revealed by the multiple regression mediation approach, a form of path analysis (see Baron & Kenny, 1986). This analysis indicated that the influence of the introduction of cooperation on more positive evaluations of outgroup members was substantially reduced when the mediating effects of group representations and perceptions of cooperation and competition were considered. Furthermore, consistent with our model, among these potential mediators, only the "one group" representation related independently to evaluations of outgroup members.

The advantage of the experimental design is that we know that cooperation preceded changes in participants' representations of the aggregate from two groups to one group and also changes in intergroup bias. Also, when we manipulated only the representations of the aggregate (i.e., in the absence of cooperation), we know that the one-group representation preceded changes in intergroup bias. Such certainty regarding the direction of causality is not afforded by our correlational studies of the effects of contact hypothesis variables on intergroup bias that we conducted involving more natural contexts. However, we can rely on the results of the experimental study to at least support the plausibility of the direction of causality proposed by our model as it is applied to the study of the effects of cooperation as well as the other features specified by the contact hypothesis on intergroup harmony in more natural contexts.

In addition, we conducted three survey studies in natural settings across different domains of intergroup life which offered converging support for the idea that features specified by the contact hypothesis increase intergroup harmony, in part, because they transform members' representations of the memberships from separate groups to one more inclusive group. Participants in these studies included students attending a multiethnic high school (Gaertner et al., 1996); banking executives who had experienced a corporate merger involving a wide variety of banks across the United States (Bachman, 1993), and college students who are members of blended families whose households are composed of two formerly separate families trying to unite into one (Banker & Gaertner, 1998).

These surveys included items (specifically designed for each context) to measure participants' perceptions of the conditions of contact (i.e., equal status, self-revealing interaction, cooperation, equalitarian norms), their representations of the aggregate (i.e., one group, two subgroups within one group, two separate groups, and separate individuals), and a measure of intergroup harmony or bias. For example, contact hypothesis items measuring participants' perceptions of equal status between the groups included items such as, "Teachers at this school are fair to all groups of students." Participants' cognitive representations of the aggregate as "one group" were measured by items such as, "Within the merged organization it feels like one group." Although the measures of intergroup bias or harmony were different across the three contexts, each study included some measure of affective reactions (e.g., feeling good, respectful, happy, awkward) to ingroup and outgroup members. Within each setting composite indexes were created for each of the major components of our model, that is, the conditions of contact, the representations and intergroup harmony or bias.

In general, the more favorable participants reported the conditions of contact between the groups (e.g., cooperation), the more the school (or company or family) felt like one group. Supportive of the model, the more it felt like one group, the lower the bias in affective reactions in the high school, the less the intergroup anxiety among the banking executives, and the greater the amount of stepfamily harmony. Recently, a longitudinal study of stepfamilies found evidence supportive of the direction of causality between the constructs proposed by our model across time (Banker, 2002). Thus, across a variety of intergroup settings and methodological approaches we have found reasonably strong and consistent support for the common ingroup identity model.

To directly determine whether a common ingroup identity can increase positive reactions to racial outgroup members, we executed two additional experiments. In a laboratory experiment (Nier, Gaertner, Dovidio, Banker, & Ward, 2001; Study 1) White participants involved in the same session with a Black or White confederate were induced to perceive themselves as separate individuals with no functional connection or as members of the same team. The results revealed that the evaluations of the other White confederate were virtually equivalent in the individual and team conditions, whereas the evaluations of the Black confederate was reliably more positive when they were teammates than when they were just individuals without common group connection.

Additionally, a field experiment (Nier et al., 2001, Study 2) conducted at the University of Delaware football stadium prior to a game between the University of Delaware and Westchester State University demonstrates how a salient superordinate identity can increase behavioral compliance with a request for assistance from a person of a different race. In this experiment, Black and White, male and female students approached fans of the same sex as themselves from both universities just before the fans entered the stadium. These fans were asked if they would be willing to be interviewed about their food preferences. Our student interviewers systematically varied whether they were wearing a University of Delaware or Westchester State University hat. By selecting fans who wore similar clothing that identified their university affiliation, we systematically varied whether fans and our interviewers had common or different university identities in a context where we expected these identities to be particularly salient. Although we planned to oversample Black fans, the sample was still too small to yield any informative findings.

Among White fans, however, sharing common university identity with the Black interviewers significantly increased their compliance (59%) relative to when they did not share common identity with the Black interviewer (36%). When the interviewers were White, however, there was no significant difference in their levels of compliance as a function of their university identity. They gained equivalent levels of compliance when they shared common university identity with the fan

(44%) as when they appeared to be affiliated with the rival university (37%). These findings together with those of the preceding study offer support for the idea that outgroup members will be treated more favorably in terms of evaluations and prosocial behavior when they are perceived to also share a more inclusive, common ingroup affiliation. In the next section, we explore whether a common ingroup identity can make an even more fundamental change in the behavior of Whites during interracial interactions.

Common Identity and Motivation in Interracial Interaction

Within the aversive racism framework, a major motive of Whites in interracial situations is to *avoid wrong-doing*. Supportive of this view, we have found across a variety of different studies that Whites typically do not discriminate against Blacks in situations in which norms for appropriate behaviors are clearly defined. Thus, Whites can, at least under some circumstances, successfully suppress negative beliefs, feelings, and behavior toward Blacks when it is obvious that expressing such reactions reflects racial bias. Unfortunately, in view of recent work on stereotype suppression and rebound (Monteith, Sherman, & Devine, 1998) it is possible that once this self-imposed suppression is relaxed, negative beliefs, feelings, and behaviors would be even *more likely* than if they were not suppressed initially.

The common ingroup identity model, because it focuses on redirecting the forces of ingroup favoritism, can potentially change the motivational orientation or intentions of aversive racists from trying to avoid wrong-doing to trying to *do what is right*. Evidence from our laboratory suggests the potential promise of a common ingroup identity to alter motivation in just such a positive way (Dovidio, Gaertner, & Kawakami, 1998; Gaertner & Dovidio, 2000).

In this experiment, White participants who were about to interact with a White or a Black confederate were either asked to try to avoid wrong-doing, instructed to try to behave correctly toward the other person, informed that they were part of the same team with their partner and competing against a team at a rival institution, or were given no instructions. The dependent measure of interest was the relative accessibility of negative thoughts, as assessed by changes in responses on a Stroop color-naming task after the interaction relative to responses on a baseline Stroop task administered before the interaction. A rebound effect would be reflected in greater accessibility (i.e., longer color-naming latencies) of negative relative to positive words on the posttest Stroop task.

We hypothesized that, because the primary motivation of aversive racists in interracial interaction is to avoid wrong-doing and thus to suppress negative thoughts and feelings, participants explicitly instructed to avoid wrong-doing and those given no instructions would show relatively strong accessibility of negative thoughts after interacting with a Black confederate. In contrast, we expected participants instructed to behave correctly and those in the "same team" condition (who were hypothesized to adopt a positive orientation on their own) would escape such a rebound effect.

The results were encouraging. When the confederate was White, the experimental conditions did not differ significantly in the accessibility of negative thoughts from one another or from baseline. When the confederate was Black, however, the increased accessibility of negative relative to positive characteristics (from the pretest to the posttest) in the avoid wrong-doing and no instructions conditions was significantly greater than in the do right and same team conditions, in which there was an increase in the accessibility of positive relative to negative thoughts. The pattern of these findings suggests that the development of a common ingroup identity can alter motivation in interracial situations from one of suppressing negative thoughts, feelings, and actions to one that is positive, more appetitive and prosocial – and in a way that does not ironically result in further increases in negative thoughts. These findings are particularly encouraging to us because they illustrate the effectiveness of a common ingroup identity for addressing individual-level biases and particularly the underlying motivational dynamics of aversive racism.

In general, when we present this work people frequently question whether the development of a common ingroup identity is a realistic strategy. Our evaluation study of an elementary school antibias education intervention attempts to address this question.

Common Identity and the Green Circle Elementary School Antibias Education Program

Several years ago, we became aware of the Green Circle elementary school-based intervention program, which is now run by the National Conference of Community and Justice of Northern Delaware that is practically and theoretically compatible with the common ingroup identity model. The guiding assumption of Green Circle is that helping children bring people from different groups conceptually into their own circle of caring and sharing fosters appreciation of their common humanity as well as respect for their differences.

In the program, a Green Circle facilitator visits each class for about 40 min per session four times over a 4-week period and shows children a small Green Circle on a felt board. The facilitator states, "Whenever you see the Green Circle, you should think about your world of people; the people who you care about and the people who care about you." A stick figure is added to the circle and the students are told that the figure represents themselves. The facilitator explains that each person has "a big job of deciding who is going to be in your circle, how to treat people, and how big your circle will grow," and engages children in a variety of exercises designed to expand the circle. The facilitator points out that, "All of us belong to one family – the human family." Paralleling the common ingroup identity model, Green Circle assumes that an appreciation of common humanity will increase children's positive attitudes toward people who would otherwise remain outside of their circle of inclusion.

This collaboration with the Green Circle staff provided an applied opportunity to test the general principles of the common ingroup identity model and also offered the Green Circle program an evaluation of their intervention's effectiveness (see Houlette et al., 2004). On the basis of the goals of the Green Circle program and the principles of the common ingroup identity model, we expected that children receiving the program would be more inclusive of others who are different than themselves in playing and sharing following the implementation of the program relative to pretest levels and also relative to children in a control condition who did not yet receive the program. To evaluate attitudes toward children similar and different in sex, race, and weight children were asked about their willingness to share with and play with each of eight different children depicted in drawings in which sex, race (Black and White), and weight were systematically varied.

Overall, our results revealed that first- and second-grade children in fairly well-integrated classrooms still had a general preference for playing and sharing with children of the same race than a different race. Nevertheless, we also found that the Green Circle intervention did lead children to be more inclusive in terms of their most preferred playmate. Specifically, compared to children in the control condition who did not participate in Green Circle activities, those who were part of Green Circle showed a significantly greater increase in willingness to select a child from the eight drawings who was different from them (in terms of race, sex, and weight) as the child they "would most want to play with." These changes involve greater willingness to cross group boundaries in making friends – a factor that is one of the most potent influences in producing more positive attitudes toward the outgroup as a whole (Pettigrew, 1998).

Conceptually, the Green Circle findings illustrate that it is realistic to operationalize the primary theme underlying the common ingroup identity model. These findings also demonstrate how interpersonal and intergroup routes toward reducing intergroup biases can involve complementary processes that reciprocally facilitate one another. That is, changes in intergroup boundaries can facilitate the occurrence of positive interpersonal behaviors across group lines such as self-disclosure and helping in college students (see also Dovidio et al., 1997) and, as the Green Circle study illustrates, preferred playmates in children.

Future Directions

The research we have summarized in this article found converging evidence across a variety of cross-sectional and longitudinal surveys, as well as laboratory and field experiments, supportive of the model's fundamental assumptions about the causes and consequences of a common ingroup identity. In particular, we demonstrated that inclusive, one-group representations critically mediate the effects of intergroup contact on the reduction of intergroup biases, including cognitive, affective, and behavioral outcomes. This effect has been obtained in laboratory and field experiments that manipulated the strength of a superordinate identity in temporary and enduring groups, in cross-sectional and longitudinal field studies of the relations between (a) racial and ethnic groups in high schools and colleges, (b) executives who recently experienced a corporate merger, (c) members of blended families over time, and (d) elementary school students participating in an antibias program (Banker et al., 2004; Gaertner, Bachman, Dovidio, & Banker, 2001; Houlette et al., 2004). The more participants reported that different groups felt more like "one group," the more positive were their attitudes toward former outgroup members.

In addition, emphasizing a common group identity between two groups facilitates forgiveness by members of the victimized group for historical transgressions by the other group and promotes intergroup trust (Wohl & Branscombe, 2004) and prosocial behavior (Dovidio et al., 1997; Nier et al., 2001). Also, creating a common ingroup identity facilitates more intimate self-disclosure (Dovidio et al.), which in turn can produce more personalized (i.e., decategorized) interactions (Brewer & Miller, 1984) that can further reduce intergroup bias.

As we noted earlier, replacing different group representations with a common ingroup identity is just one form of recategorization. Another form is a *dual identity*, in which separate group identities are maintained but within the context of an overriding superordinate identity (a "different groups working together on the same team" representation). Although the relative salience of the subgroups and shared inclusive group identities may vary in different contexts (as do figure-ground perceptions of reversible figures), both remain salient to some extent. The dual identity approach is a particular form of recategorization in which the original group boundaries are maintained but within a salient superordinate group identity that represents a higher level of inclusiveness.

Inducing this form of recategorization may be particularly appropriate when group identities and their associated cultural values are vital to people's functioning. Under these conditions, it would be undesirable or impossible for them to relinquish this aspect of their self-concept completely. Indeed, demands to abandon these group identities (e.g., to adopt a colorblind ideology) would likely arouse strong reactance and countervailing motivations to achieve positive intergroup distinctiveness, which would result in especially poor intergroup relations. In this respect, the common ingroup identity model is aligned with bidimensional models of acculturation, in which cultural heritage and mainstream identities are relatively independent (Berry, 1997; Dovidio, Gaertner, & Kafati, 2000), not with unidimensional models, which posit that cultural identity is necessarily relinquished with adoption of mainstream cultural identity (Gans, 1979). Also, the positive effects of the dual identity form of recategorization may be more likely to generalize to the original outgroup as a whole than are the effects of a one-group representation because the associative links between members present and the group are maintained with a dual identity (see also Brown & Hewstone, 2005; Dovidio, Gaertner, & Validzic, 1998). It is therefore important for practical as well as theoretical reasons to consider more complex forms of social identity in which more than one identity is salient at a time.

Consistent with our hypothesis that a dual identity represents a form of recategorization that can facilitate positive intergroup relations for minority group members, Huo, Smith, Tyler, and Lind (1996) found that even when racial or ethnic identity is strong for minority group members, perceptions of a superordinate connection can enhance interracial trust and acceptance of authority within an organization. Also, we found that students in a multiethnic high school who described themselves as *both* American and as a member of their racial or ethnic group showed less bias toward other groups in the school than did those who described themselves only in terms of their subgroup identity (Gaertner et al., 1996). Thus, even when subgroup identity is salient, the simultaneous salience of a common ingroup identity is associated with lower levels of intergroup bias. These findings are also conceptually consistent with studies that reveal that interethnic attitudes are more favorable when participants are primed with a multicultural, pluralistic ideology for increasing interethnic harmony that emphasizes the value of a dual identity, relative to an assimilation ideology, which closely parallels a one-group representation (Richeson & Nussbaum, 2004; Wolsko, Park, Judd, & Wittenbrink, 2000).

However, in contrast to the consistent, significant effect for the one-group representation across studies, the experience of a dual identity produces different effects across intergroup settings. A stronger sense of dual identity has also been shown to relate to *more* bias in our corporate merger study and to more conflict within our stepfamily study (see Gaertner et al., 2001). In addition, a series of studies by Mummendey and her colleagues indicate that making a superordinate identity salient while subgroup identities are also salient (e.g., among bikers, teachers, and Germans) increases bias toward the other subgroup (e.g., Waldzus, Mummendey, Wenzel, & Weber, 2003).

The goal of our future work is to further investigate the impact of a dual identity on intergroup relations, conceptually reconciling apparently contradictory findings (by others and ourselves) and extending the scope of the common ingroup identity model, by examining mediating mechanisms and moderating factors associated with a dual identity. In addition to trying to reconcile apparently inconsistent findings involving the dual identity representation, we will explore our trade-off hypothesis (see Gaertner & Dovidio, 2000: 148–150). Specifically, we hypothesized that as the one-group representation becomes stronger, attitudes toward immediate outgroup members will be more favorable, but because the associative link to additional members of the outgroup category has been potentially weakened (see Rothbart, 1996; Rothbart & John, 1985), these positive feelings would not generalize to the outgroup as a whole. In contrast, when outgroup members are categorized primarily in terms of a dual identity, attitudes toward those members present may not be quite as positive as with complete recategorization, but these positive responses are more likely to generalize to the outgroup as a whole. However, because the strength of the dual identity can be associated with either increased or decreased bias toward outgroup members present, this generalization can involve either increased positive or increased negative attitudes toward the outgroup as a whole, which adds another level of complexity to our future work.

Conclusion

Intergroup conflict and bias often reflects deep cultural and historical roots of conflict, the intricate nature of the political and economic relations between groups, and the complicated nature of the contemporary events initiating and sustaining adversarial relations between groups. The nature of conflict is thus infinitely variable. Nevertheless, although conflict occurs across groups, it is experienced by individuals. Because of the complexity and variability of conflict and bias, social psychology cannot offer a single, simple intervention for creating intergroup harmony. The path to intergroup harmony is likely to be as complicated as the path that led to conflict and bias. Nevertheless, social psychology does identify a number of intergroup and interpersonal processes that are fundamental to understanding group relations. These are not simply academic theories. Rather, they represent important tools for developing strategies and concrete interventions for promoting positive intergroup relations. The recipe may vary from place to place and from time to time, but social psychology can identify some of the key ingredients, which hopefully can be operationalized by people on the front lines of reducing intergroup conflict and promoting productive intergroup relations – enabling the memberships to appreciate their common humanity.

References

Allport, G. W. (1954). *The nature of prejudice*. New York: Addison-Wesley.

Abrams, D. (1985). Focus of attention in minimal intergroup discrimination. *British Journal of Social Psychology, 24*, 65–74.

Bachman, B. A. (1993). *An intergroup model of organizational mergers*. Unpublished Ph.D. Dissertation, Department of Psychology, University of Delaware, Newark.

Banker, B. S. (2002). *Intergroup conflict and bias reduction in stepfamilies: A longitudinal examination of intergroup relations processes*. Unpublished Ph.D. Dissertation, Department of Psychology, University of Delaware, Newark, DE.

Banker, B. S., & Gaertner, S. L. (1998). Achieving stepfamily harmony: An intergroup relations approach. *Journal of Family Psychology, 12*, 310–325.

Banker, B. S., Gaertner, S. L., Dovidio, J. F., Houlette, M., Johnson, K. S., & Riek, B. M. (2004). Reducing stepfamily conflict: The importance of an inclusive social identity. In M. Bennett & F. Sani (Eds.), *The development of the social self* (pp. 269–288). New York: Psychology Press.

Baron, R. M., & Kenny, D. A. (1986). The moderator–mediator variable distinction in social psychological research: Conceptual, strategic, and statistical considerations. *Journal of Personality and Social Psychology, 51*, 1173–1182.

Berry, J. W. (1997). Immigration, acculturation, and adaptation. *Applied Psychology: An International Review, 46*, 5–34.

Bettencourt, B. A., Brewer, M. B., Croak, M. R., & Miller, N. (1992). Cooperation and the reduction of intergroup bias: The roles of reward structure and social orientation. *Journal of Experimental Social Psychology, 28*, 301–319

Billig, M. G., & Tajfel, H. (1973). Social categorisation and similarity in intergroup behavior. *European Journal of Social Psychology, 3*, 27–52.

Brewer, M. B. (1979). Ingroup bias in the minimal intergroup situation: A cognitive-motivational analysis. *Psychological Bulletin, 86*, 307–324.

Brewer, M. B. (1988). A dual process model of impression formation. In T. Srull & R.Wyer (Eds.), *Advances in social cognition* (Vol. 1, pp. 1–36). Hillsdale, NJ: Erlbaum.

Brewer, M. B. (2000). Reducing prejudice through cross-categorization: Effects of multiple social identities. In S. Oskamp (Ed.), *Reducing prejudice and discrimination: The claremont symposium on applied social psychology* (pp. 165–183). Mahwah, NJ: Erlbaum.

Brewer, M. B., Ho, H., Lee, J., & Miller, N. (1987). Social identity and social distance among Hong Kong school children. *Personality and Social Psychology Bulletin, 13,* 156–165.

Brewer, M. B., & Miller, N. (1984). Beyond the contact hypothesis: Theoretical perspectives on desegregation. In N. Miller & M. B. Brewer (Eds.), *Groups in contact: The psychology of desegregation* (pp. 281–302). Orlando, FL: Academic Press.

Brewer, M. B., & Schneider, S. (1990). Social identity and social dilemmas: A double-edged sword. In D. Abrams & M. Hogg (Eds.), *Social identity theory: Constructive and critical advances* (pp. 169–184). London: Harvester Wheatsheaf.

Brown, R., & Hewstone, M. (2005). An integrative theory of intergroup contact. In M. P. Zanna (Ed.), *Advances in experimental social psychology* (Vol. 37, pp. 255–343). San Diego, CA: Academic Press.

Brown, R. J., & Turner, J. C. (1979). The criss-cross categorization effect in intergroup discrimination. *British Journal of Social and Clinical Psychology, 18,* 371–383.

Brown, R. J., & Turner, J. C. (1981). Interpersonal and intergroup behavior. In J. C. Turner & H. Giles (Eds.), *Intergroup behavior* (pp. 33–64). Chicago, IL: The University of Chicago Press.

Campbell, D. T. (1958). Common fate, similarity and other indices of the status of aggregates of persons as social entities. *Behavioral Science, 3,* 14–25.

Cook, S. W. (1984). Cooperative interaction in multiethnic contexts. In N. Miller & M. B. Brewer (Eds.), *Groups in contact: The psychology of desegregation* (pp. 291–302). Orlando, FL: Academic Press.

Commins, B., & Lockwood, J. (1978). The effects of intergroup relations of mixing Roman Catholics and Protestants: An experimental investigation. *European Journal of Social Psychology, 8,* 218–219.

Correll, J., & Park, B. (2005). A model of the ingroup as a social resource. *Personality and Social Psychology Review, 9,* 341–359.

Deschamps J. C., & Doise, W. (1978). Crossed-category membership in intergroup relations. In H. Tajfel (Ed.), *Differentiation between social groups* (pp. 141–158). London: Academic Press.

Dion, K. L. (1974). *A cognitive model of ingroup–outgroup bias.* Paper presented at the American Psychological Association Meeting, New Orleans, LA.

Doise, W. (1978). *Groups and individuals: Explanations in social psychology.* Cambridge, UK: Cambridge University Press.

Dovidio, J. F., Gaertner, S. L., & Kafati, G. (2000). Group identity and intergroup relations: The common in-group identity model. In S. R. Thye, E. J. Lawler, M. W. Macy, & H. A. Walker (Eds.), *Advances in group processes* (Vol. 17, pp. 1–34). Stamford, CT: JAI Press.

Dovidio, J. F., Gaertner, S. L., & Kawakami, K. (1998). *Multiple attitudes and contemporary racial bias.* Paper presented at the annual meeting of the Society for Experimental Social Psychology, Lexington, KY.

Dovidio, J. F., Gaertner, S. L., & Kawakami, K. (2003). The contact hypothesis: The past, present, and the future. *Group Processes and Intergroup Relations, 6,* 5–21.

Dovidio, J. F., Gaertner, S. L., & Validzic, A. (1998). Intergroup bias: Status, differentiation, and a common ingroup identity. *Journal of Personality and Social Psychology, 75,* 109–120.

Dovidio, J. F., Gaertner, S. L., Validzic, A., Matoka, K., Johnson, B., & Frazier, S. (1997). Extending the benefits of re-categorization: Evaluations, self-disclosure and helping. *Journal of Experimental Social Psychology, 33,* 401–420.

Ferguson, C. K., & Kelley, H. H. (1964). Significant factors in over-evaluation of own groups' products. *Journal of Abnormal and Social Psychology, 69,* 223–228.

Fiske, S. T., Lin, M., & Neuberg, S. L. (1999). The continuum model: Ten years later. In S. Chaiken & Y. Trope (Eds.), *Dual process theories in social psychology* (pp. 211–254). New York: Guilford.

Fiske, S. T., & Taylor, S. E. (1991). *Social cognition* (2nd ed.). New York: McGraw-Hill.

Gaertner, S. L., Bachman, B. A., Dovidio, J. D., & Banker, B. S. (2001). Corporate mergers and stepfamily marriages: Identity, Harmony, and Commitment. In M. A. Hogg & D. Terry (Eds.), *Social identity in organizations* (pp. 265–288). Oxford: Blackwell.

Gaertner, S. L., & Dovidio, J. F. (2000). *Reducing intergroup bias: The common ingroup identity model*. Philadelphia, PA: Psychology Press.

Gaertner, S. L., Dovidio, J. F., Anastasio, P. A., Bachman, B. A., & Rust, M. C. (1993). The common ingroup identity model: Recategorization and the reduction of intergroup bias. In W. Stroebe & M. Hewstone (Eds.), *European review of social psychology* (Vol. 4. pp. 1–26). New York: John Wiley & Sons.

Gaertner, S. L., Mann, J. A., Dovidio, J. F., Murrell, A. J., & Pomare, M. (1990). How does cooperation reduce intergroup bias? *Journal of Personality and Social Psychology, 59*, 692–704.

Gaertner, S. L., Mann, J., Murrell, A., & Dovidio, J. F. (1989). Reducing intergroup bias: The benefits of recategorization. *Journal of Personality and Social Psychology, 57*, 239–249.

Gaertner, S. L., Rust, M. C., Dovidio, J. F., Bachman, B. A., & Anastasio, P. A. (1994). The contact hypothesis: The role of a common ingroup identity on reducing intergroup bias. *Small Groups Research, 25*, 224–249.

Gaertner, S. L., Rust, M. C., Dovidio, J. F., Bachman, B. A., & Anastasio, P. A. (1996). The contact hypothesis: The role of a common ingroup identity on reducing intergroup bias among majority and minority group members. In J. L. Nye & A. M. Brower (Eds.), *What's social about social cognition?* (pp. 230–360). Newbury Park, CA: Sage.

Gans, H. (1979). Symbolic ethnicity: The future of ethnic groups and culture in America. *Ethnic and Racial Studies, 2*, 1–20.

Hamilton, D. L., & Sherman, J. W. (1994). Stereotypes. In R. S. Wyer & T. K. Srull (Eds.), *Handbook of social cognition* (Vol. 2, pp. 1–68). Hillsdale, NJ: Erlbaum.

Hamilton, D. L., & Trolier, T. K. (1986). Stereotypes and stereotyping: An overview of the cognitive approach. In J. F. Dovidio & S. L. Gaertner (Eds.), *Prejudice, discrimination, and racism* (pp. 127–163). Orlando, FL: Academic Press.

Hewstone, M. (1990). The 'ultimate attribution error'? A review of the literature on intergroup causal attribution. *European Journal of Social Psychology, 20*, 311–335.

Hewstone, M., & Brown, R. J. (1986). Contact is not enough: An intergroup perspective on the "contact hypothesis." In M. Hewstone & R. Brown (Eds.), *Contact and conflict in intergroup encounters* (pp. 1–44). Oxford: Basil Blackwell.

Hornstein, H. A. (1976). *Cruelty and kindness: A new look at aggression and altruism*. Englewood Cliffs, NJ: Prentice Hall.

Houlette, M., Gaertner, S. L., Johnson, K. M., Banker, B. S., Riek, B. M., & Dovidio, J. F. (2004). Developing a more inclusive social identity: An elementary school intervention. *Journal of Social Issues, 60*, 35–56.

Howard, J. M., & Rothbart, M. (1980). Social categorization for in-group and out-group behavior. *Journal of Personality and Social Psychology, 38*, 301–310.

Huo, Y. J., Smith, H. H., Tyler, T. R., & Lind, A. E. (1996). Superordinate identification, subgroup identification, and justice concerns: Is separatism the problem. Is assimilation the answer? *Psychological Science, 7*, 40–45.

Johnson, D. W., Johnson, F. P. & Maruyama, G. (1983). Interdependence and interpersonal attraction among heterogeneous and homogeneous individuals: A theoretical formulation and a meta-analysis of the research. *Review of Educational Research, 52*, 5–54.

Karpinski, A., & Von Hippel, W. (1996). The role of the linguistic intergroup bias in expectancy maintenance. *Social Cognition, 14*, 141–163.

Kramer, R. M., & Brewer, M. B. (1984). Effects of group identity on resource utilization in a simulated commons dilemma. *Journal of Personality and Social Psychology, 46*, 1044–1057.

Maass, A., Salvi, D., Arcuri, L., & Semin, G. R. (1989). Language use in intergroup contexts: The linguistic intergroup bias. *Journal of Personality and Social Psychology, 57*, 981–993.

Macrae, C. N., Milne, A. B., & Bodenhausen, G. V. (1994). Stereotypes as energy-saving devices: A peek inside the cognitive toolbox. *Journal of Personality and Social Psychology, 66*, 37–47.

Marcus-Newhall, A., Miller, N., Holtz, R., & Brewer, M. B. (1993). Cross-cutting category membership with role assignment: A means of reducing intergroup bias. *British Journal of Social Psychology, 32,* 125–146.

Miller, N. (2002). Personalization and the promise of contact theory. *Journal of Social Issues, 58,* 29–44.

Miller, N., Brewer, M. B., & Edwards, K. (1985). Cooperative interaction in desegregated settings: A laboratory analog. *Journal of Social Issues, 41*(3), 63–75.

Monteith, M., Sherman, J., & Devine, P. (1998). Suppression as a stereotype control strategy. *Personality and Social Psychology Review, 1,* 63–82.

Mullen, B., & Hu, L. T. (1989). Perceptions of ingroup and outgroup variability: A meta-analytic integration. *Basic and Applied Social Psychology, 10,* 233–252.

Murrell, A. J., Dietz-Uhler, B. L., Dovidio, J. F., Gaertner, S. L., & Drout, C. E. (1994). Aversive racism and resistance to affirmative action: Perceptions of justice are not necessarily colorblind. *Basic and Applied Social Psychology, 5,* 71–86.

Nier, J. A., Gaertner, S. L., Dovidio, J. F., Banker, B. S., & Ward, C. M. (2001). Changing interracial evaluations and behavior: The effects of a common group identity. *Group Processes and Intergroup Relations, 4,* 299–316.

Park, B., & Rothbart, M. (1982). Perception of out-group homogeneity and levels of social categorization: Memory for the subordinate attributes of in-group and out-group members. *Journal of Personality and Social Psychology, 42,* 1051–1068.

Perdue, C. W., Dovidio, J. F., Gurtman, M. B., & Tyler, R. B. (1990). "Us" and "Them": Social categorization and the process of intergroup bias. *Journal of Personality and Social Psychology, 59,* 475–486.

Pettigrew, T. F. (1979). The ultimate attributional error: Extending Allport's cognitive analysis of prejudice. *Personality and Social Psychology Bulletin, 55,* 461–476.

Pettigrew, T. F. (1998). Intergroup contact theory. *Annual Review of Psychology, 49,* 65–85.

Piliavin, J. A., Dovidio, J. F., Gaertner, S. L., & Clark, R. D., III. (1981). *Emergency intervention.* New York: Academic Press.

Rabbie, J. M. (1982). The effects of intergroup competition and cooperation on intragroup and intergroup relationships. In V. J. Derlega & J. Grzelak (Eds.), *Cooperation and helping behavior: Theories and research* (pp. 128–151). New York: Academic Press.

Richeson, J. A., & Nussbaum, R. J. (2004). The impact of multiculturalism versus color-blindness on racial bias. *Journal of Experimental Social Psychology 40,* 417–423.

Roccas, S., & Brewer, M. (2002). Social identity complexity. *Personality and Social Psychology Review, 6,* 88–106.

Rothbart, M. (1996). Category-exemplar dynamics and stereotype change. In Y. Amir & J. Schwarzwald (Eds.), *International Journal of Intercultural Relations* (Vol. 20, pp. 305–321) [Special Issue].

Rothbart, M., & John, O. P. (1985). Social categorization and behavioral episodes: A cognitive analysis of the effects of intergroup contact. *Journal of Social Issues, 41*(3), 81–104.

Schofield, J. W. (1986). Causes and consequences of the colorblind perspective. In J. F. Dovidio & S. L. Gaertner (Eds.), *Prejudice, discrimination and racism* (pp. 231–253). Orlando, FL: Academic Press.

Sherif, M., & Sherif, C. W. (1969). *Social psychology.* New York: Harper & Row.

Skinner, M., & Stephenson, G. M. (1981). The effects of intergroup comparisons on the polarization of opinions. *Current Psychological Research, 1,* 49–61.

Stürmer, S., Snyder, M., & Omoto, A. M. (2005). Prosocial emotions and helping: The moderating role of group membership. *Journal of Personality and Social Psychology, 88,* 532–546.

Sumner, W. G. (1906). *Folkways.* New York: Ginn.

Tajfel, H. (1969). Cognitive aspects of prejudice. *Journal of Social Issues, 25*(4), 79–97.

Tajfel, H., Billig, M. G., Bundy, R. F., & Flament, C. (1971). Social categorisation and intergroup behavior. *European Journal of Social Psychology, 1,* 149–177.

Tajfel, H., & Turner, J. C. (1979). An integrative theory of intergroup conflict. In W. G. Austin & S. Worchel (Eds.), *The social psychology of intergroup relations* (pp. 33–48). Monterey, CA: Brooks/Cole.

Turner, J. C. (1975). Social comparison and social identity: Some prospects for intergroup behavior. *European Journal of Social Psychology, 5*, 5–34.

Turner, J. C. (1981). The experimental social psychology of intergroup behavior. In J. C. Turner & H. Giles (Eds.), *Intergroup behavior* (pp. 66–101). Chicago: University of Chicago Press.

Turner, J. C. (1985). Social categorization and the self-concept: A social cognitive theory of group behavior. In E. J. Lawler (Ed.), *Advances in group processes* (Vol. 2, pp. 77–122). Greenwich, CT: JAI Press.

Vanbeselaere, N. (1987). The effects of dichotomous and crossed social categorization upon intergroup discrimination. *European Journal of Social Psychology, 17*, 143–156.

Waldzus, S., Mummendey, A., Wenzel, M., & Weber, U. (2003). Towards tolerance: Representations of superordinate categories and perceived ingroup prototypicality. *Journal of Experimental Social Psychology, 39*, 31–47.

Wilder, D. A. (1978). Reducing intergroup discrimination through individuation of the outgroup. *Journal of Personality and Social Psychology, 36*, 1361–1374.

Wilder, D. A. (1981). Perceiving persons as a group: Categorization and intergroup relations. In D. L. Hamilton (Ed.), *Cognitive processes in stereotyping and intergroup behavior* (pp. 213–257). Hillsdale, NJ: Erlbaum.

Wilder, D. A. (1986). Social categorization: Implications for creation and reduction of intergroup bias. In L. Berkowitz (Ed.), *Advances in experimental social psychology* (Vol. 19, pp. 291–355). Orlando, FL: Academic Press.

Wohl, M. J. A., & Branscombe, N. R. (2004). Forgiveness and collective guilt assignment to historical perpetrator groups depend on level of social category inclusiveness. *Journal of Personality and Social Psychology, 88*, 288–303.

Wolsko, C., Park, B., Judd, C. M., & Wittenbrink, B. (2000). Framing interethnic ideology: Effects of multicultural and color-blind perspectives on judgments of groups and individuals. *Journal of Personality and Social Psychology, 78*, 635–654.

Author Index

A

Abrams, D., 9, 10, 113
Adorno, T. W., 44, 46
Allport, G. W., 14, 44, 89, 93, 101,
    111, 113, 116, 121
Amir, Y., 93
Amodio, D. M., 91
Anastasio, P. A., 115, 119
Anthony, T., 69
Arbona, 20
Arce, C. H., 22, 23
Arcuri, L., 114
Argenti, A. M., 73
Armstrong, T. M., 51
Aronson, J., 16
Ashburn-Nardo, L., 90
Ashmore, R. D., 92
Atherton, S. C., 100

B

Bachman, B. A., 53, 115, 119, 122, 127
Bachman, G., 110
Baddeley, A. D., 96
Baenninger, M. A., 78
Banaji, M. R., 27, 53, 90–92
Banker, B. S., 122, 123, 127
Barkowitz, P., 93, 95, 98
Baron, R. M., 122
Bartlett, M., 90
Bauman, 22
Baylis, G. C., 71
Beach, K., 54
Benet-Martinez, V., 36
Bennett, L. B., 75, 76, 82, 88, 96
Berry, J. W., 32, 33, 127
Beschloss, M., 25
Bettencourt, B. A., 117
Biernat, M. R., 94

Bigler, R. S., 73, 74
Billig, M. G., 113
Blaine, B., 16
Blaine, B. E., 56
Blair, I., 90
Blair, I. V., 45, 54, 62, 92
Blandon-Gitlin, I., 75
Blank, R. M., 45
Blascovich, J., 90, 92, 94
Bobo, L., 27, 43, 45
Bodenhausen, G. V., 112
Boneicki, 94
Bothwell, R. K., 69, 88
Boyd, C. E., 70
Brandt, C. C., 85
Branscombe, N. R., 127
Breakwell, G. M., 16, 31, 34, 35
Brent, H. P., 73
Brewer, M. B., 12, 13, 33, 34, 93, 113,
    115–118, 120–122, 127
Brigham, J. C., 4, 5, 57, 59, 68–102
Brimacombe, C. A. E., 88
Britt, T. W., 94
Broadnax, S., 16, 56
Bromley, S., 46
Brown, L. M., 19, 94
Brown, R., 118, 127
Brown, R. J., 113, 118
Bruce, A., 74
Bruck, M., 74
Bundy, R. F., 113
Buri, J. R., 95
Butz, D., 81, 96

C

Cajdric, A., 90
Campbell, D. T., 112
Cannon-Bowers, J. A., 59

Carey, S., 71, 74, 78
Carroo, A. W., 95
Casas, J. M., 16
Castaneda-English, P., 16
Ceci, S. J., 74
Chance, J. E., 69, 74, 75, 88, 92, 95, 96
Chase, W. G., 72, 81
Chavira, V., 30
Chiroro, P., 36, 70, 80, 81, 96
Chung, M. S., 78
Clark, R. D., III, 113
Codina, G. E., 22
Cohen, L., 27
Cohen-Levine, S., 71
Coleman, H. I. K., 36
Commins, B., 118
Connell, T. P., 91
Cook, S. W., 93, 116
Cooper, C., 69
Cooper, J., 63
Correll, J., 113
Cowan, G., 27, 49
Crandall, C. S., 53
Croak, M. R., 117
Crocker, J., 14, 16–19, 24, 56, 63, 94
Crosby, F., 17, 18, 46
Cross, J., 74
Cross, J. F., 74
Cunningham, W. A., 76, 91, 92

D
Daly, J., 74
Darley, J. M., 47, 49
Dasgupta, N., 90
De Haan, M., 72
De Schonen, S., 72, 73, 75
DeBosse, H. L., 34
Decker, B. P., 53
Del Pilar, J. A., 32
Dent, H., 74
DePaulo, B. M., 100
Deregowski, J. B., 77
Deschamps, J. C., 113, 118
DeSteno, D., 90, 91
Devine, P., 124
Devine, P. G., 27, 53–55, 63,
        91, 93, 94, 99–102
Diamond, R., 71, 74, 78
Dietz-Uhler, B. L., 114
Dion, K. L., 113
Dixon, R., 81
Doise, W., 113, 118
Doris, J. L., 74

Doucet, N., 49
Dovidio, J. F., 5, 8, 43–63,
        89, 90, 111–129
Drout, C. E., 114
Duckitt, J., 44
Dunton, B. C., 27, 54, 90
Dwyer, J., 84
Dziurawiec, S., 78

E
Eberhardt, J. L., 1
Edwards, K., 115
Elliot, A. J., 27, 91
Elliott, E. S., 96
Ellis, H. D., 74, 77, 80
Ellsworth, P. C., 49, 51, 69
Ellyson, S. L., 56
Elvira, M. M., 45
Endo, M., 78
Entwisle, D. R., 74
Ericsson, K. A., 72
Espino, R., 23
Esses, V. M., 51
Evans, N., 54
Evett, S. R., 55, 93
Exline, R. V., 55

F
Fairchild, H. H., 3, 49
Fallshore, M. F., 72
Farah, M. J., 71, 72
Faranda, J., 49, 61
Fazio, R. H., 27, 28, 54, 61, 62, 90
Feagin, C. B., 34
Feagin, J., 27
Feagin, J. R., 27, 34, 43
Fein, S., 44
Feingold, G. A., 87, 95
Feinman, S., 74
Ferguson, C. K., 113
Ferguson, T. J., 86
Fiske, S. T., 8, 9, 13, 15, 28,
        29, 76, 112, 115
Flament, C., 113
Flin, R., 74
Flin, R. H., 74, 78
Fodor, J., 70
Foster, J. B., 58
Franz, M. M., 23
Frenkel-Brunswik, E., 44
Frisbie, W. P., 22
Fulero, S. M., 87, 88

G

Gaertner, S. L., 4, 5, 8, 43–63,
    89, 90, 111–129
Gans, H., 127
Garcia-Vazquez, E., 22, 23, 35
Gardiner, J. M., 81
Gary, M. L., 92
Gatto, L., 50
Gauthier, I., 70
Gerton, T., 36
Gibbons, F. X., 18
Gieselman, 70
Goffman, E., 14–16, 34
Goldsmith, M., 98
Goldstein, A. G., 69, 74, 75, 88,
    92, 95, 96
Gómez, C., 23
Goodman, G., 75
Gould, S. J., 2
Green, A. W., 32
Greenwald, A., 53, 54
Greenwald, A. G., 27, 90, 92
Guiliano, T. A., 51
Gurtman, M. B., 114

H

Hagendoorn, L., 51
Hamilton, D. L., 112
Hanson, W. E., 36
Hardee, B. B., 89
Hardin, C. D., 91
Haritatos, J., 36
Harmon-Jones, E., 91
Harton, H. C., 53
Hass, R. G., 44, 89
Hay, D. C., 70
Hebl, M. R., 58
Heider, F., 8
Heiman, R. J., 9
Henderson-King, E. I., 56
Henry, P. J., 45
Hewstone, M., 94, 114, 118, 127
Hodson, G., 51, 56, 61
Hogg, M. A., 9, 10, 13
Holtz, R., 117
Hong, Y. Y., 36
Hooper, H., 51
Hornstein, H. A., 113
Hosch, H. M., 69, 70, 93, 96
Houlette, M., 126, 127
Howard, A., 54, 90
Howard, J. M., 114
Hu, L., 68, 120
Huff, R., 84, 88

Hughes, D., 30
Hunter, S. B., 94
Huo, Y. J., 128
Hutnik, N., 7
Hyers, L., 27
Hyme, H. S., 88

I

Ickes, W., 99
Islam, R. M., 94
Ito, T. A., 28, 76

J

Jackson, J. R., 27, 54
Jackson, L. A., 50
Jackson, L. M., 51
Jacoby, L. L., 81
James, J., 93
James, W., 8
John, O. P., 128
Johnson, B., 54, 90
Johnson, C., 54, 90
Johnson, D., 30
Johnson, D. W., 116
Johnson, F. P., 116
Johnson, J. D., 50, 61
Johnson, M. H., 72
Johnson, M. K., 76
Johnston, R. A., 80
Jones, E. E., 15, 18
Jones, J. M., 43, 93
Jones, M., 92
Judd, C., 54
Judd, C. M., 68, 128

K

Kafati, G., 127
Kang, S., 34
Kao, G., 27
Karpinski, A., 114
Kassin, S. M., 69, 86, 88
Katz, I., 44, 89
Katz, P. A., 73, 89
Kawakami, K., 54, 56, 57, 62,
    63, 90, 116, 124
Keefe, S., 18, 20–22, 25, 32
Kelley, C. M., 81, 98
Kelley, H. H., 113
Kennedy, R. F., 1
Kenny, D. A., 122
Kibler, J. L., 90
Kinder, D. R., 89

Kitayama, S., 9
Klahr, D., 96
Kleinpenning, G., 51
Klonoff, E. A., 27
Knight, G. P., 30
Knight, J. L., 51
Koehnken, G., 84
Koriat, A., 98
Kosterman, R., 45
Kovel, J., 44
Kowai-Bell, N., 94
Kramer, R. M., 113
Kravitz, J., 95
Krysan, M., 27, 43
Kuhn, D., 96
Kumhyr, S. M., 57

L
LaFromboise, T., 36
Lamb, M. E., 74, 96
Landrine, H., 27
Latané, B., 47
Lavigueur, H., 96
Lavrakas, P. J., 95, 96
Lawrence, A. D., 76
Leary, M. R., 100
Lee, J., 118
Lee, J. S., 75
LeGrand, R. L., 73
Leibold, J. M., 62
Lenton, A. P., 92
Leonard, C. M., 71
Levin, D. T., 49, 78–81
Levinson, D. J., 44
Liberman, A., 98
Liberzon, I., 76
Lickel, B., 94
Lin, M., 115
Lind, A. E., 128
Lindsay, R. C. L., 70, 86, 88, 95
Lindsey, S., 54
Lockwood, J., 118
Loftus, 98
Lowenstein, G., 18
Lowery, B. S., 91
Luce, T. S., 70
Luhtanen, R., 16, 56
Lundregan, T., 84

M
Ma, J. E., 92
Maass, A, 95, 114
MacLin, M. K., 70

MacLin, O. H., 70, 80
Macrae, C. N., 112
Major, B., 14, 16–19, 94
Malpass, R. S., 69, 70, 80, 84, 92, 95, 96
Mann, J., 116
Mann, J. A., 121
Mann, J. W., 32
Mann, V. A., 78
Mannix, L. M., 58
Marcus-Newhall, A., 117
Markus, H., 19
Markus, H. R., 9, 12
Martinez, L., 27
Maruyama, G., 116
Mason, P. L., 23
Maurer, D., 72, 73
Mayzner, M. S., 95
McConahay, J. B., 45, 55, 89, 91
McConnell, A. R, 62
McEwan, T., 84
McGhee, D. E., 27, 54, 90
McIntosh, P., 12, 14
McLaughlin, J. P., 48, 54
McLemore, S. D., 2
Meertens, R. W., 51
Mehrabian, A., 56
Meissner, C. A., 69, 70, 80–85, 88, 93, 95, 98
Memon, A., 69
Mendes, W. B., 94
Mendiola, S., 27
Miller, C. T., 49
Miller, N., 28, 84, 93, 113, 115, 117, 118, 127
Milne, A. B., 34, 112
Mitchell, T. A., 88
Mondloch, C. J., 73
Montalvo, F. F., 22
Montegu, A., 5
Monteith, J. J., 91, 100
Monteith, M., 124
Monteith, M. J., 53, 63, 90, 91, 100
Montgomery, G. T., 20
Moore, C., 75
Morales, A., 35
Morris, M., 36
Mullen, B., 68, 69, 120
Mummendey, A., 128
Murguia, E., 22
Murphy, F. C., 76
Murrell, A., 116
Murrell, A. J., 114, 121
Myrdal, G., 44

N

Nachson, I., 71
Nail, P. R., 53
Nathan, L. R., 28, 91
Neimann, Y, 27
Nelson, A. R., 45
Neuberg, S. L., 115
Neufeld, P., 84
Nezlek, J. B., 91
Ng, W., 70, 95
Nier, J. A., 123, 127
Nimmo-Smith, I., 76
Nisbett, R. E., 56
Nosek, B. A., 92
Nurius, P., 19
Nussbaum, R. J., 128

O

O'Connor, E., 27
Oakes, P. J., 13
Olson, M. A., 28, 61
Omoto, A. M., 113
Operario, D., 13
Otero, L., 52

P

Padilla, A. M., 7–38
Pallier, C., 73
Park, B., 54, 68, 113, 114, 128
Paul, P. Y., 28
Pearson, A., 56
Penrod, S. D., 84, 88
Perdue, C. W., 114
Perea, J., 2
Perez, W., 9, 21, 22
Perrett, D. I., 72
Perry, B., 60
Pettigrew, T., 4
Pettigrew, T. F., 51, 93, 114, 126
Pezdek, K., 75, 76
Pfeifer, J. E., 85
Phan, K. L., 76
Phelps, E. A., 61, 76, 77
Phinney, J., 30
Piliavin, J. A., 113
Plant, E. A., 55, 91, 94, 99, 101
Platz, S. J., 70, 93, 96
Pollack, K., 27
Pomare, M., 121
Pontero, J. G., 16
Poole, D. A., 74, 96
Portes, 24

Poskocil, A., 100
Pratto, F., 10, 11, 43, 49

Q

Quinn, P. C., 73
Quintana, S. M., 16, 30, 31

R

Rabbie, J. M., 113
Randall, J. L, 1
Rattner, A., 84
Ready, D. R., 85
Reicher, S. D., 13
Richardson-Klavehn, A., 81
Richeson, J., 55, 57
Richeson, J. A., 55, 62, 128
Robinson, P. H, 49
Roccas, S., 120
Rodin, M. J., 77, 92
Rogers, S., 27
Rollman, S. A., 57
Rolls, E. T., 71
Romo, H. D., 2
Rothbart, M., 114, 128
Rudman, L. A., 92
Rumbaut, 24
Rumpel, C. M., 86
Runciman, W. G., 18
Rust, M. C., 115, 119
Ryan, C. S., 68
Ryan, R. M., 91

S

Sagarin, 84
Salas, E., 59
Saltz, E., 91
Saltz, J. L., 28, 91
Salvi, D., 114
Sanchez-Ross, M. G., 51
Sanford, R. N., 44
Sangrigoli, S., 72, 73, 75
Saucier, D. A., 49
Saxe, L., 46
Schacter, S., 18
Schaefer, R. T., 35
Scheck, B., 84
Schneider, S., 121
Schneider, W., 53
Schofield, J. W., 121
Schooler, J. W., 72
Schooler, T. Y., 54

Schuman, H., 27, 43
Schwartz, J., 54
Schwartz, J. L. K., 27, 90
Sears, D. O., 45, 89
Sellers, R. M., 27
Semin, G. R., 114
Shelton, J. N., 27, 55, 57, 62
Shepherd, J., 74, 77, 81, 95, 96
Sherif, C. W., 121
Sherman, J., 124
Sherman, J. W., 112
Shiffrin, R., 53
Sidanius, J., 10, 11, 43, 49
Sierra, A., 22
Sigel, I. E., 74
Sikes, M. P., 27, 43
Simmonds, D. C., 96
Simon, H. A., 81
Sinclair, S., 91
Singer, E., 18
Skinner, M., 113
Slater, A., 73
Slone, A., 93, 96
Smedley, B. D., 45
Smith-McLallen, A., 56
Smith, H. H., 128
Smith, V. L., 69
Snyder, L. D., 95
Snyder, M., 113
Somerville, S. C., 78
Sommers, S. R., 49, 51
Spaulding, K., 95
Spencer, M. B., 30
Spencer, S. J., 44
Sporer, S. L., 70, 77, 84
Stangor, C., 53
Steeh, C., 27, 43
Steele, C., 14, 16, 94
Stephan, C. W., 93, 94
Stephan, W. G., 93, 94
Stephenson, G. M., 113
Stith, A. Y., 45
Stonequist, E. V., 31
Stürmer, S., 113
Sumner, 113
Swart, L. A., 90
Sweeney, M., 16
Swim, J., 27
Swope, T. M., 95

T
Tafarodi, R. W., 34, 35
Tafoya, S., 23, 24, 32

Tajfel, H., 12, 14, 17, 18,
  111–113, 115, 116
Tanaka, J., 70
Tanaka, J. W., 71, 72
Tatum, B., 12, 19, 33
Taylor, S. E., 8, 9, 112
Taylor, S. F., 76
Teitelbaum, S., 70
Testa, M., 17
Thomson, D., 78
Thomson, D. M., 78
Thornton, M. C., 30
Tischauser, L. V., 1, 2
Tredoux, C. G., 70
Trolier, T. K., 112
Tropp, L. A., 93
Tubb, V. A., 69
Turmer, J. C., 7, 12, 13, 18, 74,
  113, 115, 116, 118, 120
Turpie, C., 56
Tversky, A., 98
Twenge, J. M., 24
Tyler, R. B., 54, 114
Tyler, T. R., 128

U
Udasco, J. O., 32
Urland, G. O., 76

V
Valentine, T., 70, 78–81, 96
Validzic, A., 127
Van Kamp, S., 62
Vanbeselaere, N., 118
Vance, S. L., 91
Vanman, E. J., 28, 91
Vasquez-Suson, K. A., 55, 93
Vazquez, L. A., 22, 23, 35
Ventureyra, V. A. G., 73
Vera, E. M., 30
Vescio, T. K., 94
Voekl, K., 17
Voils, C. I., 90
Von Hippel, W., 114
Vorauer, J. D., 56, 57

W
Wackenhut, J., 44
Waldzus, S., 128
Wall, P., 83
Ward, C. M., 123

Warren, J. A., 28, 91
Wasserman, A. W., 84, 85
Weber, U., 128
Weizmann, F., 3
Weldon, D. E., 96
Wellman, H. M., 78
Wells, G. L., 86, 88
Wenzel, M., 128
Wetherell, M. S., 13
Weyant, J. M., 28
Wheeler, M. E., 28, 29, 76
Whitestone, E., 50
Wilder, D. A., 114, 115, 117, 118
Williams, C. J., 27, 54, 90
Willis-Esqueda, C., 1–5
Wills, E. J., 96
Wilson, T. D., 54, 61
Winter, L. I., 34
Wittenbrink, B., 54, 128
Wohl, M. J. A., 127
Wolsko, C., 128

Woodhead, M .M., 96
Woods, B., 78
Word, C. O., 63
Wright, D. B., 70
Wyatt, G. E., 3
Wyer, N. A., 90

Y

Ybarra, O., 94
Ybarra, V. C., 16
Yee, A. H., 3
Yin, R. K., 71
Young, A. W., 70

Z

Zanna, M. P., 18, 63
Zatzick, C. D., 45
Zuckerman, M., 3
Zuwerink, J. R., 91, 100

Subject Index

A

Acculturation, as coping strategy, 34–35
African Americans, 3, 45–48, 54–60
   attention to facial features, 77
   attitudes, towards races, 88–89
   beliefs about, 27
   eye movements in face recognition
      process, 82–83
   impressions of Whites, 59
   interracial interactions, 57–58
   magnitude of CRE, as measured
      by false alarms, 81
   psychological interpretation of, 3
   recognition of facial photos, 85
   socialization culture, 30
   in United States (1800), 2
Ambiguity (tolerance), 19
Ambivalent racism theory, 89
American dilemma, 44
American Indian culture, 5
An American dilemma, 44
Anti-Semitism, 26
Anxiety, 94
Asians, in United States (1800), 2
Attitudes Toward Blacks (ATB) scale, 91
Attitudes, towards races, 88–89
Aversive racism, 90, 111–112
   in candidate selection, case study, 51–52
   early evidence, 45–49
   explicit attitudes and implicit attitudes, 53–60
   in juridic decisions, case study, 49–50
   nature of, 44–45
   persistence of disparities, 49–53

B

Bias
   common ingroup identity model, 121–124
   explicit and implicit, 26–29
   facial electromyography (EMG)
      for measuring, 28–29
   among Latinos of United States, 27–29
   pro-ingroup orientation, 114
   and social categorization, 115–119
Biculturalism, 35–36
Blacks. *See* African Americans
Brain-imaging studies, of CRE, 76–77

C

California gold rush, of 1848–49, 8
Categorization, of people-by-people,
    9–10, 111
Cautionary instructions, to jurors, 86–87
Chicano Movement, 33
Children
   CRE effect in 7-, 12-, and 17-year-olds,
      74–75
   CRE in 3- to 5-year-old children, 75
   recognition accuracy in, 75
   study of color blindness, 73–74
Chinese Exclusion Act (1882–1943), 2
Civil Rights Movement (1960s), 7, 11, 33, 43
Cognitive, perceptual, and motivational
    processes, in CRE
   attentional differences, 77
   different encoding strategies, 78
   different representational systems, 78–80
   encoding race as a pre-eminent feature,
      80–81
   facial perception, 77
Collective group membership, importance,
    12–13
Color-blind theory, 3, 121
"Coming out of the closet" announcement, 14
Common ingroup identity model
   benefits, 126–127
   causes and consequences of, 120

Common ingroup identity model (*cont.*)
  development of, 119–121
  framework, 120
  and Green Circle elementary school-based
    intervention program, 125–126
  and intergroup bias, 121–124
  and motivation in interracial interactions,
    124–125
Configural encoding, 71
Convicting the Innocent, 83
Coping strategies, during ethnic threat
  acculturation, 34–35
  establishing one's identity, 32–34
  multiple group membership, 35–37
Cross-examination, of the witness, 86
Cross-race effect (CRE), in face recognition
  for Black and White perceivers, 69–70,
    81–82
  brain-imaging studies, 76–77
  characteristics, 69–70
  cognitive, perceptual, and motivational
    processes in, 77–81
  in the criminal justice system, 83–88
  developmental course of, 70–76
  feelings of familiarity *vs.* conscious-level
    conceptual information, 81–83
  Hispanics' recognition of Hispanic and
    Black faces, 70
  impact of intergroup contact on, 95–96
  impact on individual, 99–101
  issue of improving performance, 96–98
  motivation development for, 98–99
  in prejudice and intergroup interactions,
    88–94
  and racial attitudes, 93
  and response criterion, 69–70
Cross-racial identification, 87
Cultural competence, 9, 12

D
Decategorization
  of perceived group boundaries,
    115–117
  and personalization, 117–118
Default option, of the amygdala, 76
Developmental course, of CRE
  developmental age of CRE, 72–74
  modularity hypothesis, 70–71
  skill or expertise hypothesis, 71–72
  studies on children, 74–76
Dia de los Muertos (Day of the Dead), 21
Diversity, defined, 7
DNA testing, 84

Dominative racism, 44
Dual attitudes, system of, 54
Dual identity, on intergroup relations,
  119, 128
Dual-process theories, of memory, 81

E
Ethnic threat. *See* Stigmatized individuals
European Americans, 2
Even the Rat Was White, 3
Event-related evoked potentials (ERPs), 76
Expert testimony
  and CRE, 69
  by researchers, 87–88
Explicit attitudes, 53–54, 58, 90
Eyewitness identifications. *See* Mistaken
  identification

F
Face recognition, among Balcks and Whites.
  See cross-race effect (CRE), in face
  recognition
Facial electromyography (EMG), for measure
  of bias, 28–29
Facilitated classification process, 79
Featural encoding, 71
Feature-present/feature-absent manner,
  of encoding, 79

G
Group-based social hierarchies, 11

H
Holistic processing, 71, 73
Homosexuals, 14

I
Identification errors. *See* Mistaken
  identification
Immigrants and social stigmas, 17
Immigration-adjustment process, 9
Implicit Association Test (IAT), 27, 54,
  90, 92
Implicit attitudes, 90
  and stereotypes, 53–58
Implicit memory processes, 53
In-group favoritism, 10
Ingroup Outgroup, 13, 68, 90, 111. *See also*
  Social categorization

In-group stereotypes, 25
Intergroup discrimination, 10
Internal and External Motivation
    to Respond Without Prejudice
    Scales, 91
Interracial interactions, by Whites and Blacks,
    57–58

L
Latinos, in the United States
    acculturation of, 20
    acculturation rates based on skin color,
      22–25
    coping behavior from ethnic
      discriminations, 31–37
    cultural awareness (CA), 20–21
    diversity of, 7–8
    ethnic loyalty (EL), 20–21
    feelings of perceived discrimination and
      coping strategies, 18
    measurement of biasness, 27–29
    microbehaviors, 28
    perceived discrimination, 21
    social cognitions of, 13
    socialization culture, 30–31
Legitimizing myths (LMs), 11
Lineup construction and CRE, 84–85

M
Marginal person model, 31–32
Mayflower, 8
Mexican Americans, 2–3
    feelings of perceived discrimination and
      coping strategies, 18
    socialization, 30
Mistaken identification, 69, 83–84
    safeguards and remedies, 85–88
Modern Racism Scale, 89, 91
Multidimensional face space model, 78
Multiple group membership, 35–37
Mutual intergroup differentiation,
    118–119

N
The Nature of Prejudice, 89
Nebraska Symposium, on Motivation series, 3
Negative intergroup attitudes, 89
Negative stigmatization, 19
    affects of, 14
    attributes of, 14–15
    of minorities, 15

New Jersey v. Cromedy, 87
Nonverbal behavior, in interracial interactions,
    56–58, 100

O
Old-Fashioned and Racism Modern Racism
    Scales, 55
Old-fashioned racism, 89
Outgroup homogeneity effect, 68
Outgroup homogeneity, of appearance, 88–89
Outsiders, 12

P
Parental ethnic socialization, 30
Passing strategy, 34–35
Personalization, 117–118
Pragmatism
    and cultural competerce, 9
    in social cognition, 8
Prejudice. *See also* Cross-race effect (CRE),
    in face recognition
    conceptualizations and definitions of, 89–92
    implicit and explicit, 60
    and intergroup interactions, 101
    intrepretation in United States, 1
    Nazis' rise to power in Germany,
      in context of, 44
    nonverbal cues of, 57
    overt expressions of, in United States, 45
    within psychology, 3
    threat and intergroup anxiety, 93–94
Prejudice-congruent condition, 91
Prejudice-incongruent condition, 91
Protestant work ethics, 11

R
Racism
    attitudes towards races, 88–89
    classification of African Americans in
      United States, 2
    conceptualizations and definitions of,
      89–92
    cultural and scientific notion of race, 2
    intrepretation in United States, 1
    modern, 45, 89
    within psychology, 3
    symbolic, 45, 89
Recategorization, of perceived group
    boundaries, 115–117
Recognition memory, 74
Relative heterogeneity, 68

S

Salient stigmas, 15, 17–18
Same group affiliation, 18–19
Self-categorization, in-group, 10, 13
Self-esteem, 10, 19, 24, 32
Similarity-based model, of face recognition,
        78–79
Skin color and phenotypes of Latinos, study
        of Boston Social Survey Data of Urban
        Inequality, 23
    effects on acculturation, 22
    Mexican Americans with a European
        physical appearance, 22
    occupational status and income
        differentials, 23
    self-esteem, 24
    Tafoya's survey, 23–24
    US born Latino males, 22
Social activism, 32–34
Social categorization, 9–10
    and common ingroup identity model
        (*see* Common ingroup identity model)
    mutual intergroup differentiation, 118–119
    and orientation towards others, 112–115
    recategorization and decategorization,
        of perceived group boundaries,
        115–118
    in reducing intergroup bias, 115–119
Social cognition, 8–9
Social cognition theory, 9
Social comparison, 10
Social dominance, 10–12
    concept of hierarchical consensuality, 11
    development of dominance, 11
    dominant groups vs subordinate groups, 11
    individual orientation towards, 12
    and legitimizing myths (LMs), 11
    personal and group traits
        associated with, 11
Social dominance theory (SDT), 11
Social domination orientation (SDO),
        11–12
Social groups. *See* Ingroup Outgroup
Social identity, 12–14
Social identity theory (SIT), 8, 12, 90
    on intergroup relations, 13
    and stigmas, 14–17
    uses of self-categorization, 13
Socially constructed phenomenon, 2
Social psychology, of minority group
        identification
    effects of perceived discrimination
        and ethnic threat, 15, 25–26
    ethnic socialization, 30–31

    explicit and implicit bias, 26–29
    intrapsychic coping strategies, 31–37
    social categorization, 9–10
    social cognition, 8–9
    social comparison, 10
    social dominance, 10–12
    social identity, 12–14
    social stigma, 14–17
Social stigma, 14–17
Social support, 33
The souls of Black folk, 43
Stereotyped attitudes, of stigmatized
        individuals, 25–26
Stigmatized individuals, 17–20, 29. *See also*
        negative stigmatization
    behavior of, identified with their
        group, 18
    Brown's study, 19
    effects of perceived discrimination and
        ethnic threat, 15, 25–26
    experiences attribution ambiguity, 19
    and psychological and economic costs,
        24–25
    salient stigmas, 15, 17–18
    sensitivity of, 17
    stereotyped attitudes, 25
    visibility of, 16
Stonequist's theory of the marginal
        person, 31
Symbolic Racism Scale, 89

T

Theory of ethnic identity, 21, 34–35

U

United States
    African Americans in, 2
    Asians in, 2
    diversity in, 7
    egalitarian values and racist traditions, 44
    European Americans in, 2
    Mexican Americans in, 2
    overt expressions of prejudice, 45
    prejudice and racism, interpretation of, 1
    socially constructed phenomenon,
        culture of, 2
United States v. Telfaire, 86
United States v. Wade decision, 83

V

Visibly stigmatized individuals, 16

W
White Americans, 45
Whites, 3, 45–48, 54–60
    attention to facial features, 77
    attitudes, towards races,
        88–89

eye movements in face recognition
    process, 82–83
interracial interactions, 57–58
magnitude of the CRE, as measured by
    false alarms, 81
recognition of facial photos, 85

9 780387 732343